# SIX YEARS IN MOZAMBIQUE

## Things I Haven't Told Mom

By

# Amy Gillespie

*with*

## Cheri Colburn

# Six Years in Mozambique

## Amy Gillespie

First Published in the United States of America

First Printing: July 2014

ISBN: 978-1499784053
Cover Design by Zora Knauf
Cover Photo taken by Hultink Design
Author Photo taken by Simone Severo
Website: http://www.amygillespie.com

To Contact the Author: amy@amygillespie.com

*For children and the people who help them*

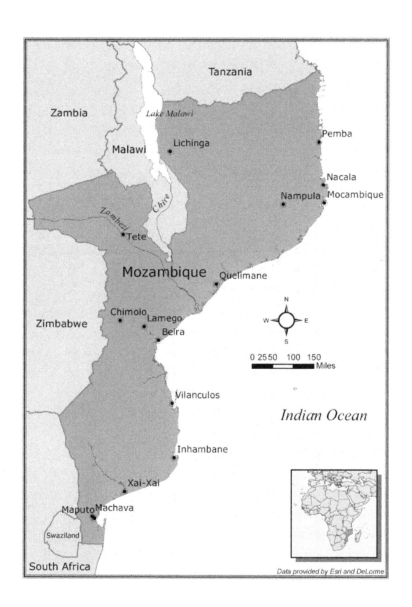

# Author's Note

This book contains personal recollections of a particular time in my life. I have shared my honest and truthful perceptions and memories, in-the-moment experiences, and the insights and reflections I've developed since leaving Mozambique. Because I've written this book from memory and personal perspective, others may have perceived things differently and some of the details may be slightly out of whack. I've done the best I can to reconstruct the story in order to share it with you.

Ultimately, this is not a book about what I did, but a book about the potential of what you could do....

# Table of Contents

# SIX YEARS IN MOZAMBIQUE:

## Things I Haven't Told Mom

# PART I:
# COMMITMENT

# 1

As I hung up the phone, I knew that my husband would soon be dead. I paced around my apartment, picking things up, setting them down, wandering aimlessly and reflecting on our time together and its tragic ending.

I'd met Bruce nine years earlier at a leasing company where I had been an administrative assistant and he had been in sales. We'd been together for more than seven years when he asked me to marry him—not just once, but three times. The first proposal had been a surprise; we were shopping for towels at a department store, and as we passed the jewelry counter Bruce said to the clerk, "The lady will need to see something... in diamonds."

Bruce was like that: enigmatic and magical. He'd grown up going back and forth between the United States and Sweden, and he shared stories of hanging out with prostitutes down at the docks in Stockholm when he was just thirteen. With his wild childhood, it was no wonder he had grown up to be a stock-car driver who shrugged off life-threatening accidents. He was blonde and blue-eyed with strong, square shoulders. I liked to think of him as *The Bruce*.

I, on the other hand, was a little less suave, and it took me a full five minutes to grasp that he was proposing marriage that day and to say yes. We bought the ring that day. Being *The Bruce that he was*, he made a second proposal that was custom fit for my practical nature. His second proposal was in writing, a Hallmark card with three handwritten boxes: *yes*, *no*, and *maybe later*. Of course I checked yes. I'd waited twenty-nine years for that moment.

Even though the ring was bought and the date was set, he had to outdo himself yet again. A few months after the second proposal, he took me on a gambling vacation to Duluth; I had never been much of a gambler, but Bruce loved the sound and action of the casino scene. At sunset on the second night, he dropped to one knee on the boardwalk and asked me to marry him. This time it felt like the perfect proposal to both of us, and the next year we got married in the little German Chapel in Plymouth, Minnesota, where we lived. After a simple ceremony that included only our closest friends and family, we all went to dinner. The next day, we had a big dance at a country club near my parents' home. What fun we all had!

Unfortunately, things changed after we were married. Bruce insisted on completely taking over our finances, despite the fact that we had been living together for three years and managing our money and home together. But that was only one of the sudden changes. *He* found *us* a job—a caretaker position at a U-Haul storage facility.

I was annoyed. I had taken a job at a rental car company as a means of getting my foot in the door to become an insurance adjuster. At that time, this was a common way for people without a college degree to enter the insurance industry. By the time I got married, I was well on my way, despite Bruce's discouraging comments, such as, "Sugarbear, you'll never be an insurance adjuster. You don't have a college degree. It just won't happen." Now he wanted me to give up the dream I'd been working toward in order to manage a U-Haul with him.

"It will be great, Amy. Monday through Saturday during the day, we will have our home and our work there. We can make some extra commissions renting out trucks, and we'll have steady income and health insurance. You can get contracts cleaning restaurants at night, and you can sleep during the day while I run the office. Maybe you can cook at the restaurants sometimes for a bit more money."

It sounded hectic, but I had grown up in a family that bonded by working. We lived on a farm, so both Mom and Dad had their work right there with us kids. We worked together as a family: painting buildings, walking beans, cleaning barns and sheds. Some of my best memories are firmly attached to working alongside my family and relaxing together afterward.

In the end, I let Bruce persuade me. I thought it might work. The only trouble was that Bruce didn't let me sleep while he worked in the office. Or maybe I should say he *couldn't* let me sleep. First, he caught a bad cold. Then he had the flu and couldn't seem to shake it. He went to doctor after doctor and even spent a week in the hospital. Nobody could figure out what was wrong with him. Meanwhile, I ran the U-Haul and worked my job cleaning restaurants.

Without any rest, I grew too weary to think straight, especially given Bruce's erratic and unpredictable moods. He smoked and drank more than ever before, and his winning record at poker was coming to a long, drawn-out, expensive end.

One time, he called me in the middle of the night, "Babe, I'm down $5,000. I'm going to try to get it back."

I couldn't figure out why he would call me to tell me something like that. "Bruce, come home. Just come home. We'll work this out. Just, please, walk away from the table now." He was gone well into morning.

Sadly, that was not an isolated incident. I tried for two months to persuade him that I couldn't cope with the situation, but nothing about his gambling behavior changed. Eventually, something had to give. I approached him in a calm moment when he was sober. "Bruce, I can't do it anymore. I'm driving all night, often in snowstorms; I'm barely awake, and all you do is drink and smoke and gamble. You aren't cutting back anywhere. Meanwhile, I'm pinching pennies and working day and night. You are sinking us into debt and you are sinking me in every way."

Bruce said nothing. In fact, "nothing" had become his standard response. I knew that somebody had to say it, so I gathered my courage and just put it out there. "I think we need to start talking about divorce."

He looked at me steadily, as if we were head-to-head in a hand of poker. He took another drag of his cigarette and gave me a long and pensive look, as if he were contemplating his next bid at the table. But I could read him better than that. His shoulders and chest fell, making him seem smaller and more vulnerable. He had always been a winner—with racecars, gambling, and life. The words were a heavy blow.

The magic of our marriage, the marriage I'd waited for and prayed for my whole life, was becoming a nightmare of sickness, fatigue, booze, and gambling. Then one night I discovered a pistol in Bruce's bed stand.

I picked up the phone. "Mom? I need to talk. Can we meet for lunch tomorrow?" She agreed without hesitation, no doubt knowing something was wrong because it was unlike me to call for help. When I got off the phone, I began dreading the next day. Talking with my parents would be excruciating, but I knew I needed their guidance.

As we sat together at the restaurant, I told my parents all the things I'd been hiding about my marriage. Dad listened but held back judgment. And I guess that first time I talked to them about my marriage (and probable divorce), Mom held back, too. They mostly just listened that day, and their relative calm helped me.

Then again, that conversation was at the beginning of the end. After a few such conversations, Mom pushed me to get off the fence. "Amy, I'm not an advocate of abandoning a marriage, especially so quickly, but you need to decide. Either you divorce, or you stay in your marriage. But if you stay, I need you to quit talking about it. It's too hard for me to listen to you talk about what's going on."

She had chosen her words carefully, to be practical and clear as was her habit. She would not make this decision for me or try to influence me by offering her opinion. She didn't need to. I knew my mom and could intuit her opinion. No matter how practical she sounded, I could hear her disappointment underneath her words.

In my family, Mom was the one to let you know if you did right or wrong, if you should feel guilty or not. Even though I was an adult, my need to seek my mother's approval had never left me, and her unspoken disappointment contributed to my overall sense of guilt, perhaps even more than if she'd yelled at me. It had always been that way. The unspoken words always affected me the most.

The fact that I was the one throwing in the towel after less than a year of marriage added to my sense of guilt. I just *knew* I was the one to blame. I wondered if I should just tell Bruce I was sorry and try again to make it work. I felt like such a coward, such a mess.

I do not remember a time before I started feeling like I'd better "get it right, or else"—whatever "it" was, whatever "or else" was. I suppose we could write off my characteristic sense of guilt to my Catholic upbringing; I will grant that Catholicism contributed. But it is more complex than that. I had been adopted as a baby, just like my older brother had been. There was a story in my baby book about my parents contacting Catholic Charities to get a baby boy for my brother to play with. The agency was out of boys, so they took me. Often during my childhood, I wondered if their first inclination had been right. Maybe a boy would have been a better fit for my brother, who didn't seem to like me very much. I often wondered if they regretted compromising and taking me instead of holding out a little longer. I wondered if the Catholic Charities people had laid some guilt on them about how this baby girl *really needed a home*.

I didn't look one ounce like any of them. My mother, father, and brother have light coloring. Mom and my brother, Tim, are blue-eyed and blonde-headed, and Dad is a blue-eyed redhead. My complexion is fair, but I'm a dark brunette. And as if that did not make me different enough, I have one blue eye and one brown eye. I never quite felt like I fit in.

Throughout my childhood, I worked hard to make up for my perceived shortcomings, always looking to Mom as my barometer for whether or not I was getting it right. My mom was not different in this way from most mothers I knew. She was practical, and she knew how to keep a couple kids in line with just a look. But I had a loving family, and Mom was no exception. Her love was always there; it was her approval that seemed conditional to me. Things were different with Dad. His approval was easier to come by, and all through the early years of my childhood, I felt secure in my relationship with him.

Then, when I was eight years old, Mom gave birth to my parents' first natural child, Kara. She was blue-eyed and a redhead, just like Dad. And she was beautiful. I tortured myself with the idea that she was their *real* daughter. From there, my insecurity with Mom intensified and spread to Dad. I was as jealous as any older sibling when a cute little baby barges into the family—and then some.

I was also crazy about Kara. She was my baby sister, after all, and I took my position as big sister very seriously. I took a very thorough babysitters' safety course in order to earn the opportunity to be Kara's babysitter. The safety course was very serious business as far as I was concerned. I still remember that classroom and all that we learned, like CPR and not to put a knife in a toaster. I was nine years old when I proudly received my babysitter's certificate. After that, I babysat Kara often while my parents were taking a paramedics course to join the volunteer rescue squad in our little town. I felt myself to be mature and trustworthy.

Unfortunately, none of that—the safety training or my sense of competence, or my experience babysitting Kara—helped the day of Kara's accident.

It was a beautiful summer day, one spent with the whole family on the farm. Dad was working on the tractor, and Mom was making lunch. I went outside to find Kara, since I'd appointed myself responsible for her.

Right away when I saw her near our camper, I knew something was wrong. As fast as I could, I ran the nearly block-long path to where the camper was parked. There she was with her head inside the camper window and her feet dangling about an inch above the step. I pulled her from the window, and as we fell to the ground, I heard a rasping exhale. I rolled out from under her and screamed for Dad. He came running and started CPR. I ran to call an ambulance, and Kara was rushed to the hospital. But nothing could be done. My sweet little sister died that day.

My brother and I had left the window open, and my attempt to help Kara had failed. Though there was no disapproving look from Mom, I knew to my ten-year-old bones that Kara's death was my fault.

Time, counseling, and an adult's perspective on the capabilities of a ten-year-old eased that sense of guilt. But it was still there throughout my early adulthood, and it was triggered whenever I made a considerable mistake.

When I left Bruce, I felt incredible guilt. Even when people pointed out his behaviors and decisions that contributed to me leaving, I still felt it was my fault. I knew that a wife stands by her man, and I had not done that. I ended up walking away from most everything we'd had together, and for a small measure of peace between us, it was worth it. I transferred to a different U-Haul facility, and Bruce simply left.

To save money, Bruce and I chose an "amicable divorce," which meant no attorneys and no court date. We simply filed some paperwork with the court and waited for the judge to sign a consent form. "Amicable" almost flew out the window when Bruce refused to sign the papers unless I took on $5,000 of his debt. I understood that he was a good man and that his previous divorces (two of them) had left him a financial mess. But this one was leaving me in that same spot and he was the one that lost $5,000 at the table. I had to do it, though. We did not have money to fight with or fight over, and I needed to make sure I got out before his gambling debt continued to grow.

One day, a few weeks after we filed the final paperwork, Bruce showed up at my apartment. He said that he was going to Texas to see his kids. We didn't talk for long before we had a kiss and a hug goodbye and I wished him well.

Shortly after he arrived in Texas, Bruce collapsed at a gas station and was rushed to the hospital. At that point—*finally*—he got a real diagnosis. Pancreatic cancer had very quickly taken over his body, and he had only thirty days to live.

He called me at home one evening, mad as hell, to deliver the news. "This is your fault, Amy. You left me in my time of need. You were a fair-weather friend. I hope you have a miserable life… and you are *not* welcome at my funeral!" Then he hung up.

The news sent me reeling. I paced around, not knowing what to do with myself. Then I sat in silence. Waylaid by shame, I could not bring myself to talk with anybody about how I was feeling. I was ashamed that I had left Bruce so that I could be safe and happy, ashamed that my marriage had collapsed in such a short time. Finally, I cried myself to sleep, miserable with Bruce's suffering and the knowledge that I had failed as his wife—the role in which I most wanted to succeed.

Two weeks later, Bruce called me again, and this time he was more loving. "Babe, I screwed you over. Would you like some of your stuff back?"

"No, Bruce. This isn't the time to quibble over towels and a few dishes. We didn't have that much. It's okay. Let it go. "

"But, Amy, I'm dying. I can't take any of it with me. A lot of it was yours, and you should have it back."

For a moment, I could not respond. The lump in my throat felt huge. My eyes were hot and wet with sadness and shame and anger. Bruce, my Bruce, *The Bruce*, was going to die. I never would have filed for divorce if I'd known he was so sick. Why hadn't the doctors figured it out sooner? During all of those months when he had been feeling so bad, I blamed it on drinking and smoking and generally terrible self-care.

His voice brought me back to the conversation. "Amy, you have to get that divorce through. If you don't, you're not only going to be stuck with all of my gambling debt but my hospital debt, too."

"But, Bruce, there isn't anything I can do. We have to just wait it out. I'll call the court again to see if I can do anything, but last week all they would tell me is that it's in process."

"Okay, Sugarbear, just try."

"I will, Bruce. Have you changed your mind about letting me come see you? Please? I'm so sorry. This never would have happened if I'd known. I'm so sorry."

"No, Amy. Don't come. I need you to stay there. I love you."

"I love you too."

I did not know it at the time, but that was our final conversation. Not long afterward, I stood with a small blue card in my hand showing that our divorce was final. I was back to being Amy Gillespie.

After all the waiting, it felt surprisingly sudden. Even though the card was basically an administrative detail, my emotions raced at the finality it represented. I had to tell Bruce so that he could rest knowing that I would be ok—and I had to do that right away, before my tears took over.

I tried to calm down, taking deep, smooth breaths as I dialed. His daughter Annie answered, and my voice shook a bit. "Annie? Can I talk to Bruce?"

"He can't talk now," she drawled. "The cancer's really deep in his throat."

"Okay. Please tell him the divorce card has come. It's final."

I heard her tell him.

"He smiled, Amy. He seems happy."

I got off the phone as quickly as I could, before the tears took over. I don't even remember offering Annie any words of comfort.

She called me the next day to tell me that Bruce had died within an hour of my call. He had been waiting. I lurched with the realization that I had been married, divorced, and widowed all within the frame of that single harrowing day.

# 2

After Bruce died, I needed to get my life in order, and that's what I did. Within a year or so, I found my way into that insurance job by way of coincidence. I was managing a gas station, and one of my customers was an insurance adjuster. He happened to mention that his company was hiring. I applied and was surprised when I got the job.

I soon established myself as a hard worker, a quick thinker, and a diplomat who could soothe disgruntled customers. During my first few years as an adjuster, I received promotion after promotion, until finally I had a proper income and career. My confidence grew. Eventually, I landed a position on the esteemed Catastrophic Team ("Cat"), where I could take home as much as $5,000 per month, traveling the United States and Canada to settle claims following catastrophic events such as floods, tornadoes, and fires.

With a good salary finally coming in, I flew to Colorado to buy a cabin. I had always dreamed of life in the mountains, and my higher income would allow me to homestead a property. Later in life, I could retire there. After signing the contract, I returned to Minnesota and submitted my request to transfer.

The next day, while I was driving across the I-35W bridge in Minneapolis, I heard Bruce's voice, just as clearly as if he were sitting next to me in the car. "I'm proud of you." I whipped my head around, barely keeping the car in line with traffic. *Where did that voice come from? Did I imagine that? My God – that was Bruce!*

Bruce had always been against everything and anything that he deemed "aerie-faerie and woo-woo." But that day—five years after his death—I heard his voice very clearly. I did not fully understand how it had happened, but I felt a new kind of hope. From that day forward, my need to reach him—to tell him how sorry I was—turned me toward an ongoing study of various spiritual practices.

In one short week, I moved to Colorado, settled into my beautiful cabin, and commenced enjoying the breathtaking views of Pikes Peak. Whenever I was home, I loved doing small renovations and working in my yard.

A less apparent benefit of my new situation was that, between work and the cabin, I could easily pretend I did not have time for dating. I hadn't expected to be thrown back into the dating scene in my thirties, and I had no applicable skillset. By keeping busy, I didn't have to consider the very likely possibility that I was simply lousy at it.

Whenever my mind wandered to the subject of men, I refocused on work. I so enjoyed making a difference in people's lives, and my reputation continued to grow. I also loved the travel. Even though I worked long days when I was on site, I managed to see a little bit of several cities: Seattle, Kansas City, Minneapolis, and Omaha, just to name a few.

One time in Kansas City, I went to a fair where there was an intuitive artist. Instead of doing psychic readings for her clients, she created psychic drawings of their angels, spirits, totem animals, or guides. I knew there were plenty of quacks out there, but I also had met some incredibly gifted intuitive people, so I was game for a $20 chance.

She spoke while she created a portrait of a little girl. "This little girl has a rattle or something, and she is trying desperately to get your attention."

I thought it was probably the spirit of my little sister. "What's she trying to tell me?"

"I can't tell… It's like she's jumping up and down and shaking her rattle back and forth for you to notice her."

When I got home from that trip, I put the portrait of the little girl on the table in my bedroom. I began to notice that every time guests walked past my bedroom door—even if the light was off—they would ask about the drawing. And whenever I walked through or past the room, I felt the girl's energy as if she were beckoning me to look at her. I felt like she might come to life, like a character in a movie, and tell me what I was supposed to know.

Since hearing Bruce say he was proud of me, I had been reading all kinds of spiritual books, including *Conversations with God* by Neal Walsh, which introduced me to the idea of automatic writing. I'd begun to practice automatic writing, especially when I was home at my cabin.

I understood the concept of writing a question and then allowing the answer to come through my hands without thinking about it, writing as quickly as I could; that part really worked for me. There didn't seem to be any way to validate that what I wrote was "received" or accurate or truthful. Still, sometimes, messages came through my hands that seemed to defy my logical mind. I asked about the little girl in the drawing and received the message, *The little girl in the drawing wishes for you to speak for her. There are many young girls in the dark place. You must light the way for the children.*

Over the course of the next year or so—right up until I left for Mozambique—I continued to receive information via automatic writing, eventually filling thirteen journals. The messages indicated I would write books, study family dynamics, talk on the radio, work with diplomats, and go to Africa. I felt as if I had stepped into the Twilight Zone. Those spiritual messages, along with other signs and my ongoing search for redemption, were the reason I went to Africa.

# 3

⊸∘⟨⟩∘⊸

On Mother's Day 2002, I was in Amarillo, Texas. They'd had quite a hailstorm, and I was there checking roofs for our claim-holders.

I was heading back to my hotel after lunch, and as I pulled into an intersection, I saw the silver grill of a Ford Ranger coming straight at my door. In a split second, I knew the driver would never be able to stop. With my foot pushed hard into the brake, I turned toward the Ranger so only the corner of his bumper would hit me.

The blow was quick and hard. It sent me straight up in the air, and I hit my head on the ceiling. The world fell silent, and time seemed to stop. I vaguely noticed the traffic light still cycling—green, yellow, red—but nobody moved.

Mom's repeat advice that I'd better wear my seatbelt flashed through my mind. I had never used seatbelts. My dad had been in a tractor accident when I was a kid. The tractor had rolled, and he would have been dead if he had not been thrown clear. That incident had left me with the belief that it was better to be thrown free of the vehicle than to be trapped by a seatbelt. I had never worn one, even after establishing my career in insurance.

I discovered that my car could still move, so I limped it over to a nearby parking lot. I sat there, shaking my head to clear the daze. Then, at some point, I got out of my car and people rushed toward me.

A baldish man, slightly older than me, shoved a business card into my hand. "That kid totally blew the stoplight. I'll testify for you. I saw the whole thing."

A slim brunette in a floral dress came running up to me, her Mother's Day corsage flying petal by petal into the wind. She was very upset. "I'm sorry. I'm sorry," she said over and over again. I couldn't make sense of her; I knew she was not

14

the person who had been in the truck. I had seen a boy or a young man.

Everything was a jumble. I looked at my car. The dash was cracked in half, and my front wheel was angled in sharply at the bottom. I wondered how I had made it to the parking lot. The daze in my head thickened as I called my supervisor, Brenda. She said she would come get me.

Finally, the young man from the truck appeared, but instead of talking to me, he turned to the woman with the corsage. "I'm sorry, Mom," he told her. "I was waving at you. I didn't see the light."

After a quick check at the Amarillo ER, I drove home to Colorado in a rental car. When I got some clarity about the extent of my injuries, the news wasn't terrible. The chiropractor said my back would need six months to heal and that I would need to see him three times a week over the course of that time. There was no way I could see the doctor that often while doing Cat work, so I needed to take some down-time before getting back into the field.

I considered making a Workers' Compensation claim. But my boss warned me that if I did, I might have trouble getting back onto the Cat team. So for a while I would be living on $3,000 less per month. I did not have savings, but between credit cards and a home equity line of credit, I had enough credit to last six short months. I recognized the potential risk of going more than $18,000 in debt. But when I got back to Cat, I could pay that money back within a year.

The truth is that the idea of being off the road excited me. I looked forward to spending more time in my lovely mountain cabin, especially now that the renovations were complete. I loved the aspen tongue-and-groove walls and floors, the luxurious views, and the big rose-stone fireplace that made up the wall between the living room and bathroom. I loved my home—and now, finally, I would have time to enjoy it.

Over the next six months I worked at my company's local office handling local claims so I could get to the chiropractor at lunch. Since the nearest office was more than an hour from my cabin, my day included a long commute. Still, the windshield time left me ample opportunity to contemplate my spiritual studies. Once in a while an inspection would allow me to slip off to the hot springs for a fifteen-minute soak on my lunch hour.

But at the end of the six months, when I was released from the chiropractor to return to my Cat job, the company had established a freeze on hiring in that department. My planned-for return to the great job and salary never happened, and when the six months was over, I called a credit counseling organization.

Their advice? "You just don't make enough money for us to be able to help you. You probably need to file bankruptcy."

I took a deep breath, got online, and found an attorney.

A few days later, as I approached the attorney's office for the first time, I was nervous. I did not have much experience with the legal system, and I had no experience backing out on my financial obligations. I showed up right on time, with my paperwork in tow.

The attorney's office was a bit...*dated*. From its hiding place behind filing cabinets, the dark paneling whispered "1972," and the flat-pile gold carpet looked to be the same vintage. Books and papers were stacked everywhere. The attorney's lack of pretention made me like him even before I really met him.

His name was Tom Wisdom. (I figured "Wisdom" was a good omen.) He took notes on a legal pad as he interviewed me. I explained how I had gotten into the financial mess, and he explained how things would go moving forward. His voice was soothing and a bit run together, like a grandfather saying the rosary—a low, steady drone that put me into a hypnotic place of calm.

Weeks later, Tom and I stood together in front of a bankruptcy judge. He must have noticed me fidgeting. "Everything's going to be fine, Amy," he soothed. "They almost never turn anybody down. The hearing is practically a formality."

But Tom's calm refused to rub off on me. *Why did I wear this suit? Will the judge think I look too wealthy to need bankruptcy? Do I look as nervous as I feel? Do I look as guilty as I feel?*

The judge's features, voice, and mannerisms reminded me of "Judge Judy." She was efficient to the point of being abrupt, and she barely looked up from her papers as Tom presented my case. She continued to look down as she said to me, "Do you understand the ramifications of what you are doing today?"

"Yes, your honor. I do." Then suddenly, as if I had startled her, she looked up at me.

I held steady and looked her in the eyes, holding my breath for whatever was coming next. Her gavel slammed down like the gavel of God, and I was the one startled.

Tom started packing up. For him it was just another day at the office; for me, it was a moment that would change my life forever.

"That's it? It's over? No more calls? No more harassment?"

"Yeah. That's all there is to it."

In something like three minutes, my entire debt—$50,000?—was just gone. There was nothing more to say.

As I climbed into my SUV and headed home, my relief quickly faded. What was I going to tell my parents? Every time I thought of them lately, my face flushed with shame. My parents believed in living within your means—and teaching your children to live within their means. Besides, Mom had worked at a bank, and money was a subject she took seriously. (In Minnesota, most people take most things seriously.) I remembered Mom teaching me, more than once, how to balance my checkbook. I felt like my bankruptcy would make them feel as ashamed as I did.

I decided I just wouldn't tell them.

# 4

After the bankruptcy, I threw myself even harder into the one thing that was working for me—my spiritual study. A friend had introduced me to Unity Church in the Rockies, and I had become good friends with the minister. He could tell a great story, and his sermons were provocative, leaving congregants no choice but to ponder his message all week long. After church hopping for years, I finally felt at home.

Unity felt like a place where I could enjoy an open and exciting relationship with the Divine. I had attended the Catholic Church my entire childhood, and I spent time at the local Lutheran Church as well, often seeking solace there during my tumultuous teen years. I loved to soak up the energy of the church building, and no wonder. My genetic ancestors (that is, my birth ancestors) had been church builders, and my family (Gillespie) had historically been caretakers of churches. When I found Unity in the Rockies, I found my spiritual community.

Lately, I'd also been meeting a lot of authors from the new-age community. At a book signing in Boulder, I met Rhonda Britten, the author of a book and life-coaching program called *Fearless Living*. The program, which focuses on living as your true, authentic self and getting out of fear-based victim thinking, really called to me. If a person follows the tenets of Fearless Living, they will move steadily toward self-actualization. I was fascinated.

I'd gone recently to the New Age Trade Show in Denver, where I met Louise Hay herself (renowned author and founder of Hay House Publishing), along with a number of other popular new-age authors (such as Doreen Virtue, Dan Millman, Ted Andrews, and Sonia Choquette) whose books share spiritual tools for everyday living.

I'd also been reading a lot of spiritual books. *The Path of Least Resistance* had presented me with the idea that I could stop fighting my life and start embracing it, even though the approach seemed to conflict with my Minnesota work ethic. Because of the ideas in this book, I was moving in a direction that felt easy and harmonic, and I was experiencing the major truth that our thoughts determine the quality of our lives.

I wanted to spend more time learning about these things. I started fantasizing in earnest about making my living as an intuitive and a Fearless Living Coach. Once again, I thought maybe I had found a career that would help me support lasting changes in other people's lives. What a life it could be!

But I didn't get too far down that road. At some point I would flash on an image of Mom giving me "the look." She had always told me I could do or be anything I set my mind to. But I am quite sure she did not—in any way, shape, or form— intend for "Psychic" to be on the list of possible careers.

One evening at the cabin, I left my laptop running while I went to take a shower. When I came back, there was Latin text on the screen—a couple pages worth. I tried but couldn't remember where I'd been online when I got up. *What in the world is this! Where did this come from?*

I copied the text and ran it through Google Translate. The translation didn't work well, but I was able to gather that it referenced the Essenes, who lived over 2,000 years ago and included (among others) Jesus, Joseph and Mary, St. Ann, John the Baptist, and John the Evangelist. The Essenes considered themselves to be a separate people because of the illumination of their inner life and their knowledge of hidden mysteries. They are widely believed to be the authors of the Dead Sea Scrolls.

I took a couple of passages from the translation and ran that through yet another Google search. It brought me to an article on a psychic/paranormal message site (worldITC.org). The information there had to do with saving children and referenced Anne de Guigné, a girl who had died in 1922 when she was eleven years old. Her messages and photo had come through people's televisions and fax machines. She discussed the responsibilities of the adults responsible for children's tragic, premature deaths and the retribution those adults would one day face.

Then an image came up. It looked exactly like the little girl in the intuitive drawing, right down to the clothes! As I searched further, I discovered Anne had been declared "Venerable" by Pope John Paul II in 1990. To me this image's similarity to the intuitive drawing, along with everything I learned about Anne, was clear evidence that God or some divine entity was trying to get my attention. I had learned a long time before this that so-called "coincidences" were always at work in my life. They were there on my path long before *The Path of Least Resistance.*

The material about Anne's concern for children matched information I was getting during automatic writing sessions. The most dramatic, and perhaps most interesting and confusing message, was a call to "help the children of darkness." As I scribbled down the words, I was flooded with emotion. Sadness and desperation took over. I knew these were the feelings of the "children of darkness," but I had no idea who they were.

Intuitively, I knew the word *darkness* did not reference race. It related to the emotions they felt, the emotions I was feeling in that moment. The darkness was a place in the hearts of these children, wherever and whoever they were. And they needed my help, so I'd better find them.

In addition, I was starting to remember more and more about childhood encounters with Spirit. When I was a little girl, lying in bed in our old farmhouse before going to sleep, I would sometimes have visions. Lifelike images of people and things came into my mind as though running on a filmstrip. Visions would disappear unless I stayed very still, so that is what I did. I did not tell anybody about these experiences. Though I had heard stories of faithful Catholics having heavenly visions, their visions seemed much grander than mine—and so far away in time and space. Those were saintly people, not little farm girls from Minnesota. I didn't think my parents, the local priest, Father Kellen, or any of the other people in my life would understand.

One vision that I had a number of times revealed an unusual staircase. The stairs were like those in a hayloft— simple and steep and open in back. The nineteen or twenty steps went up to a small landing; then the stairs went down again. I was always under them, trying to crawl through to the top, but I was too big to fit. I experienced that vision so many times that it stuck with me into my adulthood.

As spring became summer and summer became fall, I grew increasingly preoccupied with my financial situation. One day I called Tom Wisdom to find out when my house would be foreclosed on and my car would be repossessed. With alarm in his voice, he told me that he had reaffirmed those loans in the bankruptcy. All I would have to do afterward is start making payments. The only problem is that I learned that about five months too late. By that time, I was no longer invested in my former life, and the news about the reaffirmed loans was not too hard to hear. My spiritual messages were pointing away from, not toward, the status quo.

I still needed a way to get by until I figured it all out. Since I couldn't get back on the Cat teams and I was already on a salary that was cut by $3,000 a month, I couldn't afford to keep driving my SUV to the insurance office, so I quit to take a job at a hotel near my cabin. The money I had left after the bankruptcy was nearly gone, and although I had received my certification as a Fearless Living Coach, I was not yet making enough money to support myself. I badgered God for more signs, and I got them through automatic writing sessions, though much of the content continued to be vague.

When I asked, "How will I maintain my finances during this time?" I received this response: *We will guide you. All is planned and coming to you in its time.* Even as I wished for more information and clearer guidance about my financial issues, I trusted the message had come from a divine source, so I trudged forward faithfully.

One night while I was lying in bed, the weight of the message that I was to help the children of darkness just felt crushing—as though an actual weight were on my chest. I prayed: "Look, God, I am willing. I can go anywhere, do anything. But please tell me very clearly where I'm going and what you want me to do. Please tell me clearly. I can go."

The day after that prayer, I attended Quest—an ongoing class at Unity that was bringing me further into the fold and helping me explore my spiritual experiences. That night we looked at Biblical stories as metaphors that we could apply to our own lives. For example, the story of Lot's wife (who looked back on Sodom and Gomorrah and turned into a pillar of salt) reminded us that whenever we remain emotionally attached to something in the past, we get stuck.

Next, we looked at the story of David and Goliath. Our question for the week was "Who or what is the Goliath, the unconquerable foe, in your life?" I pondered this question all through the night.

The next morning was cool and fresh. I drove to Starbucks, just a few blocks from my cabin, and smiled at the continuity the building represented for me. It brought back family vacations from my teenage years (when it had been a 7-Eleven). Those memories were warm and happy, and I loved that my little town brought them to mind. I felt like Woodland Park had always been my true home. I enjoyed the majestic view of Pikes Peak and ordered up my standard Caramel Macchiato, with no thought to the weight I had been steadily gaining since leaving Cat.

As I waited, I glanced down at the newspaper stand. There was the *New York Times*. I never read the newspaper, didn't watch the news. But I was moved to pick it up, and after my fervent prayer for a sign, I did as I was told. The article on the front page spoke of thirty million Africans with HIV/AIDS and hundreds of thousands of orphans. My first emotional response was defeat. My stomach deflated, like when the air leaves an over-filled balloon. "There's Goliath," I said out loud.

"Amy?" My macchiato (which at $3.85 suddenly seemed shamefully extravagant) was ready. I set the newspaper back on the rack. I'd read only a few paragraphs, but it had been enough. I glanced at Pikes Peak, went home, and started packing.

# 5

---

Over the course of the next several weeks, I talked with friends to find a way to volunteer with AIDS orphans in Africa. I was seeking my path to help the children. When three of my contacts suggested the same organization, I took the Universe's hint. I called the phone number one of the girls had given me. Before the end of that conversation, I committed to be part of a team of aid workers going to Mozambique, Africa.

I would spend a year working for the organization in a capacity to be decided later. But first, our training would take six months, during which time we would be required to donate a total of $7,000. I gave them the money left from my insurance settlement—$3,500. So I would need to raise another $3,500 before the six months were over.

The East Coast training campus had several buildings—a couple of dorms, housing for employees, classroom buildings, and offices. Volunteers were doubled, tripled, and sometimes quadrupled in small bedrooms. Given that each volunteer had donated $6,000 or $7,000 (depending on how long they were going to volunteer), a huge amount of money was flowing through the organization.

But there was no sign of money at this facility. The buildings were not particularly well built or well maintained, and really, everything seemed to be a crapshoot. Computers didn't work, the Internet went down, we got snowed in, and cars got stuck in snow and mud. Often vehicles would have to stay at the bottom of the driveway, making it necessary to hike the mile or more to the top—in blizzards. It was brutal.

At first, I wasn't too concerned about the disarray and disrepair; I figured that most of the money should go to help people who really needed it. But my concerns kept mounting. For example, all of the volunteers were assigned chores, and the schedule was strictly imposed. But there was no quality control. One of my teammates contracted giardia, a digestive parasite that plagued her all through training and beyond. Subpar sanitation was more serious than thin walls. But I kept telling myself that this organization was my route to Africa. I hung in there.

The volunteers were from everywhere: Japan, Brazil, the United States, Germany, England, and a few other places I couldn't figure out from the accents. This was my first introduction to an international community. I had been raised in a small Minnesota town. So on one hand it was a new experience for me. On the other hand, the environment at the training facility—everyone dining and relaxing together—made me nostalgic for my hometown café.

Volunteers were divided into teams, based on where we were going. Our team had six members scheduled to leave together for Mozambique. Most of us were complete strangers, but Lindsay and Chris were a dating couple in their twenties. Both of them were experienced national and international travelers, and I would soon be very grateful for their savvy.

The rest of the team was made up of very young women: Briana, Rachel, and Terra. Briana was all peace and love; Rachel was spontaneous and in-the-moment; Terra was enthusiastic and erratic.

I was the sixth and final group member, ten to twenty years older than the rest of the team. Throughout my time with the organization, I was one of the oldest volunteers, and I felt it. In contrast with the young, lithe people around me, I felt old and fat. Yet I trusted that God had given me young teammates for a reason.

Brian, a man in his twenties who had been to Mozambique, was our coach. His role was to help us understand the country and the work we would be doing there. On a practical level, though, he mostly shared tips for fundraising. He had been to Mozambique, and he could help us tell compelling stories—or so the thinking went. I have always wished that, having been to Mozambique, he would have shared more practical information about how to live there. For example, he could have said something like, "Make sure you have a copy of your itinerary and contact numbers before you get into any vehicle." Maybe he thought we should have to figure stuff like that out for ourselves, perhaps like he had. Or maybe, like many young people, he was still a bit self-absorbed. In any case, many things would have been different if we—and probably he—had received more thorough and sensible training.

There was a curriculum for Portuguese, the official language of Mozambique, and we had lessons every day for at least an hour. Lindsay had extensive Spanish and seemed to be grasping Portuguese pretty easily, with Chris right behind her. The rest of us struggled. After one Portuguese lesson on verbs, Rachel and I asked the rest of the team, "What's a conjugation?" As if my struggles with Portuguese weren't enough, even my English grammar—or lack thereof—would prove to be a handicap.

On our own, we studied the history and culture of Mozambique. We learned about the war years—first, the war for independence from Portugal, which the Mozambicans won in 1975. The Portuguese were given twenty-four hours to get out of the country and could only take twenty kilos' worth of possessions with them. Before leaving, the Portuguese had dumped their heavy construction equipment into the ocean and poured cement into city septic systems. They were determined to not leave the Mozambicans what they had worked to build.

The government that was established following independence was communist and supported by Cuba and the Soviet Union. Their crackdown on opposing forces plunged the country into civil war lasting from 1977 to 1992. The central government executed tens of thousands of people and sent many more to re-education camps, where many thousands more died. During these wars, fighting soldiers would camp in game preserves and eat the wildlife. As a result, the wildlife populations were decimated. The People's Republic of Mozambique (which was later renamed "The Republic of Mozambique") was off to a rough start. Even now, the effects of the war for independence from Portugal and the effects of the civil war that followed can be observed on the infrastructure and environment in Mozambique, especially in the lack of sanitation and poor healthcare.

We received some information about the exchange rate—basically that it varied wildly and that we should pad our proposals for funds in order to accommodate the fluctuations. That was very important information. The fluctuations meant we never knew how much money we would have when we received donations or how far the money would stretch. It made for some difficult math whenever we applied for and/or received U.S. funds.

We were told of parasites and worms that could burrow under your skin and make their way to your heart or brain if left unchecked. We learned a bit about sanitation in Mozambique. We learned the dangers of unsafe water. Yet we didn't learn any practical information about how to deal with hygiene in the bush, where latrines are few and far between and running water is nonexistent.

We learned that we had to be cautious about taking photos in public places or we might be arrested. We learned that the buses would be exceedingly crowded. We learned about "survival mode," your body's response to being in a constant state of fight or flight. Because of this phenomenon, the average female Peace Corps volunteer misses her menstrual period for six months upon moving to Mozambique. Survival mode can also mean that you lose peripheral vision and feel fatigued.

We learned the rule, "Boil it, peel it, cook it, or forget it." In other words, if we were going to drink water that was not bottled, we had to boil it first. We shouldn't eat popsicles because they were usually made with water that hadn't been boiled. We could not eat raw food unless the food could be peeled; there were too many bacteria that were unfamiliar to our bodies. Mostly, we should rely on cooked food.

Much of what we learned about Mozambique came from casual conversations with other people who had been there:

"Be sure you study your Portuguese." "Be prepared to make up theatrical skits for teaching, as that is how they learn." This last tip became crucial to my work; there are sixteen tribal languages in Mozambique. "Theatre" was necessary for communicating in spite of language barriers.

Returning volunteers also spoke of the almost constant overt sexual invitations they received in Mozambique. They said it seemed like Mozambicans could smell a new volunteer and that a pack of suitors would appear out of the bush. Combine that with their warnings about the importance of local community practices—"Pay attention to what the local Mozambicans do. Some things are different from one place to the next. If you don't see people going into a Mozambican house, don't go in; you might get engaged by just stepping inside for a cup of coffee!"—we were beginning to see some of the cultural issues we would face.

We learned that the word *Muzungu* meant white person, or a person of European descent. The word is from the Kiswahili language and literally means "dizzy person" based on the confused looks of the first European people who came to the African Great Lakes Region. Culturally, the word also carries the implication of "rich person."

We got a lot of information, some of it confusing, but overall, I wasn't too worried. (I didn't know how much I didn't know.) As for bugs and worms, I had grown up on a farm and was unfazed by the subject. And malaria? I hadn't been sick in years. I also felt like I could handle the men; I was not a naïve twenty-year-old, and I was going there to help the children, not to find a husband. Only my struggles to learn the language really gave me pause. But I had a job to do for God. I was sure He would sort things out for me.

I took a week away from the training program to volunteer at Heifer Project and learn how to do organic farming. Milking cows, feeding goats, and gathering eggs felt grounding and nurturing. My mind was calm for the first time since I had joined Cat, more than four years earlier.

We were also offered a week's HIV prevention and awareness training with the Red Cross in Albany, New York. We had to cover the price of the training, about $70 per person, but we all felt it was imperative because we were headed to work in a region of Africa where HIV infection rates were estimated to be as high as 70%. This region was called "the corridor." It crossed the narrowest part of Mozambique and ran along Highway EN6, a very heavily traveled route from Zimbabwe to the Indian Ocean.

Trade routes and traveling truck drivers often attracted sex workers, and because of sex trafficking the corridor had a much higher HIV rate than the rest of the country. In the country overall, infection rates were listed at around 25 to 30% (depending on where you got your information). I've since learned that *the corridor* became synonymous with higher HIV rates and because of the stigma associated with HIV, the term became offensive and is now rarely used.

Before the training in Albany, I knew nothing about HIV except that it was a sexually transmitted disease. The main instructor, an African man named Julian Bane, was an engaging teacher, and the forty-hour training was very thorough. We learned all the facts of HIV prevention, statistics, and transmission. For example, did you know that you need ninety days after your most recent possible exposure to HIV before the results can be trusted? It can take that long for the antibodies to reach measurable levels.

Our instructor, who was from South Africa, felt a strong mission to help fellow Africans learn the facts about HIV so they could protect themselves from early and certain death. I felt a surge of pride as he presented me with a South African bracelet, my reward for getting the highest score on the final exam. "It's up to you now," he told me. "Go help my people."

One volunteer, headed to Botswana, purchased anatomical dolls to take with her for AIDS/HIV training and prevention. I thought it was a very clever idea, one that would provide an option less abstract than, say, putting a condom on a Coke bottle. It might even be a lighthearted way to get at the problem. But the dolls were over $200 for a family, which was out of my price range.

Sometimes I was uncertain I had gotten the original message right and uncertain whether God had intended for me to go to Mozambique. In those times, I would send up a prayer: "I said I could go if you would point me in the right direction and this is the organization you pointed me to... Please help..." God seemed to be sympathetic, sending frequent reminders of the synchronicity of the universe.

One day I decided to head into the computer room to practice Portuguese by reading some Mozambican newspaper articles. I noticed an African gentleman at one of the other computers and struck up a conversation.

His name was Jean Manirakiza, and he was from Burundi. Happily, I said, "Oh, yeah? I know some people from Burundi!" Jean didn't acknowledge my response, believing, I imagine, that I was being daft. (After all, it's not like everybody in the country knows each other.) But then I said more. "Yeah, I know the Nzigamasabo family."

Now he turned to me, incredulous. "Ernest? And Alain and Patrice?"

I nodded. "They were at my wedding."

Jean had grown up as best friends with Ernest, who my sister-in-law had helped to immigrate to the United States. We bonded over the "small, small world." This was the kind of coincidence that restored my faith that the Universe was with me.

# 6

After six weeks of training, it was time to start fundraising. Brian guided us to fill three-ring binders with photos of Mozambican children, and he helped us work out a spiel to go with the photos. We explained where we were going and why, and then we asked for donations. I was always very aware that I had to raise $3,500 in order to be able to get on the plane. I felt the pressure of that number.

Each day as we set out, the whole team would load into the decrepit sixteen-passenger van and settle in for the commute to our fundraising location. On the road, we practiced our Portuguese and got to know each other. I learned that Lindsay majored in physics and Chris in architecture. It was his dream to design "green" buildings, and he was excited to try his skills in Mozambique. I also learned that Briana had come from New Mexico, Rachel was from Oregon, and Terra's quirks were more than just eccentricity.

When we got to the site—no matter the weather—we all lumbered out of the van and started trying to get the attention of people walking by. I vividly remember one trip to Harvard. I felt like a twelve-year-old Girl Scout as I walked the streets, approaching person after person for funds. With temperatures ten degrees below zero, nobody was interested.

One gruff man added insult to injury, yelling at me, "Lady, your story is old and so are you!" Usually I am pretty resilient, especially when it comes to grouchy strangers, but I wasn't getting quality sleep and I was so, so cold. A lump rose in my throat. My eyes were already watering from the cold, and now tears of frustration and fear were adding to the mix. Then my sniffles turned into sobs, right there on the freezing streets of Harvard.

31

If the cranky man had been unkind, my inner voice was brutal. *Oh my God, I'm not going to get the money and I'm not going to Africa and I'm not going to help the children I'm meant to help. I have nowhere to go. My home is gone, my vehicle, my credit, my job. I'm going to have to tell my parents!*

The messages had told me to be alert as I looked for signs that would guide me. Not long before I had left for training, I received this message: *There will be symbols and obscure messages, like the ones from the children…Do not fear. You are well guided and protected.*

But there did not seem to be any symbols in Harvard. I was having an old-school fit, stomping my feet and crying in frustration, like a child coming in from the cold, late for naptime.

Brian rescued me, hauling me into Peet's Coffee shop, where he helped me hit the reset button. "You've got to let it go, Amy. Just relax and forget about it. Everybody has a bad day now and then."

"I know, Brian, but I've had bad days since day one. I haven't even raised $500. I'm never going to get to Africa this way. You've been there, so you have stories that inspire people. But I can't inspire people with stories about a place I don't know."

Eventually we made it back onto the streets, but I never did raise considerable funds in Harvard. In my experience, walking up to strangers was never a successful fundraising approach.

About that time, Brian brought us background on several locations in Mozambique. We got to choose which location and facility we would join. We studied the options carefully. Most of the team—everybody but me and Terra—chose to go to Lamego, a small town in the middle of EN6, the east–west road from the ocean to Zimbabwe. There, the organization has a vocational school that trains people for jobs in construction, agriculture, and animal husbandry.

I was interested in a street kids' school called *Formigas Do Futuro* (Ants of the Future), located in the city of Chimoio, a city with a population of 400,000. The city's name meant "small heart," and it is closer than Lamego to the Chimanimani Mountains that mark the border between Zimbabwe and Mozambique. The fresh, cool mountain air called to me. I knew I would never survive a sweltering humid climate, which was how Lamego was described.

*Formigas Do Futuro* is a five-days-a-week school for elementary-age children, in a city where most public schools have classes only three days a week. That piqued my interest because I imagined that, there, I could answer my call to help the children. But they didn't have any openings for volunteers.

On the same property as *Formigas Do Futuro,* there was a teacher-training college that was sending eighty to ninety teachers a year into the rural areas of Mozambique, where each teacher might have as many as seventy students. The school had an opening for someone who would go out to assist graduated teachers with their curriculum planning. I liked the idea of going into the bush and seeing rural communities. I was also excited about the fresh air and cool climate that blessed Chimoio, which had been known as Vila Pery (village of health) during the Portuguese colonization. Whether it was those things or simply God's whisper, Chimoio was the place that called to me. That was the one!

Terra also decided to go to Chimoio to help train teachers. We would be a pair.

One thing that emerged from a conversation with Lindsay was the realization that our training implied that our aid work would be a one-way exchange. Our trainers seemed to suggest that *we* would be the ones doing the giving—period. I don't recall that there was any mention that we would have a reciprocal relationship, a relationship in which we would also receive. Now I believe that representing aid work this way is a disservice to people in developing nations, undervaluing just how much they give back to the "rich" people who come to "help" them. And it was a disservice to us because it did not begin to explore the depths of how we would grow through this experience. I still wonder who lives a richer life—an American or a Mozambican.

I don't recall ever being asked to reflect on why we were going to Africa or why we had volunteered. We were encouraged to consider creating our own projects, but we were not given support to understand relationships and procedures that might be a needed part of those projects. Maybe Brian was supposed to help us with that kind of thing, or maybe it had not been considered by the organization. The thing is, it left a whole lot of "figuring it out as you go along."

Hoping for better fundraising results in warmer weather, we headed south. Our accommodations along the way were not any more elegant than our van. We stayed mostly in churches, where we shared bathrooms and inevitably ran out of hot water.

We slept on the church floors. Thankfully I had brought an inflatable mattress, the kind with a little tube that you blow into like a swimming pool floater. It gave me some protection from the ice-cold tile floor; if I had slept without it, I'm not sure I could have functioned. I took it in stride, counting the church floors and cold showers as good practice for the discomforts I knew I would encounter in Mozambique.

The ancient van labored, stop by stop, all the way to Raleigh, North Carolina. There I discovered that God had a new symbol for me. We were fundraising door-to-door, and as I walked toward my next house (still stinging from rejection at the last one), I noticed that the front door was open. A woman came to the door, and I soon found that she was South African. She was excited to learn about my trip and happy to help fund it since she knew personally of the troubles in Mozambique. She introduced me to her daughter, Malika, and gave me cookies. I left that home truly fortified; it was so lovely to be welcomed by someone—anyone—on this journey.

The open door was the symbol. Anywhere that I found a door open, I was successful. I mean this literally: if a home's front door or even garage was open, the residents donated money to support my trip. Any house that had a closed door? Well, let's just say the door remained closed.

I had received the message in an automatic writing session to not worry about money but to just let it come to me. Now that message was beginning to make sense.

My new symbol and my experience with *The Path of Least Resistance* served me well. Throughout my journey, my least effort, my most humble approach, always raised the most money. I even started having fun with the North Carolina fundraising. Since the holidays were coming, Terra and I went caroling one night and raised more money than ever before.

One night while we were still on the road, a few of us sat around talking. I told the rest of the team about Fearless Living and how each of us has a core fear that drives us. We went around the circle, figuring out each person's fear and freedom. The team laughed when I told them my fear was being ordinary and that my freedom was beauty. Another team member said that her fear was looking stupid and her freedom was trust. The other volunteers were surprised by our fears, but I knew better. A person's fears are always the thing nobody would ever guess because people overcompensate for their fears.

I told them about Fearless Living's take on the relationship between fears and freedoms: basically, that intersection is the key to the authentic living, the key that will set you free. If my teammate could learn to trust, her fears of looking stupid would diminish. She would be free. If I stopped fearing being ordinary, I would stop overcompensating for it by running all over doing *extraordinary* things; and if I could just see the beauty in every situation, I would be free.

After our talk, I had a conversation with myself. Was I operating from my highest self? Was I demonstrating my understanding of spiritual principles? Was I acting as a certified Fearless Living Coach? Absolutely not! I was a mess. I was totally operating from a fear-based place, crying in the streets of Concord, flailing through fundraising in too many cities to track. I knew I needed to refocus and set a bolder course for my mission.

On April first, I attended Sunday morning services at the Unity Church in Chapel Hill, North Carolina. It was just what I needed to catch my breath and make a new plan. Nothing could have refreshed me as much as their service that day, April Fool's Day, which they called "Funny Sunday." As the minister came out dressed like Johnny Carson with the psychic turban on his head, the choir sang, "Forget your dharma! Live your karma!" The church roared with laughter. I was restored and renewed.

After the service, the minister apologized to me for the silly antics and pointed out that the congregation's reverence was usually as intense as the laughter had been that day. He tried to explain how they had come to sing crazy songs like "How Great Thou Fart" on Funny Sunday. I laughed 'til tears ran down my face. The release was so welcome. The community felt familiar to me, like my own Unity family.

Maybe it was the contrast between how I had been feeling before the service and how I felt after; at any rate, I decided this would be my last fundraising trip. I was done with the absurd scenario of driving all over God's creation knocking on doors, hoping to pick up a dollar. Writing had gotten me out of a few scrapes in the past. I thought writing might be the answer again.

I told the administrators of the program that I was done with the door-to-door thing and that I would be writing letters to prospective donors. I didn't present the idea as a topic of conversation but as a decision. They were fine with the idea, even happy that somebody had another fundraising approach.

I began to prepare letters telling how I had come to this mission. Via snail-mail, I sent out about 400 letters, and one in ten recipients sent funds. (I kept track.) One by one, those responses came in with small checks until my $3,500 fundraising requirement was met. In just three months, I had earned the privilege to get on the plane to Mozambique with my visa in hand. Prior to the letters (by walking door-to-door and standing on freezing street corners), I had raised only about $700, with two hundred of that coming from the night we had gone Christmas caroling.

One night while we were still in North Carolina, a few of us started sharing some observations about our teammate, Terra. She wasn't doing very well. Once when she and Brian had gone to a local police station to register us as fundraisers, Terra had simply stood up and started screaming. No explanation was given, and no apology was offered. Another time while we were out door-to-door, Terra had pulled wads of bills from her backpack, saying over and over, "I just have all this money. I want to give this away. I want to give this to the children."

We were worried about her—worried that she might pose a danger to herself, the rest of us, and even the people of Mozambique. We were also concerned that if her condition worsened while she was in Mozambique, she might get herself into real danger.

Together, we decided to talk with Jytte, the headmistress, about the possibility that Terra needed to go home. Like the other Danish people I've known, Jytte was down-to-earth and straightforward. I couldn't help but imagine her as the woman Karen Blixen (*Out of Africa*) would have matured into. The similarities between her and Meryl Streep's portrayal of Blixen—same voice, similar personality—were remarkable. I had loved her from the start, and I trusted that she would know what to do about Terra.

So when we returned from the Carolina trip, we told Jytte our concerns. And Jytte understood. She said that she had seen other volunteers who consciously wanted to help, but who were actually driven by a deeper need to overcome low self-esteem.

That observation hit a bit too close to home for me. It helped me get clear that this mission of mine was not just a response to God's call (though it was definitely that). It was also about assuaging my guilt—guilt over my recent financial failure and guilt about my older, more devastating mistakes. Was I punishing myself for the bankruptcy? Was I punishing myself for not being able to help my little sister? Was I still seeking my own redemption? I saw that all of those things—to a greater or lesser degree—were in play, right alongside my mission.

Jytte was discreet, and one day Terra was gone. So then we were five. And I was the only person going to Chimoio. Though I would be alone, I was relieved. I had enjoyed Terra very much as a friend and a person, but if we had gone to the same town, I would have appointed myself her caretaker. I did not believe that was my true mission.

Before we left for Mozambique, the team compared notes about training and came to the consensus that perhaps we had not joined the most stable organization. The advertisements had been impressive—slick buildings, inspired volunteers, and persuasive information. And in fact, the organization had started with a great idea. A couple of teachers had put their money together and taken off in a bus to teach around the world. But the organization had grown too quickly. Soon they had too many volunteers and (literally) more money than they knew what to do with.

Somebody brought up the possibility of just quitting and going back to our previous lives. I said that I was definitely going to Mozambique. I had given the organization all of my savings and the thousands I'd raised. (My teammates didn't know the organization had *all* of my money. I had no previous life to return to.) Besides, I had a mission to track down Goliath, and I had been guided to this organization going to this country. There was nothing for me to do but follow the path at my feet.

The others chose the same route—to at least go and experience whatever came next. Like me, they felt that since they had invested so much time and money in the project, they should at least go see Mozambique. So, although Terra had headed home, the rest of us were going to see what we would see, experience what we would experience, and do what we could to help.

# 7

⟶⋄∘⟨⟩∘⋄⟵

Our flight from Newark brought us as far as London, where
we boarded a flight to Johannesburg. We had to travel through
South Africa so we could enter Mozambique through the
capital city of Maputo and file required paperwork. Altogether,
the trip took three days.

I was surprised that Johannesburg was so developed. The
paved roads were as good as any in the States, and American
businesses were everywhere—here a KFC, there a McDonalds.
We spent a night in a small, humble Johannesburg hotel. There
was no heat, even though it was thirty degrees outside. The
cream-colored ceramic tile floors were frigid, and the windows
were single-pane glass with wooden frames, no more airtight
than those you could have found in 1940s America. Inside the
rooms, the cement walls were painted a too-bright orange, and
my construction knowledge (thanks to Cat) told me the paint
was likely loaded with lead. The bathroom was simple but
adequate with hot, running water.

The motel had some surprising touches of luxury. The
doors were at least three inches thick, and one of the "big five"
safari animals—lion, Cape buffalo, leopard, elephant, or
rhinoceros—had been carved into each one. The headboards,
too, were ornately carved, and the beds had mattresses like you
would find in the States. It wasn't exactly the Radisson, but the
hotel was serviceable.

The next morning, Chris and Lindsay led us through
purchasing bus tickets and finding the right bus to the
Mozambican border. Our bus was a modern double-decker.
When we got on the road, I saw perfectly "American" power
lines running along the steady stream of Mercedes and Toyotas
and every other familiar make.

My thought at the time was that we could have just as easily
been driving across Nebraska. In my naiveté I was glad I had

not signed up to volunteer in South Africa. I couldn't imagine what kind of aid work they could be doing in a place that was so developed. I remembered all of the ad campaigns I had seen and the missionaries who had come to my church raising funds to help the poor in South Africa. I thought also of Oprah's school. It seemed to me that those resources could have been used to help people with greater need.

Since then, I have learned a lot about the needs of the people in South Africa, and I have, of course, come to see that although their needs are different from the Mozambicans', they are no less real. Also, now I understand that donors are motivated by different types of need, and that is probably for the best.

At the South African/Mozambican border crossing, I was reminded of a trip my family had taken across the U.S. border into Juarez, Mexico; in a matter of minutes we left every imaginable amenity behind and were surrounded by cardboard-box homes and abject poverty. Such was the case at the South African/Mozambican border. On the Mozambican side, black bicycles replaced motor vehicles. These bikes, which looked like they had been used for generations, were loaded down not only with people but also with goats and chickens. And everywhere I saw pregnant women and women with babies tied to their backs with colorful fabric.

The clamor when we stepped into the Immigration building was something like you would expect at a high school basketball game, one with a noisy crowd and lots of children. And there was a noticeable odor hovering in the air, like a blend of dried fish, perspiration, and something else—a strong, exotic, disagreeable scent that I later came to recognize as the smell of Mozambican money.

The border-agents' desks had windows like you might have seen in U.S. banks in the 1950s, but there were no orderly lines. We were propelled forward in one surging mass. Watching the exchanges between the locals and the bureaucrats, I got the impression that the locals couldn't understand what was being said to them or what they were supposed to do next. For the most part, I was probably right. Though the national language in Mozambique is Portuguese, only about half the adult population is fluent.

The air was charged with desperation—"Get it now. Now or never." Over time, I found this attitude to be pervasive. Things can be taken away from you at any time so you had better "get yours" as quickly as possible. Now I know that the people at the border crossing that day (like every day) were just hoping to get everything right because of a desperate need to cross the border and complete a mission—find a sick relative, collect a dead body, show up for work, or simply get the heck out of Mozambique.

The hillsides around the border crossing were dirt, with brush here and there. A few small, roofless structures were higher up on the hill. I had heard about these in training. They were Mozambican latrines. An outhouse in Mozambique is like a kitty-litter box surrounded by bamboo for privacy. When you enter, you find dirt to pee on. (With any luck, the last person's pee had a chance to soak in before you got there.) If you had something "major" to do, you would pay to go to a "long-drop latrine," which has no seat but instead has a foot-print on each side of the hole to show you where to put your feet when you squat.

There was a lot of small trash scattered about—nothing whole or complete like a soda can—just bits of cloth, bits of paper, bits of wrappers. Much later I realized that these bits were quite likely litter from the outhouse.

Wild dogs were scavenging among the waste. All of them were pretty small, knee high at most. I did not see any white dogs, black dogs, or even black-and-white dogs. They were all various shades of brown, with ribs emerging through their hide that made them look striped. There was no interaction between the dogs and people. It was as if the dogs didn't exist for the people and the people didn't exist for the dogs. I felt like the dogs must be the product of my imagination.

Miraculously the whole team, which had been separated by the crowd inside, came out of the building at about the same time. We got back onto our bus, which now seemed quite luxurious, and settled in to enjoy our little box lunches and the fact that the chaos and panic were behind us.

It was well after dark when we arrived in the capital city of Maputo—or rather, its suburb, Machava. Once again, thank God for Chris and Lindsay! We never would have found the bus stop without their excellent command of Portuguese. Because of them, we ended up in the right place, an unremarkable cement building along the road, indistinguishable from dozens of others.

If Africa is "the dark continent," then Mozambique is the dark country. Outside lighting is virtually nonexistent. From the bus stop, we stumbled and fumbled through the streets. Around us, people were speaking languages I couldn't understand, none of which sounded like Portuguese. The murmur sounded like several different dialects; one group was speaking one language and the next group was speaking another. It made the darkness even darker.

A car came and whisked us away. I have no idea where it came from, if Chris and Lindsay had arranged it, or if it was a taxi sent by the organization; I was simply thankful to be back in a vehicle that felt familiar. After driving through the dark, dark streets for a few minutes, we arrived at a set of white cement buildings. The owner of the establishment shuffled us into a small cottage, where we found single beds and foam mattresses on the floor. The walls were dingy, but otherwise everything was clean.

I for one had no idea exactly where we were or who had been driving the car that brought us there. I found the thought a bit disturbing, but I didn't worry for long. Exhaustion took over, and I fell gratefully into bed.

# 8

In the morning there was a knock at the door. Two Mozambican men were looking for me! Reverend Zaccharias Gode, a man with a huge toothy smile, had come with his assistant to invite me to speak at the Unity Church in Maputo. I was very surprised to see him. Was this what they meant when they said that when we arrived, people would appear instantly out of the bush?

Rev. Gode and I had corresponded by email a few times, but I had told him only the date we would arrive, not where we would stay. I never learned how he figured out the details and appeared our very first morning in Machava to invite us to Sunday services the next day. We accepted, and a plan was made.

Early the next morning, Reverend Gode and his translator arrived in a white *chapa,* or passenger van, designed to carry sixteen people. It was a thousand times nicer than the one we had used fundraising in the States, and we were excited to get in. In Mozambique, chapas routinely hold thirty people; they are not full until someone's knees and elbows are poking you, or your lap is filled with a baby, a package, or a chicken. To drive around Mozambique with a half-full chapa is very rude because many people need a ride and giving them one takes nothing from you. Looking back, I saw that by only having seven people in that van, Reverend Gode was showing us a great honor—even though it cast him (and us) in a bad light with people who saw us.

As we drove along, I pointed out that each woman had a brightly colored piece of fabric, either securing her baby or tied around her waist. The translator explained that these were *capulanas,* a very important garment for women in Mozambique. Capulanas could be used to secure babies and other burdens, to provide warmth for the women and their children, and to afford some privacy, like a curtain, when privacy was called for.

Children were everywhere, and at least every third woman was pregnant. Many—or maybe most—of the women and girls (as young as five years old) had babies secured to their backs. Several women had five-gallon water jugs, firewood, or baskets of cashews on their heads in addition to babies on their backs. Even with their burdens, every woman I saw possessed remarkable grace.

We passed one tiny cement building after another, and the translator told us they were homes and shops. Otherwise, the streets were lined with little bamboo *bancas* (selling tables), some of which had plastic tarps stretched across four poles to make a bit of shelter. We gaped at bicycles laden with goats, bananas, chickens, firewood, and five-gallon jugs labeled "World Food Program."

Lindsay gasped, "Look. . . is that what I think it is?" The hand-painted sign read *Curandeiro*. Our translator explained it was the sign of a local witch doctor. (*Curar* means to heal or to cure.) He said that a curandeiro is typically a good guy, a holistic natural plant healer that people could afford. My pulse quickened, and the whole team perked up. We were getting to the "good stuff," stuff we had seen in movies or on *Mutual of Omaha's Wild Kingdom*.

We saw men casually holding hands on the side of the street. Sometimes one man would hold another man's wrist, as if to keep him safe from stepping out into traffic. These were acts of brotherhood, demonstrations of fellowship. The odd thing I noticed was that men and women weren't interacting physically at all. In fact, in all the time I spent in Mozambique, I rarely saw a man and woman holding hands or enjoying physical connection. Once in a while, teenage couples would show affection for each other, but that was it. I later learned that in Mozambique's war years, it was dangerous to be known as a wife. Raping the wives and daughters of an enemy was common. Still, I noticed that the lack of public affection between men and women conveniently hid people's marital status as well.

As we got deeper into the *bairros* (the neighborhoods), we encountered women wearing head-to-toe white: simple long-sleeved jackets puffed at the shoulders and drawn in at the waist, pencil skirts, pumps, and hats that brought to mind a baker. We asked our translator what it meant, and he said they were from the Zion church. I couldn't get my head around it. They were spotless, despite living in mud huts surrounded by mud streets. I shook my head in disbelief.

We saw no sign of a clinic, hospital, or school, but we did see a lot of young people. At that time, 60% of the population of Mozambique was under the age of sixteen—*60%!* This statistic, one effect of the HIV epidemic, stared us in the face as we drove on.

It was getting warm in the chapa, and the road dust from outside was beginning to find its way in. We took many, many turns, and an uneasy nervousness passed over me as I once again realized that we had gone to a country where we could barely communicate, gotten into a vehicle with a man we didn't really know, and driven for many miles through a big city from an address-less starting point toward an unknown place. During those last few miles, I felt a little sick. I could imagine the headline: "American Volunteers Disappear, Presumed Dead."

Finally we stopped. We got out of the van and were promptly ushered through two steel gates. Inside we found a church unlike any we'd ever known—just a cement pad between two buildings. Forty or fifty white plastic chairs were lined up in rows, and every seat was taken; the women toward the back and the men and children in front.

A black plastic tarp stretched from the roof of one building to the roof of the other, covering the parking pad. Shade was the obvious intention, but the tarp was full of holes from being used in sun and rain, over and over. The shade it provided was too broken to be useful. Besides, the black plastic absorbed heat and trapped the dust at nose-level rather than allowing it to rise up and away. Maybe they knew better than I did, but I felt like the plastic was making things worse.

Although we attempted to slip into the back row of the congregation, we were promptly ushered to the very front. My team was not happy about being front-and-center, a fact I gathered from their glaring looks. They had imagined, as I had, that we were just going to a nice church service and would get to experience something new and exciting in Maputo, and they blamed me for the assumption that we—that *they*—would participate. Nonetheless, we sat behind a long altar-like table, facing the rest of the group.

Reverend Gode was a small man, a characteristic highlighted rather than obscured by his oversized suit. Every once in a while, I noticed a look of concern or worry flash across his face, and given his sunken cheeks and bony frame, it occurred to me that perhaps it was hunger. Yet he emanated a heart energy that took over the entire space; the smile I had noted earlier now eclipsed his face. And that spirit seemed to infect the congregation, whose equally broad smiles revealed flashy white teeth.

Reverend Gode began to explain to the congregation that they would sing and dance and speak the word of the Lord for us. (I knew this because of the translator—and only because of the translator.) Then our group would share some songs from our church. As the translator delivered this last bit of information, I got some even more intense glares from my teammates. I fully understood where they were coming from: none of us went to the same church or were likely to know the same songs.

The children danced for us, and the congregation sang songs (though of course we didn't understand the words). Everybody in the congregation smiled and clapped and expressed a joy and gratitude that most Americans rarely witness, let alone experience. They had no idea who we were, but they were so glad that we were with them. A few adults stood up to speak their gratitude for our visit and for my coming to teach them about Unity, their wonderful faith.

46

Never mind that I had *just now* become an official member of Unity; to them I was the expert about to teach them the power of their faith.

The women were wearing dresses and skirts that appeared to have come from the clothing donations collected in the United States and Europe. Most everybody wore flip-flops, and some of the children were barefoot. Still, the people had pride that showed they had worn their Sunday best. Meanwhile, there I stood in my purple-and-pink floral sundress, with three days of jetlag wearing on my face. I felt overweight and worn out, especially in light of their enthusiasm.

When it was our turn to sing, we fumbled for a song we all knew, finally resorting to "Yes, Jesus Loves Me." Then we squeaked out "Hallelujah." All in all it was a laughably pathetic effort, especially compared with the amazing performance the Mozambicans had just given.

Now (with more perspective and experience) it seems to me that when you put Africans together to sing, they are somehow in exact harmony. But when you put Americans together, there are bound to be sour notes. Maybe Americans are more self-conscious and their anxiousness keeps them from staying in the moment and in the song. Mozambicans grow up with less criticism, so they don't hold back their singing, which allows it to flow and harmonize. That's my theory.

I was quite relieved when the singing was over, even though it was time for me to speak. During Reverend Gode's sermon, I'd had time to think about what to say. The reverend had mentioned that the congregation had been spending time in the community, sharing the good news of Jesus and bringing new people to the Savior at Unity. I couldn't help but notice that I had gone from "How Great Thou Fart" to proselytizing for Jesus in just a few weeks. The thing is that Unity does not support proselytizing. I thought about mentioning that fact, but I did not think it would be gracious to do so.

I decided instead to teach the congregation about the beginnings of Unity and about the power of prayer for self-healing, which is the foundation of the Unity movement. I had already learned that Mozambique had one doctor for every 39,000 patients, outrageous child mortality, and astronomical HIV rates. It seemed like information about self-healing through prayer might be useful.

I spoke slowly and clearly so my interpreter could relay the story. I told how Myrtle Fillmore had been about forty years old when she was diagnosed with tuberculosis and given thirty days to live. She had opted to heal herself spiritually, through prayer and with the power of God. She sat every day and repeated the mantra, "I am a perfect child of God and therefore can inherit no illness."

Within those thirty days, she was completely cured of her TB. Her husband, Charles "Papa Charlie" Fillmore, was not a religious man. In fact he was a bit of a scientist. He wondered at his wife's healing. How had it happened? Was it the words she'd been speaking? Had it been that she sat in the same chair every day? Had it been the emotions she felt while saying her prayers? He decided to set up an experiment to study the power of prayer for healing.

He used himself as the test case by trying to heal a limp caused by a childhood ice-skating accident. Well into his forties at the time, he used Myrtle's techniques to cure the limp. From there, the Unity Movement began, based on the power of prayer to help us heal ourselves.

I explained that there was a town in America called Unity Village and that in that town was a very special chapel, Silent Unity. At Silent Unity, someone has been praying nonstop 24/7 for the past 111 years. When you submit a prayer request to Unity, somebody at Silent Unity prays for your success continuously for thirty days.

I felt like I had done a pretty good job representing my faith, but it was clear from the exchange of looks that the congregation suspected the translation was wrong, and repeating the story did not help. Perhaps up until then they had thought that Unity celebrated the suffering of Jesus for our sins (like many churches do), rather than the joy of co-creating with God. I could feel the gap between my message and their understanding, but I did not have tools to bridge it.

After the service, we were invited into the home behind the altar table, where drinks and snacks were served. Chris engaged in a discussion with Reverend Gode, who said that many people didn't take his church seriously because it was just chairs in an alleyway. In Mozambique, everything is based on how serious people are, and this is often determined by appearance and economic/material investment. That made sense to me—not necessarily the economic side of it, but the respect for serious people. I felt the same way.

Reverend Gode explained that they already had a small piece of land and could construct a church for about $900. Chris, ever the architect, was amazed at how inexpensively such a life-changing structure could be built. In our minds, $900 was nothing, especially to construct a church, and we all began to envision the great things we could do with very little money. It was an optimistic time for our team, part of our honeymoon period in Mozambique.

# 9

We woke very early the next morning and left at 3AM to get to the bus stop on time. That is how buses work in Mozambique. In the wee hours of the day, people gather at the bus station, which is typically a dirt parking lot with a bunch of buses, people, and carts. Everyone loads onto the buses through the actual door or, for latecomers, through the window to avoid unloading and reloading passengers. The buses leave by 4AM, which helps them take advantage of the cooler parts of the day and allows time in case the bus breaks down, which often happens.

Whether accidentally or on purpose, I had been booked on a separate bus from the rest of the team. They would be going directly to Lamego, and I would be going alone to Chimoio. We were all a bit distraught about the change in plans, but we went along with it. What else could we do? Our tickets had been bought, we weren't carrying our own travel money, and we couldn't communicate effectively with the man who had arranged our travel. Anyway, the rest of the team had each other. I was the one with a problem. I told myself it was just a bus ride, and took comfort in the fact that the automatic writing had not indicated I would be killed on my first day. I got on the bus.

It was something like an old Greyhound: blue on the outside with red fabric seats. Where the aisle would be on an American bus, drop-down seats had been welded in. After both sides of the row were filled with passengers, these jump-seats could be dropped into the center so two passengers could sit in the aisle. I got on the bus and was told to sit in one of the jump-seats, third row from the back.

Before we even pulled out, there was an elbow in my rib cage. I wiggled, trying to get some relief, but there was none to be found. I sat there, uncomfortable, and wondered how I had gotten such a terrible seat. Had somebody saved money on my ticket, perhaps keeping the difference? Were the seats a free-for-all instead of being assigned? Or had some Mozambican taken my hypothetical window seat at the front of the bus, figuring (rightly) that I wouldn't have the language skills to complain?

Row after row filled with six-to-eight adults, plus young children. People with packages held them on their laps or stashed them under their seats. People with children (or chickens) were going to have a lapful of wiggles, making the ride even more uncomfortable. In my row, which in the U.S. would have held only four people, there were eight adults and a baby. I was in full body contact—hip-to-hip and shoulder-to-shoulder—with the person on my left and the person on my right. I couldn't even see the front of the bus. I am only five feet four inches, and my knees were jammed up against the seat in front of me.

The atmosphere was a little bit noisy and a little bit sweaty. It was pitch black outside. And although lots of passengers tried to talk to me, they couldn't understand a word I said. I was suddenly and painfully aware of how much I had come to rely on Chris and Lindsay's mastery of Portuguese.

We headed off, and I tried to figure out how to nap in the jump-seat. I was going to be in this hot, smelly, cramped environment for the rest of my very long day, and dozing was the only way I was going to make it through. Since I could not rest my head to the right or the left and since I couldn't lean it back because the jump-seat was too short, I ended up using my backpack as a pillow and leaning forward to rest.

When I woke I couldn't see the road, but I could see lush green on both sides of the bus. Bushes, trees, and plants I didn't yet recognize walled us in, thick and green. There were no visible pathways, driveways, or trails leading away from the road; in fact, I couldn't see a single man-made object outside the bus. The United States would have phone towers, mile markers, reflectors, and road signs, even deep in the middle of national parks. But here there was just the road, which I

51

couldn't see, and green banks running miles and miles alongside. They reminded me of snowbanks from my childhood.

Each time we stopped, the unloading began. The jump-seats in the first row were emptied and the people from both sides filed out. Then the first-row jump-seats were lifted so the second row could unload. This process played out row by row, all the way to the back, where I sat. The people with seats in the front of the bus not only had the luxury of getting out to use the latrines first; they also got to stay off the bus longer than everybody else.

After about twenty-five minutes of unloading, it was finally my row's turn, and I could stand up and stretch. I could also use the latrine—eventually. Because I was at the back of the bus, I was about the 180th person in line.

This was my first latrine experience in Mozambique. Even cleaning barns had not prepared me for that smell, which sent a shudder through my every cell. Imagine an outhouse used by thousands of people each day in intense heat and humidity. I don't have the words to adequately describe it.

There was a latrine house with one side for women and the other for men. Everybody had to pay the attendant ten meticais (about thirty cents) to use the latrine. The attendant allowed each person to go in for the allotted time. Then she went in behind with a ladle and a water bucket to clean up.

I paid the woman and went in, discovering that this was a long-drop latrine. There were footprints carved in the cement where the seat should have been to keep you from sliding around and to show you where to hover over the latrine hole. As you can imagine, this system isn't always sanitary— people who have been drinking, people who are sick with malaria, and young children miss a lot of the time. (Hence the woman with the ladle.)

I had a really hard time peeing. I was nervous that someone was going to walk in or that I might miss the hole. But it was more than that. I was having a visceral reaction to the entire scenario—a reaction that made me want to go find any other place else in the world to pee, rather than wiggling back and forth, trying to center over the keyhole cut in the cement. The thought of *anything* splashing made me shudder and cringe. Why hadn't they told me to pack sanitizer?

I thought of the female Peace Corps volunteers not having their periods for six months after entering Mozambique; that is another kind of pulling back, like life itself receding. And right about then I realized that no menstruation would probably be a wonderful benefit of the stress. No American woman—probably no woman of any nationality—would want to be menstruating on that bus or in this latrine. Eventually I managed to pee. I survived the latrine and made it back on the right bus at the right time, without having to go through the window.

It was still well before noon, but people started drinking Wild Turkey. Like people in 1940s America, Mozambicans tend to drink whiskey or bourbon. It's much cheaper and more efficient than beer.

The next time we stopped for a bathroom break, we were in the middle of the bush. The bus driver simply pulled over and stopped. Some privacy was established by the ladies going behind the bus and the men going in front, but nobody was going off the road behind a tree or bush—probably due to snakes, bugs, and whatever else lived out there. (I didn't know yet about the land mines.) I couldn't ask anybody what to do, so I watched.

The women, who all had capulanas tied around their waists, simply pulled down the clothes they were wearing underneath. Then they could relieve themselves in relative privacy. I would have given nearly anything for a capulana— or to be wearing my purple dress from the day before. But I had gotten no warning about this process.

Of course I didn't have a capulana. I couldn't ask anybody for help, and nobody offered any. Those women must have thought I was just another idiot aid worker, which is pretty much how I felt. Here I was the only white person on this bus carrying 200 people, and now I had to pull down my pants on the side of the road and bare my thirty-eight-year-old white ass in front of everyone.

Thankfully, survival mode decreases the likelihood of any serious bathroom needs. I did learn to pee when a stop was offered, and that was a very good thing because there was no stopping the bus for one person's bladder.

That first roadside bathroom break was when I realized how much I had to learn about African hygiene. How do you go to the bathroom when there's no toilet? No toilet paper? No running water of any kind? How do you wash yourself in a place where the water is as brown as tea? I watched one lady grab a stick from a bush to clean her child's bottom after he had gone #2 along the road. I had a lot to learn.

This was yet another sign that I was ill-equipped for this journey. My confidence in my aid organization continued draining away. Nobody had told us, "Hey, the first day, when you get to Machava, make sure you buy a capulana and wear a skirt with no underwear on the bus." Nobody in Machava had told us, "You will want to buy a capulana here in the market today for your trip tomorrow." I wasn't the first person the organization had sent to Chimoio, and I was willing to bet that I was not the organization's first volunteer to bear her white ass in plain view along that road. My white ass might have been the oldest, but it wasn't the first.

Twice we stopped for just one person to unload. The first time, the passenger opted to climb out the window, sparing us (and him) the time and trouble to unload. The second time, the unloading passenger was sitting three rows from the front; he simply climbed over the rows between him and the door. I tried to imagine where he was putting his foot on each row. Could there have been some kind of magical space up there, or was he stepping on the people?

In the heat of the afternoon, the voices rose to a bantering clamor. I closed my eyes and listened closely, trying to pick out the words. But I only understood about one word in ten. Was this Portuguese? It certainly wasn't the Portuguese the Brazilians had taught us in Massachusetts. I longed for a window seat, if only to crack open the window for a little fresh air—something nobody else on the bus had done.

Just as daylight, my last comfort, was disappearing, I noticed a hand-painted wooden sign on the side of the road. I made out a few words: *perigoso*, *risco*, and *estrada*. I knew for sure that *perigoso* meant "danger," which led me to see that *risco* probably meant "risk." The sign was essentially saying, "Travel this road at your own risk." *Fabulous. Just great.*

I was grateful that I couldn't actually see the "dangerous" road; feeling it was enough to tell me that it was riddled with potholes. The people sitting around me were getting louder and drunker, stomachs full of nothing but Wild Turkey. Over the next couple of hours, the volume continued to rise, and so did the tension as people got a bit surly.

One woman nearby had been friendly from the start. She was patient with my Portuguese and smiled warmly. Her wavy hair looked like it had been set on rollers, and she wore a white-and-black button-down blouse along with her capulana. I could not see her feet, but I imagine she wore rubber flip-flops like most Mozambican women do, especially for traveling. She looked to be about thirty-five, roughly my age. Like many women on the bus (and many women across the whole country), she carried a basket made of heavy vine-like material the color of dried cornstalks. These baskets are very strong, strong enough to carry groceries.

Early in the day, I had eked out enough Portuguese to ask her if I could use her cell phone to call the director of the school in Chimoio. She had told me very clearly that I could use it, but now she was being evasive.

We stopped here and there to let people off. Some people went through the window. Some went over the seats to the front. Sometimes we unloaded row by row to get people out the door. Nobody squabbled or seemed to mind the people stepping over them; this was clearly how it was normally done, and nobody seemed to be concerned about protecting anyone's personal space.

We must have made six or seven stops, and by this time it was pitch black out. The lady with the cell phone was now drinking Wild Turkey with the people next to her. The group was getting punchy.

I began to feel like the road was not the only danger. In my imagination, people were plotting against me. *She doesn't have a cell phone. She doesn't speak the language. She's not sure when to get off or who's meeting her. Let's get off with her and grab her bag. Surely the Muzungu has many valuable things.*

As the bus emptied, I tried to console myself by moving from the jump-seat to a roomier normal seat, a relative luxury. But I couldn't shake my visceral dread. Yet again I had driven off with people I did not know and couldn't talk to, without the information I needed to take care of myself. I was pretty annoyed at this point, and I vowed to never let this happen again. From now on, I would have all the details.

Nothing had been familiar in the daylight, and I was even more disoriented now in the dark. I've always thought that the darkness just after sunset has a different quality than the darkness just before sunrise. Moving into darkness is a heavy feeling; as you move out, the energy gets lighter. This darkness was heavy indeed.

The voices blended into a dull drone, but the higher pitch of suggestive laughter and flirting had dropped away. Now the drone was irritated. Gruff. The man next to me shifted, and I felt his elbow hard in my ribs. Oh, I was so tired of this! *Really, God? Is this the bus to help the children?* I tried to snooze, but it was useless. I hadn't gotten any deep, rejuvenating sleep since leaving the United States.

I noticed the road began to feel smoother and figured we had returned to pavement. Every once in a while, the bus would hit a huge pothole (or maybe a small hippo?). We jostled into each other's laps and sometimes bumped heads. The bus windows remained closed, as they had been all along. The walls were closing in.

The next time the bus stopped, around ten or fifteen people needed to get off, and most of the bus unloaded yet again to give them a path. After the long day, I was thankful that I was near the back!

With that stop, the bus had gotten quite a bit quieter and emptier, and the air had become more charged with threat that I did not fully understand. It didn't help that the woman with the cell phone had clearly decided she wasn't going to let me use it, though she never admitted it.

I would ask, *"Telefono?"*

She would say, *"Sim, Sim, em um pouco."* (Yes, yes, in a little.) But even as she was saying the words, she pulled the phone further from me.

I got the impression that she might be plotting with the man next to her to do me some kind of harm. I tried to tell myself that I was being paranoid, but I also understood that if something felt wrong, it probably was wrong. I remained wary.

The bus driver announced, "SOALPO." I had no idea what that meant, but a lot of people got off, and the woman with the phone began an earnest conversation with the man next to her, clearly avoiding me. I was deathly afraid of getting off at the wrong stop: Alone. In the bush. In the dark. Unable to communicate. My sense of frustration increased with my fear. I wanted to throw up, but I did not want to be sitting in vomit.

*How much longer?*

I'd been on the bus since 3:00 in the morning, it had to be nearly 10:00 at night, and it had been at least five hours since our last bathroom break. Why hadn't anybody told me how long this ride would be? Even a vague, "It usually takes about sixteen hours to get to Chimoio," would have been helpful.

I leaned over to the next nearest person to me and said, "Chimoio?" to which he nodded joyfully, *"Sim, Sim em um pouco."* That was confusing. It could have made sense—he could have been telling me that, indeed, we would be to Chimoio "in just a little." Or like the woman with the phone, he could have been brushing me off as politely as he could.

Once the people had unloaded at "SOALPO," the bus driver closed the doors once again. I had been too scared to get off the bus to relieve my bursting bladder. The bus was much emptier now, and it might easily have left without me, taking my luggage with it. As the bus lurched into gear, I sat very still and tried not to throw up.

# 10

<img> ~~~~oᴄᴥᴐoᴄ~~~~ </img>

Just as the bus driver was about to pull away from the SOALPO stop, I heard someone yelling, "Amy, Amy! Get off the bus! Amy, get off the bus!" Two volunteers from the teacher-training school had come to get me and weren't going to let the bus leave with me on it. First I was relieved— seriously relieved. But then I realized that my suspicions of the woman with the phone were probably right: she had known this was my stop.

But my mind let that go in pretty short order. I was grateful and relieved to be hearing my name in English. I gathered my things and climbed off the bus into the safe hands of my new colleagues.

That night, the director of the teacher school in Chimoio gave me a tour. We walked to a small, round hut that had a toilet and shower. She told me that such huts were called *rondavels*. I was amazed to learn that there would be only one toilet, sink, and showerhead for twelve volunteers. Then she quickly walked me through another, larger hut that was the eating and socializing area; it had a fridge, a hot plate, a stainless-steel sink, and a cement counter. There was a wooden cupboard where we could store our own food and a long picnic table where a communal lunch would be served each day.

She took me to the volunteer hut where I would sleep. *Finally.* I'd been on that bus for more than fifteen hours surrounded by people I didn't know, speaking a language I couldn't understand, driving across miles of unmarked land, where I had no reference point. I made my bed quickly and fell into it. In no time, I was fast asleep.

The next morning, I woke to a surprising chill. I had known it would be winter when I arrived, but I had no idea Mozambique could get so cold. I shivered and wiggled deeper into my sleeping bag until I could no longer resist the growing daylight.

When I finally coaxed myself out of the bed, I got a glimpse of the breathtaking terrain of Manica Province. It was something straight out of *Genesis*. Misty haze hovered near the ground. Here and there the tip of a small mountain popped out above the haze, and it seemed these must be new mountains just being born. I half expected a dinosaur to walk by.

On one of my first days, I asked Pazit, my volunteer mentor, if these were new mountains being born or old mountains wearing down.

She answered flatly, "I think if you ask people this question, Amy, they will think that you are a crazy woman, and they will not work with you."

So much for poetry!

Pazit was the first Israeli I had ever met. She was about my height, but smaller than me, with long hair that was very dark except for a few white strands here and there. I could not begin to guess her age.

On my first day of work, I shadowed Pazit. The campus driver dropped us at the chapa stand so we could catch a ride to the village of Macate (which means "market"). We were going to supervise student teachers and help them improve their curriculum and materials.

When the pickup truck chapa arrived, Pazit and I climbed in the back and waited while it filled. The process took at least forty minutes, and twenty-six people (not including babies) jammed themselves into the bed of the truck before the money-collector decided it was full. Then the driver jammed the truck into gear and lurched forward. I struggled to hold my balance, even though I was one of the theoretically lucky ones with a seat on the outer edge of the truck's bed. I say "theoretically" because the people standing in rows—whose arms were holding each other's waists and forming a web— might have actually had more stability. The ones who were most in danger were sitting on the edge of the closed tailgate.

Chimoio could have been Anytown, U.S.A., circa 1965. The five blocks of Main Street were lined with 1960s architecture, still standing from before the Portuguese departure. Everywhere there were relics of a long-ago, abundant, and peaceful time. It is difficult to say whether people had lived better during Portuguese rule if there had been more jobs, more amenities. One had to assume that there was a revolution for a reason, yet evidence of the opulence of the life in Chimoio in the sixties was apparent and surprising.

The school in Macate looked just like many others we had passed along the road: a rectangular building, about sixty feet by fifteen feet, with a corrugated asbestos roof. Next to the school was a library building. We stepped inside, and Pazit showed me books—boxes and boxes of books—many of them still wrapped in plastic, others water-damaged or moldy. "They were a donation," Pazit explained. My gut knotted up as I looked at the rotting books. *What a waste of resources!*

Now, with more aid-work experience, I see those stacks of rotting books as a small example of a big problem. Organizations often receive more donations than they are able to handle. They don't want to turn money away, lest it is not offered again. So they are forced to spend, in a rush, whatever money is left at the end of the funding year.

During my stay in Africa, I saw many donations (made as a tax write-off, most likely) that were not useful and some that were even dangerous. Making these donations was a way for people in other countries to dispose of things they could no longer use. For example, certain models of semi-trucks from the 1970s were determined to be dangerous after decapitation accidents in the United States. Many trucks of those models were donated to Africa, even though the steering wheel was on the wrong side, which made them even more dangerous. I had heard that vaccines that were about to expire were sometimes sent to Africa, even though, once expired, they could be as dangerous as the diseases they were intended to prevent.

After our workday, Pazit and I walked back toward the road. All along our path, women were grinding corn into flour with mortars and pestles that were waist-high. Their muscles rippled. Other women were hoeing gardens or carrying water on their heads and/or babies on their backs. I almost never saw a man working in a field or caring for children. That was woman's work. The men were supposed to have *real* jobs—as guards, tailors, and bus drivers, for example.

We stopped at the building that housed Macate's Development Committee (Comité de Desenvolvimento). There, Pazit showed me a list of more than 150 orphans' names—pages and pages of names, which had been compiled by the Committee. These were Macate's orphans. Next she introduced me to the Development Committee director, Senhor Chimoio, a man with a modest demeanor and a modest life. The building held small offices for him and his secretary, along with a functioning preschool.

When we reached that preschool, Pazit said, "I would like to help these people. I have some money left. I think I might get them some goats, like Heifer Project." I knew that livestock from the Heifer Project had to be managed; the organization didn't just plunk goats down in the bush. Besides, goats at that time cost $150 each, and they had to be purchased in pairs. Then somebody had to be chosen to receive the goats. Who would get them? Who would train the recipient? How would the community or the children benefit? I felt like Pazit hadn't thought her plan through.

She would be leaving in a month after a whole year in service, and at first I was puzzled about why she had waited so long to create a lasting project. Then I saw the way she had thrown herself into the local culture, and I saw how much she loved her Mozambican boyfriend. In many ways, she came across as a Mozambican woman. She looked perfectly at home in her capulana, and she moved with quiet grace from one task to the next. Most impressive, when she demonstrated her African dancing skills, she moved just like a Mozambican. I laughed at the idea that I might learn to move like that or look half as graceful attempting to move like that.

At the time, I felt a bit critical of her priorities and wondered why she had waited until her last weeks in Mozambique to get started on a lasting project. Now I would say that she was just enjoying her life and that her intentions were good. I might say that she lost track of time, or that the money had just arrived recently. But that day, I made a mental note to myself. *I will not get distracted playing around. I will figure out what I'm called to do. I will do it. Then I will go home and get on with my life.*

When we got back to the campus, I reflected on all of the dangerous situations I had witnessed that day. There were twenty-six people in the back of our chapa and roughly the same number in all of the other chapas on the hazardous roads. I wondered how often people were injured or killed in chapa accidents. How often did a tailgate latch loosen, dumping people in the street to be run over by the vehicle behind? During our evening conversation, I shared these concerns— and more general concerns about safety and first-aid training— with the other volunteers and the teachers in training.

I found that one of the teachers was proud to show me his skill in first aid. He kindly showed me how he had been taught to assist a choking victim. He turned his volunteer victim upside down, placing one of the victim's feet over each of his own shoulders. Then he began to shake the victim and pound on his belly. It looked something like a circus act—or maybe a position from African Twister. My mouth was hanging open by the time the demonstration was done. I was dumbstruck.

Right then, I started to see my path of least resistance in Mozambique. It was clear to me that I could help save lives by simply teaching survival skills, like the safety and first-aid I'd learned before age ten. These are skills that can be taught through theatre, which all Mozambicans love. I figured my terrible, no-good Portuguese wouldn't get in the way of teaching the Heimlich maneuver! My original thinking was that I could teach survival skills to the teachers-in-training, who would then go into the bush and teach the skills to kids and villagers. I had a kind of exponential chart in my head that showed the skills spreading through villages and into the bush until they reached every last hut in the country.

# 11

One night I lay in my bunk thinking about the miles I'd traveled—the flights to Johannesburg, the border crossing, the harrowing bus ride to Chimoio, the chapas into town and back. Even my bones felt tired. Every night, I fell into bed exhausted but couldn't get to sleep. In the mornings, I stayed in bed as long as I could, burrowing deep into my sleeping bag, seeking comfort.

Then, weirdly, I started having muscle spasms in my legs. *What in the world?* I didn't think I could have a nutritional deficiency after just a couple weeks. And why was I shivering?

The program director noticed the effects of my insomnia.

"You look tired, Amy."

"Yeah, I can't sleep at night. I keep getting these weird tremors in my legs—like muscle spasms."

"Oh. That sounds like malaria." She said it like we might say, "Oh, that sounds like a dog barking."

"I don't think that can be it. I have been taking Lariam, and I've only been here two weeks."

"Still you better take a test."

Pazit went with me into town and walked me to the back of the clinic building, where we climbed a narrow staircase to the clinic. Every stair required huge effort, and I still remember that there were twenty-six steps in all.

The clinic was shockingly clean, and the building had electricity. There was even a television in the lobby.

I'm betting the lab tech had done thousands of malaria tests. In no time flat, he wiped my finger with alcohol, cut the tip, and pressed the blood onto the slide. Done.

An hour later, we returned to find out what we already knew. I was in the midst of my first bout with malaria. Along with my medicine, I got some information. The most common kind of malaria in Mozambique, 1+ malaria (also known as resistant malaria) is the most drug-resistant strain in the world. It is low-grade, but symptoms can return up to fifteen years after the first exposure. (The Mom in my brain shot me "the look.")

Nevertheless, most people in Mozambique treat malaria like an allergy; people are expected to just deal with it. If you think about the high rates of malaria in Mozambique, this might seem like a healthy emotional adjustment. But the fact that a single bout of malaria usually kills anybody who is HIV-positive—well, that puts a different spin on their casual attitude.

For me, malaria didn't even warrant a day off. The day after I was diagnosed, the director's assistant called me to the office to help sort something out with my stipend.

"You look tired, Amy. Is everything ok?"

"I've got malaria."

"What? You haven't even been here two weeks. Please, sit down before you fall down. Can you sign this?"

I managed to do as he asked and then stepped into the sunlight. After that, I don't remember anything until I heard someone calling my name. "Wake up. Amy, wake up!" My left arm was jerked into the air, and my body was being jostled over dirt and grass. Evidently the Genesis of Manica Province had a few cavemen. The gardener was dragging me across the yard in an attempt to bring me back from blacking out. "Wake up, Amy. Wake up."

Eventually, though I don't know how long, his technique worked.

*God, Really? Was this really what You had in mind for me?*

About the time malaria was behind me, the ring-toe on my right foot started itching. I figured I had pressed my foot against the mosquito net in the night and had been bitten. But it seemed to be getting worse rather than better. Day by day it got more swollen, and it was taking on a yellowish tinge. I couldn't see it very well in the dim lighting of the hut, but it seemed like something was really wrong.

66

I told the other volunteers about the problem. They said we should ask the Mozambican housekeeper. She gave me a grim but resounding, "*Sim.*" (Yes.) It was definitely a worm or maggot under my skin. Then she continued, as one of the Finnish volunteers translated. "She's saying it's a worm and sometimes they work their way up to your heart or your brain. You have to get it looked at." Again, dramatic and disturbing health information was delivered calmly—slowly and smoothly with no hint of urgency. Even though a maggot could be on its way to my brain.

I was ushered back to the clinic to see a "doctor"—or at least a man in a lab coat. I could not communicate with him, could not agree or disagree with any plan of treatment. I was at his mercy. His back was slightly hunched, and he moved in an excited, jerky way—like a mad scientist. To me, he will always be "African Igor."

He was putting on quite a performance as he opened the glass hutch and clanked about the dark brown bottles inside. He picked up the first bottle, held it up in the air, and looked through the glass. Then he made a chuckling sound, as if he were mixing a fine martini and was quite tickled with himself and his choices. *You gotta be kidding me.*

With dramatic flourish, he set one dark bottle and then another on a silver tray, alongside tools that he had arranged as though for surgery. He motioned for me to sit back on the exam table with my foot propped on a gray rolling stool. With my leg (whose whiteness was jarring even to me) propped up for him, he began mixing.

When the concoction was done, he dipped two gauze pads into it and then picked up what looked like a steel shish-kabob skewer and wrapped the pads around the end. Then he poked the instrument into my toe. Really, though: He poked my swollen wound with a sharp stick that had been dipped in God-knows-what. Some kind of poison, I'm pretty sure.

As the pain shot through my entire body, I grabbed the exam table. Igor grinned gleefully. *"Dor? Dor?"* he taunted. (Does it hurt?)

Hell, yes, it hurt, but I was in no mood for conversation. I just wanted to get out of there before something really bad happened. What a nightmare! He bandaged the wound, and I left.

After that incident, the other volunteers told me that many of the Mozambicans practicing medicine weren't really doctors. During the war, some of them had been in jobs somewhat related to healthcare (like ambulance driver)—but they were not doctors. If you wanted a real doctor, you'd probably need to see a foreigner, usually a Cuban.

Couldn't they have told me that sooner—like *before* Igor?

By the next morning, the burning pain in my toe had become excruciating. The bandage only exacerbated the pain, so I pulled it off. What had started as a simple itch under one toe was now a three-leveled blister extending over three toes. I could barely walk. I was pretty anxious as I headed back to the clinic, the *same* clinic, the only clinic for miles around.

This time the doctor (?) was a tall, slim man who looked like he might be East Indian. He sat me down and took a look at my toe. His face wrinkled into a grimace, which made me think he saw a real problem, not a hypochondriac Muzungu. He seemed concerned.

He was also very obviously interested in a male/female kind of way. Back then, moments like that still shocked me. I was sitting there in pain with my hideous foot up in his face. Yet his mind was on sex.

Well, mine certainly wasn't! I was not at the clinic to find a date, I was there to keep my toe—and in that moment, the main reason I wanted that toe is because losing it would surely mean having to go home and abandon the mission... and tell Mom about the whole sordid situation.

He led me to the same exam room I'd been in last time. I thanked God that the tech who came in was not Igor. This guy, too, was speaking a language I couldn't understand, but this time it didn't matter; he gently cleaned the wound and covered it with waxy layers of gauze and a soft bandage. His hands seemed confident, and I felt like he understood that I was in a pretty bad situation. He gave me a piece of paper to get antibiotics next door and instructed me to come back the next day to get new bandages. Eventually, my foot healed from the chemical burns of Igor's medical martini.

Unfortunately, those very uncomfortable early days in Chimoio had a little more in store for me. Not long after the dreadful toe incident, I had another telltale itch. This one was on my right hip, under the waistband of my panties. Over a day or two, the little itch turned into a bump with what looked like a very large pore at one end. When I noticed the pore, there was no more denying it: the egg from a putse fly had gotten into my clothes and now a maggot was growing under my skin. The maggot appeared to be thriving, actually. *Ewwww.*

Even farm life had not prepared me for maggots burrowing into my skin. Later I learned that this was a fairly common problem in Mozambique. Nobody has a clothes dryer, so clothes are dried on a line—or worse yet, on the grass roof of a hut. In the clothes, putse flies lay eggs that are too small to see. To kill the eggs and prevent the maggots from getting under their skin, Mozambicans iron their clothes—*all* of their clothes—usually with very hot charcoal-filled steel irons (think antiques). Apparently our housekeeper had not been careful enough.

At that point, I fully understood why the book *Where There Is No Doctor* was a must-have for aid workers. I grabbed my copy and pondered my options. I could smother whatever was in there by covering the pore with oil, but then I would have something dead inside my skin. To me that seemed to be the worst option.

If I didn't want to kill it by smothering (which I did not), I had to let it grow big enough so I could squeeze it out. If you do it too early, the delicate baby maggot can get smashed and turn to dead mush under your skin—*disgusting* dead mush under your skin—which (go figure) can lead to infection. But if you wait, the maggot gets a little sturdier, and you get out the whole thing, *alive.* I thanked the good Lord that it wasn't in a place more intimate than my waistband and gave it a few more days. Getting the whole, entire thing out of me would have to be worth the wait, the excruciating wait.

When the day finally came, I holed up in the training center bathroom, with one thumb on each side of the bump. I pushed in to get under the maggot. Then I pushed my thumbs together slowly, moving them toward the surface of my skin to force the maggot out. A very fat, white blob-ish *thing* started to emerge. *Ohmygod, ohmygod.* I had never seen a maggot, let alone touched one, let alone (most of all!) had one come out of my body. But, just as I had been promised, the thing popped right out. For a few heartbeats, I looked at it wriggling there on the floor and debated whether it was innocent or deserved to die. Then I squashed it with my shoe.

A South African friend of mine later told me a story about staying at a hotel and noticing that the sheets were a bit damp. A day or two later, his back was itching horribly. Seventeen maggots had burrowed into him. He told me, "Forget the cute Columbia sports clothes, Amy. If it can't be ironed, throw it away. Or sell it and let it be somebody else's problem." After my run-ins with the maggots, I always took that advice.

# 12

One day the director of the organization told me and another volunteer that we were being assigned to the village of Dombe for a week to work on site with the teachers. I didn't know anything about Dombe except it was in the bush—really in the bush—and that we might see elephants there. I was excited about the trip. In addition to working with the teachers, I was hoping to develop the content for my first-aid and safety-skills training.

The director also told us that Jorge Lampião would be in Dombe while we were there. Jorge, who I had met previously at the teacher training college, always had an air of wisdom about him. He was tall for a Mozambican, probably close to six foot, and a few years my senior. His English was perfect, and during our early conversations I learned that he had adopted two orphans. I found him to be a generous man with a good heart, and I had an immediate sense that I could trust him.

Jorge was the director of OSEO <sup>*</sup>, an organization concerned with women's empowerment, as well as clean water and improved sanitation, particularly in rural areas. He was more educated than I was, with a college degree, and he was so very wise. Like many Mozambicans, he had this way of listening: he waited for every last thing you had to say and then he would breathe for what seemed like two minutes before giving a response. It was a patient and respectful way of letting people present their case before making any kind of comment or passing judgment. It struck me as a tribunal way, and I always admired it.

I looked forward to seeing Jorge again as the other Dombe volunteer and I set out early one morning with a driver from

---

* Oeuvre Suisse d'entraide ouvriere (Swiss Labour Assistance)

our organization. We needed our own vehicle so that we could bring bicycles, enough drinking and bathing water for the whole stay, and some of the food we would need. What a blessing it was to need all that cargo, which spared us a long, uncomfortable ride in the back of a chapa.

At one point along the way, we stopped because the driver spotted some elephant scat—and it was fresh. (*Scat* is an awfully small word for the steaming pile we saw alongside the road!) The mere possibility of seeing a wild elephant was exciting; unfortunately (in spite of the poop), we didn't see any elephants.

Later, the driver shared with us that Dombe still had a leper colony. It was across the river from the village. He said that the treatment at the facility was free and that, unlike what most people think, leprosy can be cured if people get treatment. I had no idea anyone still had leprosy. In my mind, it was a thing of the Bible. My curiosity tugged at me, and I kind of wanted to go see the people across the river. Then I thought of how I would feel if some curious foreigner came to see my mottled skin, and a wave of shame passed through me.

After five long hours on treacherous and dusty roads, we finally arrived at the school, a cement building with four classrooms. The windows had wooden shutters that could be left open to allow for air and light, and there was a latrine in back where we could bucket-bathe with the water we had brought from Chimoio.

The village itself was nothing more than a few buildings along a dirt path—very much like Macate. For a Mozambican town, Dombe had a lot of trees, some of which were big mango trees.

On our first day in Dombe, we saw a big, black selenopid spider. Selenopids look like they come out of a Barrel O' Monkeys, and if you blow on them, they spin down the wall in a blur. We decided without any debate that instead of sleeping on the floor, we would sleep on the school tables. I resolved within an hour of arriving never to drink anything after four in the afternoon; that way, I wouldn't have to wade through spiders to use the latrine in the night.

I tried to keep myself from wondering if the children who had been introduced to me in my automatic writing, the children of darkness, were in the leper colony on the other side of the river. After the trials with creepy crawlies, my appetite for adventure was low; the last thing I wanted was a medical event. I'd heard that just three years earlier, because of shortages and despite the ever-increasing HIV rates, the clinic in Dombe had been reusing syringes. Who knew what the shortages were now?

The town of Dombe had a single, and in many ways unconventional, restaurant. Lunchtime depended upon what time the policeman wanted to eat, and with the exception of the day's meat, he also got to choose what food would be offered. We had to reserve our meals a day in advance so that the right amount of meat would be on hand. There was no way to store leftover meat, because the electricity was on only a few hours a day. If more than four people were coming to lunch, they might prepare a goat; otherwise, they would almost certainly prepare chicken.

Before lunch each day, we gathered with the school's teachers to review their curriculum. With an eye for the upcoming term, we talked about what they were teaching and what they might add, as well as what was working and what was not. Then we tried to offer any useful ideas that came to mind. To be honest, I didn't much know what I was doing. I had never developed curriculum. I had never been a teacher. But we traded ideas, and I believe the other volunteer and I managed to be useful.

It was wonderful to see Jorge again and to learn all I could from him. That trip to Dombe was when I first shared with him my vision of teaching survival and safety skills to children. I was so excited that I spilled the whole plan out to him while he waited for the last bit of it in his patient way. "I want to make actual safety-skills centers for children, teaching accident prevention, safe water, sanitation, and hygiene. I also want to teach income-generating skills to the girls because they don't have as many opportunities as the boys. I'm thinking the young ones can learn simple things like knitting potholders to prevent burns. The older ones can make more complicated products like solar cookers. I'm thinking of calling it *Treinamento Internacional para os Órfãos e Sua Sobrevivência* (International Training for the Orphans and Their Survival). Then we can call it TIOS for short."

"It's a good idea, Amy. These things are very necessary here, and they seem to have fallen between the cracks. You will need to set yourself up as an association." He went on to give me some warnings about the inefficiencies and challenges of working with some of the local regulating authorities, though he avoided calling anything corrupt or wrong. (He simply said that perhaps working with them might get "complicated.") He was truly a fountain of insight on the subject of development work in Mozambique because of the successes and failures he had witnessed.

Jorge invited me to teach first aid to his women's empowerment group there in Dombe, and of course I said yes. The women came in skirts and blouses with capulanas tied about their waists. Some had children secured on their backs, and others came alone.

My teammate and I worked well together. She did most of the verbal teaching, while I demonstrated, and we both knew enough first aid that we were able to demonstrate things pretty smoothly. We needed volunteer victims, and at first the women were shy about it. They seemed engaged, nodding their heads as we explained what we would be doing, but when it came time for a volunteer, nobody raised their hand. Finally, we selected a woman from the audience and began to bandage her. Once they realized we weren't going to hurt anyone, everything loosened up. Now I see that they probably didn't understand our Portuguese enough to know what we were going to do until we actually started doing it.

After the bandaging demonstration, we showed how to wrap a splint. For this demonstration, we tore up a capulana to show that everyday things (or parts of them) could be used as bandages. I was especially careful to show how to make a bandage snug but not too tight. (My gory toe was still fresh in my mind.) Next, I demonstrated how to lift an accident victim while minimizing the chance of spinal damage. Theatre came in very handy for that one.

Things were going well, but we decided not to demonstrate mouth-to-mouth or CPR. Given the language barrier, one woman putting her mouth over another's or putting her hands between another's breasts could have been disastrously misconstrued. Anyway, the women in the group seemed a bit nervous about all of the content, so we didn't want to push them too far. I remember thinking that if I had purchased the $200 dolls in training when I'd had the chance, they might have come in handy.

After several demonstrations in front of the group, we had everyone participate by practicing on each other. As the women demonstrated their new skills, they began to stand a little straighter and move with more purpose. Soon, all of the women were seeking new victims to bandage. After two hours, the *machessa* (meeting house) was filled with light banter and smiles and a lot of laughter. When our time was up, nobody wanted to stop.

I have very warm memories of the time I spent in Dombe. The first-aid class really helped me develop the content of my classes, and the days of working with the teachers went well enough. But my most heartfelt memories of Dombe came from the time I spent with the orphans.

After the hot, muggy days, the fresh evening breeze drew me out onto the veranda at the school. Every evening, one or two orphans would come, all curious and wanting to see the Muzungu. I knew by then that most orphans (in fact, most children in Mozambique) owned only one or two sets of clothes. So each evening when a child climbed into my lap, I pulled out the traveler's sewing kit that I had made with my grandma and repaired the child's clothes, very gingerly, while the child still wore them.

Though I did not know it at the time, my opportunities to enjoy the children in Mozambique would be rare. I ended up spending the next six years helping the children, but I rarely had time to *enjoy* them. Those twilight sewing sessions are a treasured memory.

At one point, I rode my bicycle out to the Catholic Mission on the far side of town to visit the Irish priest. His brogue was easy to understand, and our conversation led us to the topic of orphans and their care.

"Do a lot of the orphans get adopted?" I asked.

"Orphans here are handled much differently here than in most other countries. Adoption is strictly regulated. International adoption of Mozambican children requires the parents to live in-country with their new child for six years before the child can leave. This way the Mozambican child will be tied to his or her homeland and might come back to help. Because of these requirements, few Mozambican children are adopted internationally."

I was surprised. I had heard there were tens of thousands of children orphaned by AIDS in Mozambique. As an adopted child, adoption had always seemed like the answer for children whose birth parents couldn't take care of them.

I hesitated. "What happens to all of the AIDS orphans?"

"Keep in mind that children in Mozambique are called orphans even if they have lost only one parent. It's so difficult for one parent to care for a child alone that children in single-parent families are considered orphans. This way, they are eligible for whatever donations might be available to orphans, such as food from World Food Program."

"But where do they stay? I have not seen a single orphanage."

"Well, in Mozambique there are no orphanages in the Western sense of the word. Orphans are simply absorbed by the community. If a child's second parent dies, family is expected to take the child in, which they do, usually without hesitation or complaint. If no family is apparent, the government launches an exhaustive search for extended family, and the extended family always takes the child, whether they've met before or not. We do have a few orphans that truly have no family. They are called *abandonadas*, which means "abandoned ones." Another family in the community will usually step forward to take those children."

I was learning about Mozambican generosity. No child would be turned out to strangers unless absolutely necessary—and when it was necessary, the child would be welcomed into the strangers' home. Upon being given a piece of bread, even very young Mozambican children (say fifteen months) share what they have with the next child. Hungry little children break their bread in half and give part away.

The entire time I was in Mozambique, just as the priest had said, I saw very few homeless children. Unlike some impoverished countries, especially those with high HIV rates, Mozambique has very few true abandonadas. You might see what look like street kids begging for change, but most of them go home to one or both parents at night. They've just seen that they can beg and get money. You can't always tell the difference between who is begging because of need and who is begging just because they know it works.

I liked the idea of no orphanages, but I still knew that in many ways, Mozambican orphans had desperate lives. Not enough food. Scarce opportunities for the future. Very little healthcare. I decided early that I had to keep my wits about me in order to be of any use to these children. For me that meant I needed to stay a bit at arm's length emotionally so that I could get some things done. There was no room for a soppy Amy in Africa.

So I decided to treat Mozambique like a huge hurricane Cat site. After big disasters, adjusters are sent out immediately—often to neighborhoods that have been reduced to rubble. There is no time for panic or tears or even a sense of the enormity of the problem. You have to keep your wits about you and your mind on the work at hand, leaving your heart for later. You have to be resilient, creative, and patient in the face of chaos.

I could do that.

# 13

━━━━━━━━━━━━━━ ∾○〰○∾ ━━━━━━━━━━━━━━

Joe, a fellow volunteer who was about to leave Mozambique, was trying to talk me into helping him with a project. "Why couldn't you help me? You've got the money!" Like Pazit, he very much wanted to create a project that would outlast his time here, and like Pazit, he had waited until the last weeks of his stay to get things started.

Joe wanted to create a preschool in the village of Mudzingadze, and though I could see the need, it looked like a difficult project to manage. First, the village was pretty far into the bush, a seven-mile walk over goat paths. But Joe assured me that I would seldom need to trek out to the village because a local man had volunteered to be the teacher. "They even have a building that only needs renovations. We only have to get the ball rolling."

One thing I found appealing is that it sounded (given the local man who would teach) like the community had ownership of the project. Already I knew that local ownership was crucial if a project was to last. So I said I would at least take a look at it.

Joe and I made our way along the goat trail toward Mudzingadze. The path wandered through high grass and over rough rocks. We crossed a number of dry riverbeds that would be treacherous during the rainy season. Sometimes I heard snakes in the grass, but thankfully we didn't see them. In fact, we did not see any wildlife at all. Because of the wars, there was none.

As I set eyes on Mudzingadze for the first time, Joe announced, "We're here!"

"Here?" I asked. "Where, here?" There was nothing but six big branches stuck in the ground with a grid of sticks across the top that might have once held up a roof. A bit past the sticks I could see a single, small, mud-covered brick house. We had also passed an abandoned soccer field on our way. That was the entire village so far as I could see.

As we walked up to the sticks—which turned out to be the "building," by the way—I shook my head firmly. *No, No, No... You've got to be kidding me.*

I knew the apparent lack of development could be deceiving; what looks like a clearing in the bush could be the meeting place for hundreds of people if that's where they determined to meet, but there was no evidence of foot traffic. My investigative, insurance-adjusting mind kicked into gear, saying, "If it looks like fraud and smells like fraud...." But I pushed those thoughts aside. It was possible this really was a meeting place.

That day, several community members were on site to meet with us: the local *regulo* (official or leader), the man who had volunteered to teach, and maybe twenty (obviously very poor and somewhat disinterested) mothers and grandmothers. They were there to petition our assistance to rebuild this preschool. They explained to me that I was seeing a building that had been donated by a former volunteer from my organization and that they had used the building as a preschool and meeting place for some years.

I tried not to roll my eyes. It didn't take an insurance adjuster to see it had been *a long time* since anybody had used this, uh... structure.

The teacher was very determined. He made a bit of a theatre demonstrating his curriculum. He intended to teach phys-ed, math, and basic Portuguese. These are the subjects routinely taught in Mozambican preschools because they can be demonstrated, bypassing the need for a common language. Most Mozambican children speak tribal languages at home, so the first three years of school in Mozambique focus on teaching one common language that all the students can learn with: Portuguese. At my request, the teacher also agreed to teach gardening, another skill that could be taught using theatre and that could be used to teach Portuguese vocabulary.

Joe was at least as determined as the teacher. He said that he would take care of the renovation (i.e., the rebuild). He estimated it would cost $150. Only $150 to build a serviceable school! When working Cat, I had once spent that much on a single pair of shoes.

In the end, I agreed to fund the project using some of my own money and some money left at my discretion by another volunteer. I was also going to buy a chalkboard and some classroom supplies.

I was satisfied that we had figured out the details. Even if the preschool failed, it was a better investment than a pair of shoes, though I glanced around and wondered if it would last as long as those shoes—which were safely packed in storage, waiting for my return.

Joe was excited about the project and worked tirelessly. After just a few weeks, construction was complete. We now had an actual building, with a new grass roof that would probably last ten years. If we had given the roof a higher pitch (causing the rain to run off instead of soak in), it would have lasted twice as long, but a higher pitch would have been more expensive. We also built a latrine so we could teach sanitation and hygiene.

Shortly after the structure was complete, Joe returned home. Now that he was gone, it was up to me to figure out how to sustain the project. I was beginning to learn that projects in Mozambique often fizzle for predictable reasons: funding disappears; organizations get too big too fast; money is mismanaged or embezzled. In this situation, as in many others, the volunteer most interested in the project (Joe) had gone back to his life. But I was on Joe's side, and I did my best to figure things out. Besides, those children, many of whom seemed to sense they were a burden to their grandparents, had won my heart.

My idea to help sustain the project was to provide the mothers and grandmothers with income-generating projects or a skill so they could earn the money to pay the teacher's stipend. That would give them control over the teacher and the school. I was pretty sure I had it figured out.

I trudged back to Mudzingadze, this time with my friend Manuel, who owned a local taxi service. We had met and become friends not long after I arrived in Mozambique, bonding over our mutual interest in helping the children of his country. Manuel was one of the most socially concerned Mozambicans I ever met, and his understanding of Mozambican culture was a great benefit to me. On this day, because of his curiosity about my survival skills programs, he had agreed to come to Mudzingadze to translate.

When we arrived, thirty women and their children greeted us with a demonstration of gratitude (like at the church in Maputo—except that, thank God, they didn't ask me to sing). After that, the regulo and the teacher began their plea: basically, they wanted me to pay the teacher's salary.

When they finished, it was time to share my idea (via Manuel). "It's better if you mothers have control of this teacher. We could start you with a personal business making something at home—baskets or whatever you like. Then you would have the money to pay this teacher far into the future. You could also make money for your family."

Every face had glazed over by the time I finished speaking. The only thing that was clear to me was that this conversation was way overdue. We should have figured these things out before the first stick was pulled out of the ground and reset. Beyond that, I was confused. Maybe, as a woman, I was wrong to have talked back to the regulo by suggesting an idea different from his. Or maybe I was another Muzungu who did not understand the community's needs. Maybe they didn't understand what was being said, or maybe they just didn't care about the preschool. The most troubling possibility of all is that the mothers were acting as pawns of the regulo and that all along he had simply been angling for a new building; however, there would be no way to uncover a truth like that unless I came back with a translator chosen especially to build trust with the mothers—probably a Mozambican woman.

Later I realized that they expected me to pay the teacher because I was a white woman, thinking something like if I had the money to build this school, I should have the money to pay the teacher. I thought the mothers would want the control they'd get by paying the teacher and the opportunity they'd get with the income-generating skill.

Manuel looked more and more concerned as he listened to the regulo's response. "He's saying these women already work very hard just to feed their families. They have no time to do another income-generating activity. They are asking you to set up a small *banca* (selling stand) for this teacher. His wife will run it, and that will supplement their income so he can teach here."

Then I started to get it. I should not have been suggesting that mothers and grandmothers should work even harder than they already did in order to fund my project. After all, I was (theoretically) the one who had wanted the project.

Nevertheless, when I heard that banca proposition, up from the depths of my belly came the knowing, *Oh, that's such a bad idea!* Now I see that I probably should have left right then. If they weren't ready to take responsibility for a school, they weren't ready to have a school. But I did not want to let Joe down—or the children, even if their parents did not seem particularly concerned.

I tried one more time to explain my perspective, especially how my plan would empower the mothers, and Manuel tried to help me. But it was hopeless. After an hour and a half, I gave in and agreed to pay for a small banca so the teacher could set up his own business. In return, the teacher agreed to stay for three years. I couldn't get past the gnawing feeling in my gut that this banca thing was a bad idea, but the building had been built, and I had said I would work out the ongoing operations at this preschool. So that is what I would do.

On the walk back to Chimoio, Manuel shook his head. "You know, Amy, I don't know why you are so insistent to help these people. They are not interested in educating their children. They just want food on their table and money."

"But Manuel, an education can give them that."

"Not necessarily. This isn't America, or even Malawi. An education alone won't get you a job. You need contacts and a vocational skill to survive in Mozambique. What you call a diploma has no value here."

"Well, I'm sure you're right, Manuel, but everybody needs basic skills. We can help them have better lives in simple ways, like teaching them to germinate avocado pits so they can grow some of their own food. Besides, this is Joe's project, and I promised him I'd look after it. I will keep doing what I can."

# 14

About this time, I learned that the WK Kellogg Foundation (a huge U.S.-based philanthropic group) was looking to fund projects that promoted health and safety in rural areas. I asked our director what kind of project she would be submitting, but she said she didn't really have time to write a proposal.

As soon as I recovered from the director's decision to pass up this opportunity, I saw an opportunity of my own. This could be just the thing that would help the children. I sat down at the computer and began typing. I didn't know anything about writing a proposal, but the instructions were easy to follow, and I was inspired. The words tumbled forward effortlessly, with as much speed and ease as they had during my automatic writing experiences.

It was a simple idea, designed to expand the current curriculum, which we were already delivering to eighty-some teachers every year. I named the program after my grandma, CLARA—Children's Lives Are the Responsibility of All. Teachers-in-training would receive instruction in the areas of first aid and basic accident prevention. In addition, this plan would provide teachers with an additional income-generating skill—gardening of medicinal herbs. Teachers could use the herbs to improve their health, and they could sell them to other community members to earn money.

I made a simple budget, which indicated that the training would cost almost nothing. To teach first aid, we would need only a capulana, a five-gallon jug to carry purified water, and a few bits of clean gauze. Seeds and starter plants for the teachers' gardening projects would cost almost nothing. The total cost of the plan was $800 for each location.

I was quite pleased with myself and confident that I had come up with a great plan to help people. But when I presented the plan to my director, she looked mildly disgusted. "I just don't know why you think we have to do all this work with first aid and accident prevention."

Though I was temporarily dumbstruck, my reasons stampeded through my brain. *Because there is no medical care here. Because there is one doctor for every 39,000 patients. Because there are no ambulances. Because 80% of the fewer than one thousand doctors in the country are a thousand miles away in Maputo. And because you are sending able-bodied, trainable people into rural areas where there are no doctors!!*

But she was the next one to speak. She flat-out refused to present my proposal to the Kellogg Foundation. Mute with shock and anger, I threw my hands into the air and left her office.

Though I trusted that God had put me just where He wanted me and had a hand in the development of my safety-skills focus, I did not think He wanted my hands tied like this. I became convinced that if I were to fulfill my mission, I would have to leave the teacher-training school and the organization that had brought me to Mozambique.

As I was solidifying those plans, the Mudzingadze teacher came to see me. A few weeks prior, he had brought evidence of how hard he was working, and his need for additional money (for supplies). With a feeling of dread, I had given him the funds, expecting him to return soon. Now I saw that I had, unfortunately, been right. He needed more money. He said that he needed more supplies and to replace his goat, which had been stolen. Even though I hadn't bought the goat (and wasn't even sure if he had ever owned a goat), he seemed quite sure I would help him by replacing it. I could see no end in sight when it came to his ongoing financial pleas.

Again, he had brought the curriculum and attendance records to show what he was teaching and just how valuable he was, but already I had doubts as to how long he would be there and how long the little preschool would last.

I decided to sneak out to Mudzingadze to check the situation for myself. By now I'd been there several times and could navigate the goat path on my own: two lefts, a right at the tree house, another right where the dam used to be, across the creek, and up a hill.

That day in Mudzingadze, thirty-five children were learning to plant vegetables. The age-range was supposed to be four to nine, and I was a bit distressed to see older children who should have been at regular school in town. I could see the mothers' reasons for sending them here: planting vegetables was a practical skill that would benefit the family almost right away. Compared with sending their kids to learn to read books in Portuguese (which few of the parents could do), gardening easily won out. You can't eat books.

For the most part, the children in Mudzingadze looked healthy and well fed, although a few had what we called kworshi (more formally called kwashiorkor), a distended belly caused by insufficient protein. But I knew their health was threatened by more than just hunger. Accident prevention and first aid were almost unheard of. Though I wanted very much to bring that information to the village of Mudzingdaze, adding new material was out of the question. Already, the teacher was barely doing as much as he said he would; no way would he accept more responsibility... at least not without more "help."

# 15

————————<br>—◦◦◦◦◦————

At the end of the term, the teacher-training school held a ceremony for graduating teachers. I was excited for the ceremony because I was pretty sure my Portuguese was good enough that I would understand the gist of the speeches. But just in case, I sat next to a friend who could explain things.

Midway through the evening, a doctor stepped up to the podium. As he was speaking, the volunteers around me bristled. The doctor was saying the graduates should take their new role seriously and dress seriously. He said they should dress like Barbara Bush. *You have to be kidding me.*

But the clincher was this: He said he didn't believe in HIV, that it was something made up by outsiders. That comment is what caused the real uproar among my teammates.

Unfortunately, misinformation was often spread by people in respected positions. It was obvious at least to the outsiders that they were never going to get HIV under control in Mozambique if supposedly educated people were spreading rubbish. I noticed many of the attendees were nodding their heads in agreement with the doctor... after all, as a doctor, he would know.

When I had been in training in the States, a Mozambican named João Da Cruz, had visited to share about his country and to learn about ours. One evening, Da Cruz and I were having a chat in the dining area. The subject of HIV came up, and I mentioned an article I had read about the African potato. "Oh," Da Cruz said, "you mean the cure for HIV?"

I was shocked. There was a cure? A local plant cured it? How did the world not know about this? "But, Da Cruz, why aren't people planting this and selling it?"

"It's better to grow a food crop, like carrots or peas. To try to grow something and sell it is much too uncertain. Better to make sure you can feed your family." I was blown away.

I shared the story with the rest of my team. We were all afire with an urge to know more about this plant and how we might spread information and get people to grow more of it. We were disappointed when our research showed that the African potato only grows in the wild. And we were very disappointed to learn that the studies showed that much like an anti-retroviral, it minimizes or hides symptoms, makes people gain weight quickly, and returns people to a normal, healthy appearance in a matter of days. But with the African potato, the symptoms inevitably return with renewed vigor. The African potato leaves people believing they've been cured; as a result, they think they cannot infect other people, so they often go on to do just that.

It can be argued that the HIV virus is wiping out a large portion of the Mozambican population, orphaning thousands of children per year and causing Mozambique to have one of the lowest life expectancies of any country in the world. (A child born in Mozambique in 2013 has a life expectancy of fifty-two years, putting Mozambique tenth from the bottom on this measure of health—213 out of 223 countries in the world. The good news is those numbers reflect a ten-year increase in life expectancy since 2009.)

However, in Mozambique (and in many other developing countries), HIV is almost never listed as a cause of death on a death certificate. One reason for this is that people with HIV are usually killed by malaria or by opportunistic infections such as pneumonia—diseases that can't usually get a foothold in people with uncompromised immune systems. In addition, antiviral medication is widely available in urban areas of Mozambique where HIV rates are highest; these medications often prevent HIV from evolving into full-blown (lethal) AIDS.

But don't get the wrong idea. *Plenty* of people in Mozambique die directly as a result of HIV/AIDS. Social stigma is another reason that HIV is not listed on death certificates in Mozambique: even when HIV evolves into

AIDS and is the direct and unquestionable link to a person's death, nobody wants the family to live with that stigma.

The fact that deaths caused by HIV are not attributed to HIV obviously makes reliable statistics difficult to capture, a problem compounded by the fact that Mozambique is quite underdeveloped when it comes to recording births and deaths. These events are recorded only when somebody makes it into town, waits in line, and pays to register the event at the notary building. Many births and deaths are never recorded, and even when they are, the record-keeping (notes scrawled on the pages of paper books) leaves something to be desired.

Another problem with reported HIV rates is that those numbers are derived primarily from testing pregnant women, who are required to take an HIV test when they go to the doctor. However, plenty of Mozambican women—especially rural women without complications—never see a doctor during their pregnancies. Last but not least, most sex workers avoid pregnancy by using birth control and avoid the required HIV tests that come with pregnancy. These factors remove this incredibly high-risk population from the data virtually altogether.

Perhaps the thinking is that the HIV infection rates among pregnant women can be extrapolated to include their husbands—because theoretically that is where the women get the virus. But many Mozambican men—especially those who are employed many miles from home and return only occasionally—have multiple sex partners. A man could easily have sex with five different women during the year, infecting them all, while getting only one pregnant.

In addition, a husband might have the infection for some time before his wife contracts it, and again she would only get tested if she happens to get pregnant from intercourse with him, goes to the doctor, and the doctor administers the test. The result of the test would only be recorded if the doctor accurately reports collected data to a reporting agency that captures the numbers.

Men aren't the only ones spreading the virus, of course. While men work on the road, many of their wives end up trading "favors" for things they need. Imagine a woman with no viable income being left home with multiple children for six months while her husband is away working. If she needs to pay the doctor for malaria medicine for her child, for example, her only choice might be to exchange a sexual favor for that money.

So denial, myth, misunderstandings, and social customs often work against efforts to measure (let alone lower) HIV infection rates. In this environment, determining an accurate HIV rate is an unreachable goal.

As you can imagine, the situation can get discouraging. I remember the first time I noticed a funeral procession passing by the teacher-training school. I noticed another one about fifteen minutes later. Then again fifteen minutes later. Four times every hour of every workday, a funeral procession headed toward Chimoio's cemetery. The realization turned my stomach. Mourners traveled in what looked to be grain trucks; forty or fifty adults and children stood up in the back. The sight brought to mind Jewish people crammed into railroad cars, a thought that made me sicker still.

I spoke with one of the campus guards about it. He told me that the mortuary, which acted as the funeral chapel, hosted fifteen-minute funerals all day long. (Sadly, funerals in Chimoio were much like weddings in Las Vegas.) The result was a steady stream of vehicles making the circular route to the cemetery for a quick burial and then back to the mortuary for the next load. All. Day. Long.

# 16

I no longer slept well. Night after night I lay in my bed, tossing and turning, tired but unable to sleep. Though I had only been there five months, I knew I needed to leave the teacher training college. There was no sign of the children I was called to work with there, and no apparent interest in providing health safety to the people through newly graduated rural teachers. I was looking forward to the Christmas break and pondering my options; I hoped to have something figured out by the time we rang in 2005. Where could I go? I was here alone.

Great, I had God and a whole bunch of angels, or spiritual sponsors if you will, but I had nobody physical at my side—no partner to share this daunting task, if only in conversation at the end of the day.

That loneliness was not the whole story of my insomnia. Though I tossed and turned and tried to redirect my thoughts, it turns out that when the human body is under chronic stress or in chronic danger, the laws of nature say, "Hurry up and perpetuate the species; you're about to die!" You might say my loneliness was multi-layered.

Sex was in the air in Mozambique. Imagine it: the country is populated primarily with uneducated, poor people who have very few diversions even in the daylight hours. Because Mozambique is near the equator, the sun sets at 6PM all year round. For the most part, there are no computers, no TVs, no radios. Even the lucky few who know how to read probably have no light beyond a twenty-cent candle purchased in the market.

So you see, not much to do except... you know. Maybe not everybody's like me, but I can say what I would have probably been doing, had I been the average Mozambican.

The female students at the teacher-training college often joked about every Mozambican woman keeping three men: one to be her husband and the father of her children, one for transportation, and one *apaixonada*—the object of her passion—the one she was really in love with.

For aid workers from the United States, the situation is further complicated by the concept of the "blue passport"—marriage to, or shared children with, a U.S. citizen. A couple of students at the teacher training school had expressed the opinion that if a Mozambican could form a family bond with an American, the U.S. family members would surely want to know and help their Mozambican family members. This possibility added to the general atmosphere.

There I was, a thirty-eight-year-old formerly married woman. I knew what I was missing, and I knew what I was wanting. My ramped-up appetite was brutal. I ruefully and repeatedly remembered that the average American woman is in her sexual prime when she's thirty-eight years old.

Throw all of that in with the fact that men continually offered to help me—as in, "Amy, nobody can live without sex. It's impossible. I can help you. I can make a baby for you."

Not that I was even vaguely interested in being intimate with most of the men making these offers. My understanding of HIV pretty much killed the impulse to actually act. Nevertheless, this particular distraction was a smoldering, smoldering thing. It seemed doomed to never quite flare up and to never be quenched.

I distracted myself by trying to focus even more on my mission. Things were starting to unravel in Mudzingdaze, and I knew I could not stay at the teacher-training school much longer. My hands were tied there, and I knew the director was unlikely to ever support my ideas for safety and first-aid training.

I spoke with one of the Peace Corps volunteers about the situation, telling her that I wanted to leave the teacher-training school, but I did not know how I could do it because it would mean finding a new place to live and getting together the proper documents I would need in order to stay in-country without the sponsorship of the aid organization. She said she would introduce me to her British friend, Helen, who ran a backpackers' lodge and might be able to help.

Helen Large, the proprietress of "The Pink Papaya," and I hit it off right away. She had a feisty personality, a sassy bobbed haircut, and a trim little figure. Most every day, she wore at least a smidgen of pink, her signature color. She was full of incredible stories of adventure and exotic tales of love lost and found again. She was a brilliant hostess, able to create delicious food accompanied by plenty of socializing and adventure, all on a backpacker's budget.

Helen had started her life in Mozambique as an aid worker, but she had become disillusioned. She said that, of the hundreds of aid workers who had come to the Pink Papaya over the years, she could recall only a handful that had been successful in their attempts to make a difference. She believed that "trade not aid" would help Mozambique stand proudly on its own, without leaning on other countries. In particular, she felt that the tourism industry could be key to rebuilding the national economy. She made sense to me.

As we sat there having a cup of tea on her charming veranda, I felt right at home. At some point I mentioned that I had done a bit of palm reading back in the States. She immediately stretched out her hand to learn of her fortune and fame, and I read for her the lines of love lost imprinted on her hand. I only knew the basics, and had even brought my books with me to learn a bit more, but reading palms was (and is) something I do with a light spirit, just for fun. It certainly worked that night. Our laughter rang through Helen's house.

Like many houses in Chimoio, the Pink Papaya was surrounded by an eight-foot wall and blanketed in bougainvillea. The house was actually a duplex, with three bunk beds in the ladies' bedroom and two in the men's. All told, Helen could accommodate nine guests, plus herself.

She said I could work for her at the Pink Papaya, checking in guests, helping them with tourism information and directions, and taking their payments. In exchange, I would sleep in one of the bunk beds. This plan still left me time to oversee the preschool at Mudzingadze, and time to get started on a new orphan resource center I wanted to develop in Macate.

With the teacher-training college graduation behind me, the school was on end-of-year break and I was allowed an exploration somewhere in Mozambique. I decided some time away to sort out my plans for leaving the school (especially on the school's tab) would be refreshing. So I made a plan to go to Quelimane to visit my friend Naomi, a woman I'd met while volunteering at the training campus. She was Irish and Swedish, with blonde hair and blue, blue eyes. She moved with ease and grace, even in the craziest upside-down moments. After spending only a little time together after meeting at the teacher-training campus, we quickly dubbed each other "Sis" and exchanged cell phone numbers. And she invited me to Quelimane.

Like Maputo, Quelimane is a coastal city, but it is more difficult to get to, so it's not a usual tourist destination. As a result, Quelimane always felt to me like a retirement community. Contributing to this general atmosphere was the absence of the crazy-making chapas and their boisterous, edge-of-disaster cargo. Instead, Quelimane has bicycle taxis. Passengers ride on the back luggage rack like in movies from the forties. The stunningly beautiful Indian Ocean, which you can view as you travel along "the marginal"—a road and footpath that runs the entire length of the coastline—make Quelimane a bit of a haven.

The travel to get to Quelimane was grueling; I forged the great Zambezi River and slept outside with strangers. Luckily, by this time I had gotten somewhat used to the discomfort and danger that were part of everyday travel in Mozambique.

"Omi," as I came to call her, was all the things I was not. The epitome of a socialite, she had worked out some insane plan that we would go out on nine dates in three days. I hadn't had nine dates in three years! She was crazy, and she was wild.

95

But nobody would ever have said Omi was "loose" or a runaround. She was classy, for sure, and great at stirring up adventure. I was amazed. If I could have one ounce of what she had going on, my dating life would click into gear.

Off we went to coffee with a CEO. Then we met up with an Australian named Paul. Bachelors one and two were certainly nice, but bachelor three sounded much more interesting. His name was Daniel, and Omi said that in the three years she had known him, he asked her to coffee several times. But she had been a little nervous. She said she had never seen him with a wife, but she had seen him with a pretty little Mozambican girl with clips in her hair. So Omi had kept a cool but friendly distance.

Finally (since I was coming along) she had said yes to the coffee date, and she took me along. Daniel brought his brother Geoffrey, who was maybe eighteen and completely silent lest he be disrespectful to his brother, the alpha. Daniel's English was perfect, which was a wonderful relief to me. He was communicative, playful, and non-threatening. Even his church sounded friendly and welcoming. Though I wasn't particularly attracted to him, my mind couldn't help but tick off the checklist; nice guy, fun, nice energy, taking care of his brother, youth group leader, spiritual, plays basketball, has good job taking care of orphans (no less), intelligent, educated, friendly… hmmm.

Besides, he had a car and a motorcycle. I couldn't hide my smile as I remembered the female students at the teacher-training college telling me they kept one man for transportation… I nearly laughed out loud. I felt myself becoming more Mozambican by the minute. *They might have something there.*

Our group departed the coffee shop with a plan to meet later that night at the Riviera, a club that Omi said welcomed the wealthiest locals, along with diplomats, visitors, and volunteers from aid agencies.

The gathering was striking. Black and white tile graced the floors as black and white faces graced the tables. Omi was magical, bringing our worlds together and creating a lovely atmosphere for getting to know each other.

As we were sipping an after-dinner drink, I noticed a man in a crisp white shirt with epaulettes on the shoulders. He came in the door and quickly approached the bar. He said something to the bartender, who nodded in understanding. Then— although there had to be at least fifteen international tables in the small restaurant—he walked up to us directly. "Identification please," he said. He examined our papers, one by one, and when he got to mine, he looked at me pointedly and said something I couldn't make out. Eventually, with Daniel and Naomi's help, I understood that the certified copy of my visa stamp was expired.

Daniel took the situation in hand, as a man in a position to do something. "Look," he said to the Immigration official, "I will take her into custody and bring her to you in the morning. There has been a mistake."

I was so grateful. Even though I didn't understand everything that was happening, it was clear that I'd almost spent my evening in a jail cell rather than this lovely restaurant. I was so grateful for Daniel's help (and for his obvious clout).

Daniel was handsome by any standard; dark chocolate brown with broad shoulders and a full build. He had a bit of a tummy—as men should in my opinion. I very much liked his energy. He was playful and light, with an endearing way of shrugging up his right shoulder when he was "blowing something off."

Even with the Immigration scare, we soon returned to our lighthearted conversation about the experience of living and working in Mozambique. The fact that each of us had a very different perspective was fodder for conversation late into the night.

In the morning, my dread over the immigration paperwork returned with vengeance, and it got worse when I thought about calling my parents to say I was coming home: "I'm headed out in the morning, Mom. Yes, that's right:

Immigration is kicking me out of the country. By the way, I have no money. Can I come live with you and Dad?"

I made some calls to the organization I was working with, and they sent a copy of my passport to Daniel's office. When I got there around 10:00 the next morning, he had the papers in his hand. We went together to Immigration.

The Immigration office was in better shape than any office I had seen in Chimoio; its newer wooden furniture and crisply painted white walls were a soothing sight during that tense moment. (I couldn't follow what Daniel and the Immigration officer were saying, so I had plenty of time to take in the décor.)

Daniel's Portuguese was different from what I had heard in Chimoio, some reflection of the Chuabo and Lomüe languages he had grown up with. I did catch a bit at the end of the conversation—Daniel saying that he would bring the officer a case of beer for his assistance. I thanked the officer, and once we were safely outside, I thanked Daniel. Then we parted ways, agreeing to meet later for a drink.

I headed for the market in Quelimane, where I found beautiful capulanas. They had a silkier texture and fringes at each end, resembling an Indian sarong. I could only afford three, but I vowed to come back for more. As I walked with my treasures in hand, I soaked in the ocean breeze and reveled in my relief that I would not have to tell Mom about the Immigration snafu.

Then I happened to look up the road just in time to see an accident. A man riding a bicycle was a little too far into the street, or maybe the car was a little too close to the edge. The car's mirror just tapped the bike's handlebar, but it sent bike and rider careening into the curb. The man's head hit the cement.

Somebody pulled the cyclist from the street, with the bicycle still balanced between his legs. Then a bystander had the man sit up on the curb while blood poured from his forehead. I was a short distance away, perhaps a block or so.

*"Abaixo de cabeça! Abaixo de cabeça!"* I began to yell. (Lower his head! Lower his head!) By now a crowd was forming. One man seemed to be trying to figure out what to do. The rest appeared to be queasy about the blood and stood back.

When I reached them, I said again, *"Abaixo de cabeca!"* Then I pulled one of my new capulanas from my bag and put it over the wound. The man who had been trying to help took the capulana and began wiping the blood away. My heart was pounding *"Pressão! Pressão!"* I said, not sure of the Portuguese word for pressure. I showed him what to do. Then I left the man holding the bandana in place as I ran to the hospital, which was only a block away.

I burst through the door calling *"Ajuda! Help me! Ajuda!"* Nobody moved. They all looked at me like I was crazy. In my still-pathetic Portuguese, I tried to get across that there had been an accident with a bicycle and that somebody needed help. Nobody would come.

I ran back to see how the first aid was going, but the man was gone. Someone had taken him to the hospital, and I had missed him in my panic. All that was left was blood—a stain on the sidewalk and a pool in the street. One woman who had been at the scene was still nearby. I asked her what had happened and she said flatly, *"Morreu."* The man was dead!

I was horrified. I couldn't breathe. I couldn't sit still. I began to walk very briskly back toward the apartment where I was staying. I needed to walk. And I needed to wash off the blood.

There was no reason for that man to be dead. This was the stupidest thing I'd seen so far. A simple little accident, a simple little cut, just one block from the hospital—and now he was dead. *What is wrong with these people? What is wrong with this place?*

There were at least four million-dollar aid agencies within a block of this accident, but as far as I could see nobody was teaching accident prevention, first aid, or even water purification. They were all about HIV, but when I looked around, I thought it was a miracle that people were living long enough to get HIV!

When I got back to the apartment, I stripped off my clothes and took refuge in the blessedly warm water of the shower. I tried to let my frustration flow away with the man's blood, but my head would not clear. In my mind, the incident was convoluting itself with my sister's death.

I had been the same distance—about a block away—from the bicycle accident as I had been from Kara, when I saw her hanging from the camper window. Both times, I had run toward the problem and then left to get an ambulance. When I came back to Kara, she was gone. Dead. The same as with this man.

Throughout my childhood, nothing—not even the counseling my parents sent me to—had released me from the sense that my mishandled first aid had somehow ended my sister's life. If I ever had come close to forgetting it, Catholic Mass gave it new vigor every Sunday as we prayed in chorus, "I confess to almighty God and to you, my brothers and sisters, that I have greatly sinned in my thoughts and in my words, in what I have done and in what I have failed to do." The familiar refrain turned my stomach every week as I faced my brother and my family, knowing that they were aware of *what I had failed to do* and that I was the reason my sister was gone.

I hated that the bystanders on the street in Quelimane had been as helpless as my ten-year-old self. I wanted them to be able to save their loved one and themselves. And I wanted to earn redemption for my own mistakes. I stood under the shower until the water was gone.

Once I was dressed, I needed air. I burst out the door and headed toward the ocean. A text came. "Wait for me." It was Daniel. He had seen me from his office window. I waited as he caught up. I told him about the accident.

"It's normal," he told me. "We say, *'Fazer o que?'* What to do?"

That phrase was one I would come to know well, and for a long time it enraged me every time I heard it. It is an expression of powerlessness. It reminded me of the Crusades cry of "God wills it." Both phrases basically mean that we are not responsible—this is up to God.

"Normal? That man's death could have been prevented at least three different ways." Daniel stayed calm and patient as I went on and on about how this shouldn't have happened. I had never been so grateful for common language, and I poured my heart out.

Eventually we found our way to the machessa, this one an oval structure with a thatch roof that housed a restaurant. The walls were only waist-high, which allowed in the meager breeze (and also, unfortunately, the mosquitos). By the time we finished our second drink, the sun had gone down and so had the pitch of my emotions. If I wasn't exactly calm, at least I was tired.

Daniel walked me back to Omi's apartment with his arm over my shoulder, which felt more like a comfort than a come-on. I liked it. As we walked he asked me, "Why aren't you married?"

I told him about Bruce dying and about the trials of working on the road. Then I said, "And you know, I'm not really all that pretty, and certainly not very polished at dating or social things."

He stopped on the sidewalk and turned to me like a protective older brother. He looked down at me and said, "Amy, all women can be beautiful." He said it in a way that was long and thoughtful, like the wisdom of the ages coming from this man, seven years my junior.

Then his face shifted ever so slightly to that playful part of him as he said, "Some are only beautiful for one night..." And then he laughed. It was deep and rich and fun.

We got to the door, and when he kissed me goodnight—and then kept kissing me some more—I collapsed into his arms. Like an accident victim being wheeled into an ER, I felt a surge of relief when Daniel whisked me into the bedroom. In that moment, HIV was the furthest thing from my mind.

The room had two single beds latched together to make a king, but the mattresses kept sliding apart. With one flick,

Daniel threw a mattress to the floor, and we continued getting to know each other. Hours flew by.

Late in the night he began to tell me stories of his life as a single parent in Quelimane. He said his son's mother had not wanted a family life and had moved to the city of Beira. Before I could wonder what that meant, exactly, Daniel began to tell a Mozambican bedtime story that he often told his son. It was called "The Fat Goat and the Skinny Pig." Daniel's voice changed for each of the characters in the Dr. Seuss-style story, and soon I was laughing from the depths of my belly. As I dozed off to sleep, my concern over his son's mother was long gone.

In no time, it was 2AM, and Daniel walked me to the bus stop so I could head back to Chimoio. (This time I had my capulana and hand sanitizer, by the way.) I was so relieved when I discovered that Daniel had gotten me the front seat. Relatively speaking, I would have a lot of space, and I might actually get some sleep. Daniel knew about these things— moving people, dealing with Immigration, getting the best seat on the bus. I felt less alone (and more supported) than I had since leaving Cat. *Thank God for Daniel.*

# 17

⊸∘C∕⟩∘⊶

When I got back from Quelimane, I started organizing my strategy for funding and building my survival-skills training centers. Teaching safety and first aid would require almost no money—just enough for a capulana, some sticks for splints, and a few bandages. My Portuguese was still bad, and most Mozambican kids aren't fluent in Portuguese anyway. So the teaching would rely heavily on theatre.

The other thing I needed was kids. Where would I find them without falling into a situation like the one in Mudzingdaze, with the teacher continuously needing more money? I would also need interested parents. This time I would make sure the parents knew it was *their* project and that they needed to support it—with both money and participation. Otherwise? No project.

I decided to start my own school rather than risk getting tangled in a program that had already been established, but I needed a location. I recalled the Development Committee in Macate where Pazit had taken me and the approachable, hardworking director, Senhor Chimoio.

The building already hosted a preschool, so I thought they might be open to upgrading it to be a full orphan center offering survival-skills classes to children of all ages. The preschool was already attended by local children, whether orphaned or not. The center could address safety training for kids of all ages and teach income-generating skills for older girls.

The building was beyond simple—just cement floors and walls and a tin roof—but the location was perfect. I already knew there were 150 orphans in the area who could benefit from an orphan center. It was an ideal situation for creating and testing my program.

103

Along with Manuel, who had agreed to translate, I traveled to Macate to meet with the mothers, city officials, and children. With the issues at Mudzingadze fresh in my mind, I was confident that this time I would get it right. I began my speech (with Manuel translating).

"I am not here. You must treat me as a ghost. I will help you to set this up, but this belongs to you. Anybody can die, including me. In one month or one year or two years, I will be gone. You must be prepared from the first day to run this orphan center. Only then can I agree to help you start it."

They agreed to those terms. Then I shared a couple more concerns. Community meetings were held in the building on Wednesdays, during the same time we planned to have children attending. And there would be some overlap between the preschool and the orphan classes. The committee assured me, "That will be no problem."

*What could go wrong?*

It was May of 2005 when we agreed that I would support the Development Committee and the local parents in creating a center for orphans and other vulnerable children. I would apply for funding from CNCS * (the National Council to Combat HIV/AIDS), and we would renovate the building (which had no electricity or running water) so it could better accommodate and serve children.

In order to apply for CNCS funding, I needed a list of orphan names, and I knew I would find a list at the Development Center, so I traveled there to copy the list. The day was hot, and the building was hotter. I began writing down the names as an administrative task. In the sweltering heat, I would have given almost anything for a photocopier.

But then, after two or three pages, the names became real. Each name was a child—a motherless and/or fatherless child. And even though I did not know any of their voices or faces, I related to them as fellow displaced children. I had been put

---

* Conselho Nacional de Combate ao HIV/SIDA (National Council to Combat HIV/AIDS)

up for adoption as a baby, and I ended up in a home where I was loved and well cared for. As Mozambican orphans, most of them were in good homes, too. I felt like our emotional struggles might be similar, though their practical struggles were so much more severe.

There were *so many* orphans on that list! Emotion started to rise in me, and tears stung my eyes. But I didn't dare cry. In Mozambique the fastest way to lose people's respect is to cry or in some other way get out of control emotionally. I needed another way to express what I was feeling. I reached for a piece of paper, and words began to flow:

### Who Will I Grow Up To Be?

Who will I grow up to be?
Will someone ever care for me?
I'm only a child whose parents are gone.
I don't know why; what did I do wrong?

Will someone care enough to be smart?
Teach me a skill or to do my own art?
Then I won't have to beg in the street.
I can have my own life, full and complete.

With knowledge enough to grow up with health,
With skills enough to earn my own wealth,
With inspiration enough to share what I've learned,
I will see that your gift is returned.

I'll return it to others, also in need—
By my own hand and by how I lead.
With donations you've sent and skills that you've taught,
Sharing all the great things your gifts have brought.

Who will you help me grow up to be?
That I may share what you've given to me?

105

As I finished the poem, a bit of sweat ran down my forehead. I tilted my head back to brush it away and saw *Unity* stamped on the sheet-tin roof panels. It was the name of my church, above my head all along. For a moment I felt at peace. Silent Unity was certainly out there saying continuous prayers for these children and for my mission.

I went back to copying the names, but they were more than names now. They were children I could help. I could teach them skills that would help them survive. I had finally found my children of darkness.

# PART II:

# RESILIENCE

# 18

<hr />

Helen Large was Chimoio's socialite, which was great for me while I lived and worked for her at the Pink Papaya. I accompanied her to many dinners with other aid workers, white Zimbabwean farmers, and international visitors to Chimoio. The year that I lived at her place, she invited me to the Zimbabwean Farmer's first annual Christmas party. I enjoyed the Zimbabweans very much, so it was a pretty exciting idea—until she said, "You'll need a proper dress. This is a black tie affair." *A black tie affair? In Chimoio?*

I went to a market on the other side of town that was renowned for ball gowns and little black dresses and proper dress-up shoes. There was no facility to try anything on (and I didn't want to risk putse eggs anyway), so I went from dress to dress, sizing up how each one might fit or look once it was on my body. I chose a beautiful silver-sequined dress.

But then, when I got it home and put it on, I had to question if it was a teeny bit too tight or ever so slightly too revealing or entirely too shiny! I had never bought clothes without trying them on and checking them in a mirror. It would take some getting used to. But I would have been laughed out of town if I'd gone back asking for a return. Things like that just don't happen in that market. So I figured I might as well wear it.

I wore black heels and kept my lily-white legs bare. I felt like the ensemble announced that I was a bit of a social clod or that I did not have a mirror. It probably even said that I did not have any close friends—nobody close enough to share a frank opinion, like: "Oh, Amy, maybe a different dress would be better?"

I rode to the party with Helen and her boyfriend. December is rainy season, and as I made my way up the driveway, my shoe got caught in the thick red mud. The heel broke off, and I hobbled into the party feeling like Cinderella—except her shoe trouble was at the *end* of the evening!

Two hundred people decked in their smartest evening attire were sitting at cloth-covered tables adorned with formal place settings and floral ornaments. Each guest had a table gift—a mini-bottle of either Baileys or Amarula. Drinks were flowing. Everyone was given champagne and wine, and the bar was open. Dinner was served by waiters and waitresses: ham, roast beef, and all of the fixings you would expect in the States. They also had chilled butter packages. You couldn't even buy fresh milk in this country; how did they get Land-o-Lakes butter foils? I understood very little about the country I was living in.

At some point in the evening, Helen mentioned that I could read palms, and before I knew it, people were lining up four or five deep. I grimaced at the memory of Mom saying, "Why are you taking that palm-reading book with you? You aren't going to teach children *that* are you?" That was never my intention, obviously, but it sure turned out to be a great way to meet people!

After that party, I spent quite a bit of time with Helen and the white Zimbabwean farmers. She and I would load into her little Suzuki and head out for a "sundowner," a customary evening drink at a friend's house. Sundowners began around 5 or 6PM and often ran long into the night. Most Zimbabwean children were in boarding school Monday through Thursday, so their parents were free to live it up—or at other times, to drown a few tears.

The Zimbabwean farmers had moved to the area after being booted off their farms in Zimbabwe. Michele, a Zimbabwean-born Portuguese citizen, told me the story of leaving Zimbabwe with her husband, Scott.

"We were mostly escaping an untenable political situation. The government was broke. Our dollars were worthless, and we were second- or third-class citizens with no right to justice, which is still the way today."

"Scott was chucked off his farm and had to make a new plan to earn a living. The rest of the farming community was much the same. For those of us near the commercial center, farming was more of a plan B in case things got worse, but most farmers didn't really have a place to go. They were being run off their land and killed.

"Having said that, after the crap treatment received by most of the black *and* white Zimbos, we were happy to go. And for the most part Mozambique welcomed us with open arms. Mozambicans treat us with great kindness to this day. Scott and I have been lucky. Some farmers didn't make it out."

While I was getting to know the Zimbabweans, I was building another social life with the Mozambicans. At the local bar, I would go back and forth between the Mozambican table and the Zimbabwean table. It reminded me of going back and forth between the Catholic and Lutheran Churches as a child. Customs and attitudes changed with the venue.

As I spent time with Helen and the Zimbabwean farmers, I came to the realization that I spoke "American" and not proper English. I was delightfully entertained as I learned new words like *spanner* (wrench), *pram* (baby stroller), and *bakki* (pronounced *buckie*, a little pickup truck). I would often have to ask them what a word meant, especially when they began to use African English words like *mushy* (cool or nice) and *chuffed* (a slang term used something like we use *stoked* in the States). I also learned that *pissed* meant drunk in Africa, rather than angry as in the United States.

Zimbabweans had experienced an incredible amount of trauma in their lives and often shared stories about getting out of their country and generally how difficult life could be. Most of the Zimbabweans had built good lives in Mozambique, but it was still not their home. Sometimes they would talk about "bloody Mozambleak!"

Whenever I would cross to the Mozambican table, the group would kindly switch to English. The fluency and ease weren't the same, but the content of the conversations was lighter. The Mozambicans never—never!—complained

110

because they considered it rude to do so. At their table, I picked up odd (and, as I found out recently, inaccurate) trivia, like Nike is the only American company that has never made anything in America and Pepsi is older than Coke. I learned some history as well. South Africa and Mozambique were closely bound: The former first lady of Mozambique had married Nelson Mandela.

I enjoyed listening as they shared information and perspectives about my home culture. They spoke of how they hoped America would get a female president because sometimes a woman could smooth out the mess created by a former male president. I liked that perspective, and I suspected that people in other countries might have a similar opinion. When George W. Bush was reelected, I saw a few Mozambicans in tears. I was amazed at how much our politics meant to them when apathy often reigns in our own country.

Still, there was one thing I learned about Mozambican life that I never understood. It seemed many of the Mozambicans had more than one name. For example, my friend Tonga was also known as Tchaba.

He explained it to me. "You see, it's like this, Amy— sometimes we use different names in different circles. It gives you a place to conceal yourself sometimes." Tonga went on to talk about corruption, but I always related the swapping of names with hiding things, like one's marital status. That is speculation, though. I'm not sure I ever fully understood the custom.

I learned firsthand a couple things about crime in Mozambique. The first time I had a cell phone stolen, a friend suggested I go to the market to buy it back or have somebody make a few calls and try to find it. But I did not have to do that. Somebody contacted me to see if I wanted to buy it back. He said he had bought it on the street and wanted to do the right thing, but he spent 1,000 meticais to buy it and couldn't afford to lose that money. "Perhaps you have another phone you can give me? No. Well, perhaps you could reimburse me the money I spent for this phone."

I knew that he had stolen it from me! But he made a good point—if I bought it back, I could at least retrieve my numbers. I agreed and re-purchased the phone.

But sometimes even in Mozambique theft had a tragic ending. One night a Zimbabwean businessman, Brenden, told us the following story.

"We were pretty proud of ourselves. These kids had jumped over the half-wall and snatched a lady's purse. We took off after them. We caught 'em too. They tripped and fell in a ditch in the dark. We called the cops thinking they would take the kids off to jail, but it was absolutely shocking what they did to those kids. They shot 'em! One in the hand and the other in the foot, saying they would never steal again."

The whole group was appalled.

"Evidently it's an embarrassment thing. If the kids had just stolen the purse, it would be one thing, but they had gotten caught. With that, they had embarrassed the cops.

"Sure, they won't steal again, but what kind of job can they get? Now we'll have to give them money every time they are begging because we got them into this bloody mess. They're ruined for life. Next time we'll just give them a walloping ourselves and let it go."

"You'll probably get thrown in jail for that," I said.

"Maybe, but at least kids won't get shot."

It was easy to see how a kid could fall into crime in Mozambique. There were not a lot of opportunities—especially for kids whose parents did not have resources to help them get started. When I was still working at the teacher-training center, I met a real street kid (who sometimes lived with his older brother). His name was Nelson, and he was thirteen or fourteen when I first met him. He sometimes attended *Formigas do Futuro*, the street-kid school next door to the teacher-training center.

I believe the car ride I gave Nelson one afternoon was his first; he was terrified. (Either it was his first ride, or he thought I was going to kidnap him!)

Nelson had a big grinning smile, a gentle presence, and a driving need to find work. I had no problem with that. He just wanted to carry water for three meticais a bucket or do some cleaning or some work so he could have a bit of money. I vowed to myself that if I ever had a real job available for him, I would find him.

At this time, I had a couple different jobs myself, though my job at the Pink Papaya was so enjoyable it could hardly be called work. I spent many an evening sharing a bottle of the Manica beer that Mozambique is renowned for. A one-liter bottle would be opened, poured into old-school four-ounce juice glasses, and shared among whoever was there. Sharing kept the beer from getting warm, a happy side effect of this Mozambican custom. Sometimes Nelson would bring new guests from the bus stop to the Pink Papaya. He would collect five meticais (about thirty cents) from Helen for walking the guests directly to her place.

Visitors came from all over the world to stay at the Pink Papaya: Israel, Spain, Australia, Japan, Austria, America, and Brazil, to name just a few. Many were aid workers, traveling through from one African destination to another. Many were tourists. The natural environment of Mozambique is enough to overcome many adventurers' concerns about malaria and putse flies and all the rest. Bazaruto Island, just off the coast near Inhassora, has some of the best manatee watching in the world. Isle de Moçambique, near Nacala, has a beautiful historic fort and breathtaking ocean views.

Thanks to Helen's wonderful housekeeper, Lina, my part was easy. All I had to do was schmooze the guests with entertaining stories and explain Mozambican culture.

Between my shifts at the Pink Papaya, I had time to attend to the school in Mudzingdaze, organize my thoughts and plans for the orphan center in Macate, and work on my ideas for safety programs. I felt like I was fulfilling my mission, or at least moving in the right direction.

After my surprise visit to the Mudzingadze school, the teacher had begun visiting me weekly (first at the teacher-training campus and then at the Pink Papaya), each time making a new plea for more money. I held out for several weeks, but I could see that if I didn't pay, he would leave the position. I still didn't want to let Joe down, and I didn't want this to contribute to any stories beginning with, "You know these white people…" or "You know those volunteers from the training campus…" I was concerned that if I did not make every possible effort at follow-through, the aid workers who followed in my footsteps would have even more trouble.

Though he had promised three years, it was soon clear that the teacher wasn't going to finish the first one unless he got more money. So I caved in. I knew the situation couldn't last, but I couldn't bear to let it go just yet. I had foreseen these funding problems. I shouldn't have funded any of the renovations until there was buy-in from the community to make the project self-sustaining. I should have refused from the start; that was when I'd had leverage. Instead I had ignored my intuition and moved forward with my fingers crossed. Still, it was the right thing, this preschool, and I had to admit I was pretty proud of what we had built with so little money.

About a year and a half after the preschool opened, I met with the regulo one more time to try to figure out a solution that would make the school self-sustaining, but it was hopeless. By this time I was pretty sure that classes had already stopped—probably months before, during the rainy season.

At the end of the meeting, we shook hands, and the regulo sighed and said, "*Fazer o que?*"

There was that phrase once again! "What to do?" It is such a self-defeating expression. So disempowering!

As far as I was concerned, Mudzingadze went down as my first failed project. In the year or so that classes had actually been held, maybe a few kids learned usable skills. Maybe the introduction to Portuguese would help them later. But other than the building, which wouldn't be standing for long without maintenance, nothing lasting came of the project that I could see. My $150 shoes had outlasted my $150 preschool.

Though I don't know how much the children learned, one thing was certain. I had learned a lot from the experience. I was infused with a sense that I had to be smarter and more practical in my attempts to help these children. I pinned my poem above my bed, reiterating the phrase over and over, "Does someone care enough to be smart?"

Daniel came down from Quelimane to see me a couple of times at the Pink Papaya, and he was like a fresh breeze blowing into town. One time he brought me a fish—it must have been eighteen inches long and an inch thick, and it was covered in very hard scales. I couldn't imagine how to get the scales off, so I wrapped the whole fish in tinfoil, with onions, carrots, potatoes, olive oil, and seasoning. Then I prayed it would be perfect. It did taste good, but the scales were quite a problem, an unfortunate circumstance we ignored (in true Mozambican fashion) as we raved about the flavor.

Daniel and I didn't get together often—maybe eight days in six months at that point—but I experienced a deep connection with him. I wondered about who he was, why he had come into my life, and what would become of us. I wondered if there really was an "us."

I was enjoying a glorious day at the Pink Papaya when I experienced what could only be called a premonition. The sun was bright and warm, and there was a refreshing breeze. I happened to glance at the fire pit and recalled my half-successful attempt to cook fish and how gracious Daniel had been.

As surely as if someone had just punched me hard in the gut, I heard a whisper, "There's a woman." The pounding in my heart turned into a silent scream. *There's a woman— something's wrong.*

Less than three minutes later, my phone rang. It was Daniel. "Amy, I have to tell you something. It's a little bit difficult."

Yes, there was a woman. The mother of his children, who had been away, had returned to his home to take care of the children.

Relationships can be complicated even under the best of circumstances, and they always seemed so in Mozambique. On some level I understood, and I was trying to be compassionate. But the news upset me.

From there my relationship with Daniel turned into a supportive but distant friendship, based mostly on texting. There was an undercurrent of sadness between us; I sensed that we both felt we had missed something that could have been great.

I was grateful that shortly after that conversation my schedule filled up, leaving me little time to think about Daniel. Between my job at the Pink Papaya, the struggling school in Mudzingadze, and the orphan center in Macate, I just got down to work.

My mind was filled with visions of the space that was coming together for the children in Macate. I grabbed a few buckets of paint and headed to the orphan center. On the walls, I stenciled numbers, along with the Portuguese name for each number and an illustration of the number. For example, the numeral 3, with the Portuguese word *três,* appeared next to three ducks, along with the Portuguese word for duck, *pato.* I also included the Portuguese alphabet and the names of all the letters. I focused on animals for the illustrations because, sadly, most of the children in this area had never seen animals (other than goats and wild dogs), and many had not even seen pictures of animals. Also, with this educational information on the walls, even adults sitting in meetings could practice their Portuguese.

I painted circles on the floor to create a Twister board because the game would help me teach children the Portuguese words for left and right, hand and foot, and so on. I had an idea for making the game-board dial using handprints, so I asked Sr. Chimoio if we could use one of the children's hands to create the dial. He readily agreed.

I thought we would just grab a random child. There were certainly plenty available. But, no. This became a political affair. Sr. Chimoio said that we had to choose "just the right hands." I waited an hour with increasing annoyance and irritation while he was gone looking. The little girl he brought back was probably his own relative or the child of a director who might repay him with a favor.

The child was terrified—she nearly cried—and I had the clear sense that she had no idea where she was going or why she had to talk with this Muzungu. The poor thing was probably traumatized for life. We eventually got the job done, though.

Accident prevention was at the top of my priority list for this orphan center. At that time, 25% of Mozambican children were dying by the age of five from curable diseases and preventable accidents, like falling into wells and being hit by cars. I had three goals: First, I wanted to teach them how to avoid accidents. Next, I wanted to teach them how to do first aid if there was an accident. Finally, I wanted to make sure they all had at least one vocational skill so they could have some options in life.

Whatever was necessary to survive—especially skills their parents might not know—that would be my curriculum. I would teach several types of safety: water, snakes, land mines, and dogs. I would teach first aid, including how to stop bleeding, bandage cuts, treat burns, assess and move an accident victim, splint a broken bone, and treat head injuries.

I decided, as I had in Dombe, not to teach mouth-to-mouth resuscitation or CPR. Again, cultural issues and the lack of a common language complicated things. My process for all of the classes was simple: start with the straightforward stuff. There was plenty of that to be taught.

# 19

---

In June of 2005, I made my first trip back to the States. My purpose was to establish a nonprofit organization and to raise enough money to operate for a year. Nonprofit status would benefit my efforts in a few different ways. It would let me apply for funds from other agencies, and I would be able to get a resident visa and stop leaving Mozambique to renew my tourist visa every thirty days.

In addition, friends and other contacts in the States had expressed interest in funding me and coming to help me. Nonprofit status would let them write off their contributions on their tax returns. Nonprofit status was necessary so people could come to Mozambique to help me. In order to get a visa for Mozambique, you have to have a reason for being there. Nonprofit status would mean that I could be that reason. In addition, as with the organization I had traveled with, I could host paying volunteers.

I left Mozambique using my return plane tickets from the previous year, with only $150 in my pocket and a plan to establish a survival-skills training center for orphans. I flew from Chimoio to Maputo to catch the bus to Johannesburg. I made my way through Immigration with the resounding "bang" of the stamp on my passport.

So far, so good. Another couple of hours on the bus to Johannesburg and then the flight out. *What could go wrong?* As we all stood waiting to climb onto the bus, I noticed a white gentleman, his Mozambican wife, and their two children standing near me. The woman and I were talking when word came that the bus had broken down. I glanced at the clock and felt like everything would be fine. There was plenty of time to get to Johannesburg.

The woman introduced me to her British husband. He was having a bit of an anxiety attack about this bus situation, and after half an hour, so did I. After all, I only had $150 for this trip home, which needed to include starting a nonprofit.

About then, a big black Mercedes pulled up. The husband climbed in front with the driver, and his wife and two children climbed into the back seat. "Hop in!" the woman called to me. I felt self-conscious about getting in this luxurious car to go to Johannesburg while everyone else was stuck waiting for the bus to get fixed, but I had a mission. I hopped in the back seat, and the little girl moved onto her mother's lap. We passed the time to the airport making small talk. It was a comfortable and enjoyable ride.

As the car sped along the highway, we agreed my contribution for the car hire would be $70. But I didn't have change—only a $100 and a $50—and by the time we got to the airport, I didn't have time to get change. I handed her the $100 bill. I estimated that I had just enough time to make it through check-in and (hopefully) get the cappuccino I'd waited for all year.

As I arrived at the coffee house and began reading the list of cappuccino delicacies, I heard a woman beckoning, "Lady, Lady!" It was the Mozambican woman from the car. She ran up with my $30 change. I gave her the most grateful hug, and she sped off to catch her own plane.

Suddenly I was grabbing a cappuccino in one of the most beautiful international airports in the world and heading to my plane on time—with nearly $80 in my hand, not less than $50. And I was about to be wined and dined by British Airways during the eight-hour flight to London.

The rest of the trip to JFK Airport in New York City was a blur of naps and snacks. I took a commuter bus from there to Port Authority—cumbersome, overloaded, and exhausted. (I was pretty impressed I accomplished all the travel without Chris and Lindsay!)

From Port Authority, I took the bus to Shelburne Falls, Massachusetts, where I was going to meet Carol Kelshaw, the Minister of Unity in the Pioneer Valley. She had invited me to return to her church to update the congregation, who I had met during my training when they responded to my fundraising letter.

When I got off the bus, Carol greeted me warmly, "Our congregation is so excited to have this opportunity to hear about your experiences! We all want to know what we can do now to help the children in Mozambique." I told her about my big plans for establishing a nonprofit and all that I was hoping to create in Mozambique (even though by now—because I had paid some locals for a quick ride that saved me two hours of waiting—I was back down to $50).

Shelburne Falls was a town with quaint little shops and a footbridge that crossed over cascading waterfalls. The mood of the place was directly from the pages of *The Hobbit*. I had gone from a corrugated tin shack to a gingerbread house. Talk about a change of scene!

After talking awhile with Carol and her husband, Will, I went upstairs to the guestroom, got into my pajamas, and collapsed into the luxurious down comforter. The room was a bit cool, and after three long days of traveling, I quickly fell to sleep.

I woke early but had a hard time surfacing from my deep sleep. For a minute I considered having a bit of a "lie-in" in the cloud-like bed, but felt like it would be bad manners. So I changed into something presentable and found my way to the kitchen by following the smell of breakfast.

Carol had already talked with Will about my vision of creating survival-skills training centers for children and my need to set up a nonprofit. When I arrived at breakfast—which was simple and wholesome and delicious—they were excited to tell me the news. For the past thirty years, Will had been a lawyer who specialized in setting up nonprofits! (I was in awe at this Divine Coordination.) Not only that, he would be willing to donate his time to do the necessary paperwork if I could raise the $800 for the IRS filing fee.

Will's appearance in my life, with his particular skillset, was not the first miracle in my experience. God/The Universe/The Great Spirit/The Divine had been supporting me all along.

Still, Will was one of the most distinctive miracles I'd experienced up to that time, and I felt very blessed by his efforts.

My nonprofit was created while I slept. I would emerge from napping in the guest room, and Will would ask me questions about what we were going to do at our orphan centers, what our mission was, and who we would serve. I would answer his questions, eat something, and go back to bed.

After each nap, I awoke to find that Will had crafted several more pages of the Internal Revenue Service application and had more questions for me. I gave him my answers, and he translated them into IRS-speak.

At some point, Will and Carol and I discussed my need for a board of directors. We decided I would be president, Will and Carol would be on the board, and several of Carol's congregants would round out the group. The only hiccup in the paperwork process was figuring out the organization's name.

I had explained to Will that in Mozambique we were known as TIOS, an acronym for *Treinamento Internacional para os Órfãos e sua Sobrevivência*, which more or less meant International Training for Orphans and their Survival. Will told me that name was too vague to work with the IRS and that submitting the paperwork with an unacceptable name would slow things down. We needed a simple, straight-forward name that told exactly what we would be doing. Will chose "AIDS Orphans Skills Centers" (AOSCI). He explained that starting with an "A" was always good because it put you near the top of every list. Besides, he said, this name told the IRS exactly what we did.

Who did we work with? AIDS Orphans.

What did we do? We ran skills centers.

I reluctantly agreed to the name, and Will was right. It got us up and running quickly. But I never liked it. Labeling children as orphans is stigmatizing enough but labeling them as AIDS orphans was even worse. If that had been our name in Mozambique, the whole community would have assumed that the children coming to our classes were from families that had AIDS, and no family would have wanted to send their kids to our program.

For the most part we resolved that issue by not using the AOSCI name in Mozambique. (We used TIOS instead.) Yet there was often confusion between the two names. Generally, the only time we used AOSCI was in the States on my fundraising trips. Each year it became more difficult to remember what our legal name was, and I would frequently fumble over the name in fundraising talks. So we ended up changing the name of the U.S. organization to TIOS— Training, Ideas, and Opportunities for Success. By then it was an easy change to make, just as Will had predicted.

On Sunday morning, Carol and I headed off to the church service at Unity. I could not wait to share how my calling, barely a whisper in 2004, had turned into a roar. Carol's church was at "The Grange," a simple old building with high-up windows. I was curious about the name, and much later I did some research. A group known as "The Grange" was established in the late nineteenth century by American farmers; it was a social group, a political group, and a community service group. Perhaps they had once used this building. But the term also refers to a country house, so who knows? I wish now that I had asked Carol at the time. In any case, The Grange was a simple place, with a stage for theater and music and hardwood floors throughout. I appreciated the lack of pretention in both the church and the service.

During training, I had observed Brian's ability to inspire people with stories of Mozambique. Because he had been there, his stories came alive. Now it was my turn. I told of the first preschool built with little more than $150. I told of the orphans who lived in the rural areas of Macate and kids who couldn't get across the riverbeds during the rainy season to get to school. I told of kids like Nelson, the street kid who just wanted an opportunity to make enough money so he wouldn't have to beg. I shared my conviction that all children deserve the skills to protect themselves and their siblings, along with opportunities to make a better life.

The congregation seemed to especially like that I was collecting materials to take back with me. I told them I was looking for how-to books on almost any subject, along with knitting needles, crochet hooks, glass cutters, embroidery thread and needles—basically anything left over from any hobby that had ever been abandoned. I told them that their castoffs could be used to teach young Mozambican women marketable skills that could help them build a thriving life.

I told the congregation what I knew for sure: There was no turning back. There was no stopping. Then I read my poem. After that, there was no stopping their enthusiasm and conviction to help me reach what had become *our* goal. There wasn't a dry eye in The Grange by the time I was done talking.

The congregants in Carol's church—and the many people who have donated money and materials over the years—liked knowing that contributions of castoff items and small amounts of money could be used to change lives. A lot of times when people donate to huge organizations, it can be difficult to see where the money goes.

I created TIOS with the intention of running it like I would my own business by keeping the expenses as low as possible. Another thing I did with a mind toward a business approach was to focus my spending first on items needed for income-generating activities—sewing machines and the like. Only when we had secured the ability to generate income did I move on to buy other things. My plan all along was to create a sustainable project that would far outlast my time in Mozambique.

Will and Carol lived in the same area as my training teammate Lindsay, who had by this time returned to the States. We met for coffee and chatted like friends do, about life and work and mutual acquaintances. She said she would be marrying Chris soon, and of course I was happy to hear it. They made a great couple. I was struck by how different her life was from mine. From where I sat, she looked squared-away and picture-perfect—way more so than I was, and I was at least ten years older.

I told her a bit about what was happening with my projects. She was very engaged in the details of my story, and it was refreshing to talk with somebody who knew some of the context (and especially the subtext) of aid work in Mozambique. She asked me how I was getting back and forth to Macate (chapas most of the time and a driver when I could afford it). We chatted some about the chapas, and then at some point she revealed the real reason she had asked for the meeting. Her father had a trust and had given each of his children the opportunity to donate some money to a worthy cause. Lindsay wanted to donate some funds to me!

She said she was quite sure it would be more practical for me to have a vehicle of my own than to keep riding chapas. She thought $7,000 could cover that expense. I was speechless. *A car!* I was so grateful that day and even more grateful each time I got into the little Mitsubishi I purchased on my return to Mozambique.

On my final night in Shelburne Falls, I met with my new board of directors for the first time. They had no more idea what they were getting into than I did, but they trusted that it was a good thing, a right thing, and that someday they would look back on it with pride. I agreed.

# 20

⇒○C/⌒⌒○○⇐

I was officially on my way to being a one-woman NGO[*], and soon IRS documents would arrive to show it. Even though the CNCS funding had not yet arrived for the project in Macate, I knew it would not be long. I continued making small improvements to the space—like the animals I painted on the walls—while I waited for the funds.

The limits on how I could spend that money were pretty clear. It would cover the building repairs and one manual sewing machine. The rest of what I needed (crayons and knitting needles, for example) would come from the material donations I had been given on my fundraising trip. I had collected almost fifty boxes of used materials, $800 a month salary to cover my living expenses, and about $7,000 for projects. It was enough for me to run the established projects and to start creating the safety curriculum, which I hoped to distribute nationwide.

The Macate renovations would benefit the Development Committee for a long time to come. The building was going to have electricity, and a washstand would be built behind the building so everybody could wash their hands and we could capture the gray water for our plants. Security bars would be put on the doors and windows. A local engineering firm generously agreed to build little tables for the children's workspace.

The people of Macate were most excited about the purchase of a large television and VCR. We would use them to show health-safety training videos and the HIV prevention videos created and distributed by CNCS. When the TV and VCR were not in use for the prescribed purposes, the committee could turn the building into an evening movie

---

[*] Non-governmental organization

house, which was bound to be popular since the TV would be the only one for at least twenty miles around. The committee would be able to charge ten meticais (about thirty cents U.S.) per person per movie, which would generate money for the center. They could also sell photocopies from the printer.

One caveat on the CNCS funding was that we had to spend the money within twelve months of receiving it (by July 2006). If we used the money correctly (which mostly meant using it completely), the following year we could apply for up to $20,000. But if we did not use every last penny, we would return the excess at the end of the year, causing a paperwork nightmare for the funding organization. If that happened, the organization would not fund us the next year because giving money back meant we could not administer a proper budget. Other funding agencies would be watching, too; if we mishandled the CNCS money, it would affect our ability to get funds from other groups as well.

I was very excited by all the potential. (I was already imagining how many kids I could help with $20,000 next year.) But after I received the funding, Helen warned me to be careful because aid projects could be smothered by complicated reporting paperwork. "It is easy enough to administrate a small project with a small budget. But when a new organization receives a large grant, like $20,000, they might have a tough time keeping up with the paperwork." Because I trusted Helen, I was careful to keep her advice in mind.

The plan and the budget were in place. Manuel drove me to Macate once again—this time to discuss the project with the local government official, Edalina Gavumunde. She had summoned me to meet with community members and officials so they could hear about my plans and ask questions. That seemed reasonable enough, and of course I agreed.

Questions came from community members as to what this program would do for their children, and I answered to the best of my ability. Then Edalina started speaking, and I noticed Manuel's face darkening as he translated. None of his words were upsetting. I could tell he was leaving out part of the communication.

Edalina said that my plan must include a snack for the orphans. She said I must feed them, that I could not expect them to come to this project famished and undernourished! She worked herself into a lather, raising her voice louder and louder. "Aid projects don't consider the needs of the children! Aid workers don't think about the real needs of the children they are supposed to help! What are you doing working in this country if you don't have enough funds to feed the children while *you* are drawing a salary here?"

I watched as the once-welcoming parents became disgruntled and then mutinous. They evidently had forgotten my original "I am not here" speech. On the other hand, Edalina was right that I had forgotten to include a snack in the budget. And now it was too late; I was required to spend the money the way I'd said I would. I prayed I would have the right words.

I spoke slowly and purposefully, hoping to sound confident. "Your children don't have to come to this project. This program is not meant to replace regular school; it is a place where kids can come and learn about safety. They can also learn some income-producing skills, and if those programs make money, we can spend it on snacks. We will work to earn money to buy food, just like you do at home. If children are given everything without earning it by skill or trade, they will learn to beg, and I will not support that."

Manuel and I made it through that brutal meeting, and the community approved the project. Of course they approved it; they were getting a newly renovated building, electricity, television, and the chance to be a movie house for the community. All of that would be at no cost to them; they only had to provide space for the school.

Unfortunately, from that day forward, Manuel was less available for driving. In particular, he would not return to Macate with me again. He knew how dangerous it could be to get on the wrong side of a government official, especially if you owned anything of value. Despite Manuel's deep commitment to helping the Mozambican children and in spite of how far we had come together—working in Mudzingdaze, developing the training programs—he withdrew from our work and, sadly, from our friendship.

# 21

⋯◦◦◦⋯

My vision for the programs and their potential reach continued to evolve. I decided that the way to reach the most kids with the lowest investment would be to create safety curriculum materials, like a safety manual and videos. I could teach one child or one hundred children—maybe even a thousand children if given enough time. Yet a safety manual that contained all kinds of accident prevention and safety information—road safety, land mine safety, water safety, fire safety, train safety—could reach more than a million children, and a video could reach even more. It seemed to me that the materials would be affordable and simple enough to develop.

In addition, I had started teaching HIV prevention. An older group of kids who wanted to participate at the Macate center began attending art classes and learning safety skills. Because they asked questions (and because I knew the information was important), I was soon teaching them HIV prevention. I had not really wanted to get too far into HIV (beyond the video screenings required by my grant) because it seemed like every organization was already teaching it; I wanted to stay focused on children's safety, which was not being addressed anywhere that I could see.

For the safety materials, I intended to save money by not re-creating the wheel. I knew that there were agencies nearby who had some safety materials on file, and I figured I could use them as a starting point in my efforts to develop safety curriculum for children. So I made a plan to talk with an official at the Driver's License Bureau to see if I could look at (only *look at*) their materials, get some ideas, and create our own materials in alignment with local standards and practices.

Moisés, a Mozambican who had experience making videos for NGOs, offered his skills as a graphic artist, and we went together to the Driver's License Bureau, which turned out to be the most technologically advanced government building I had seen in Chimoio. The workers there were all using computers, whereas right next door at the Notary building, births and deaths were being recorded in a book. We made our way up the stairs toward the director's office, an island of clutter in that sea of order.

I explained the project. Our plan was to produce a children's book that would teach all aspects of safety and highlight the work of local programs related to safety, including hers. I shared my thinking that if everyone could work together (not the normal Mozambican way, but what did I know?), we could produce effective materials without investing a lot of resources. We ended by telling her that we would publicly thank and promote her department for helping us.

She was icy. "You have some funds for these things, yes?"

"Well, yes, a bit. But we are not like a big funded organization. We are just small and trying to help children to stay alive."

"You should pay some money. These pamphlets and manuals are expensive. You should contribute some funds, like $1,000 to pay for them. You buy them from us and then *we* will come teach the children. This is not for you. This is for me. Do you understand? Not for you. For me."

*Really?* We just wanted to *look* at her materials. The department wasn't being asked to give up any funds or other resources. She was guarding her gold mine of safety books and posters in her very full cabinet, waiting to share them with someone who showed the right amount of "appreciation."

I was flustered. "We don't have $1,000. We are looking for a cooperative agreement to bring all aspects of safety to the children!" *What is wrong with these people?*

"You don't have $1,000? Who let you in this country? What are you doing here? Who signed your documents? What kind of organization are you that you don't have $1,000 to spend on your programs?"

"Thank you for your time, *Senhora Directora*," I said. Moisés had the same worried look on his face that I had seen on Manuel's after the Macate meeting. We left.

When I got home, I realized that having bad feelings between myself and the director of the Driver's License Bureau left me in a precarious situation. My project was American, which meant money, which meant opportunity, which meant "Amy needs to show *appreciation* for local assistance." And I had refused to do so. The director was in a position to confiscate my car or my driver's license. I hid my car in the garage, considering the director a bigger threat than the rats that might chew a few wires.

Unfortunately, Moisés left before the safety manual really got off the ground, but over the next few months, a young Mozambican/Zimbabwean named Yuri helped me. He was a talented artist, as the drawings showed. But we couldn't seem to get an effective layout, and the information came across as disconnected. I kept trying to make it happen, but the manual was never completed.

You might think—given the behavior of the director of the Driver's License Bureau—that her materials were being used for something. You might think that the children had received some safety training, at least around traffic issues. But that was not the case. It never ceased to amaze me: lack of road-safety training struck me as one of the most glaring oversights in Mozambique. Children—and even some adults—simply didn't know how to cross the street.

One time I had seen a woman with a baby on her back and a basket of bananas on her head hunch up and start to run across the highway. She got nearly to the middle lane before she realized that she was about to be hit, made a small scream, and ran back to the edge of the road. Bystanders laughed—not nervous laughter, mocking laughter—the same laugh that erupts in middle school lunchrooms when somebody drops their tray. Once I recovered from my near heart attack, I was puzzled by the incident: Did she just not know how to cross a street? Had she just come into town from the bush? Had she never seen cars before? And what was up with that laughter?

The next near miss I saw involved a young boy. The way he prepared himself for the crossing caught my eye. First, he froze. Then he hunched up; that's when I really started paying attention. Next, he balled his hands into fists and seemed to squeeze his eyes shut. Then he darted into the road. Like the woman, he was in the middle of traffic when he realized a car was coming too close and too quickly. He kicked in a burst of speed, nearly falling as he reached the other side. But he made it. God had been on his side.

On my next visit to the U.S Embassy in Maputo, I told my friend Aissa about the people who nearly died crossing the street. I liked and trusted Aissa, who was the picture of honesty and efficiency. Like most Mozambican women, she was serious. She believed in the possibility of helping her people and was determined to make an active part.

"I've watched them," I told her. "They go to the side of the road, drum up some courage, squeeze their eyes shut, and run as fast as they can." Then I told her about seeing a kid who ran in front of a pickup truck and got hit. Bystanders picked him up, threw him into the back of a truck, and drove away. I still wonder what happened to that little boy.

"It's a big problem here, Amy." Her voice was always gentle and soothing. "I recently read a study that was done in South Africa. They found that when the babies are tied on the mother's backs, which is for their first two years, they are normally positioned with one cheek flat against the mother. This lets them see with only one eye at a time. Because of this they don't develop their... what do you call that?"

"Depth perception?" I asked.

"Yeah. That's right. They can see the car, but they can't determine how far away it is or how fast it's going or just how soon it will reach them... and maybe kill them."

At that point, I knew I had to double my efforts to teach road safety. I began teaching it anywhere I could find someone who would listen. And during my next trip to Macate I did a demonstration with the teacher, using sticks to build a practice road in the driveway. After the kids had some practice, we went to a real road. I drove my car slowly back and forth so the kids could practice walking along the road and then practice crossing the road safely, with both eyes wide open the whole time.

The Macate kids were always open to this kind of learning. In fact, they were very eager for whatever experiences we could offer. Most of them had been coming from miles away, and they were always happy to be there. Even though most of the children did not yet speak Portuguese or, like me, did not speak it very well, we were impacting lives.

I continued to watch for needed safety skills and added them to my program. At one point, one of my Mozambican staff members mentioned that she had only climbed stairs a couple of times and they were frightening to her, so we started teaching stair safety. It was fun having this level of program freedom. If I decided one day I wanted to teach a class on fire safety, I would grab a capulana and a book of matches and teach it. The language barrier didn't matter because I was teaching through theatre. It soothed my right brain and my heart to have some time with the kids.

Because the children were all terrified of dogs, thinking of them the way U.S. kids think of rats, I brought in my three-month-old puppies to teach dog safety. The children ran away crying and screaming. In Mozambique, dogs carry disease, especially rabies, so on one hand the kids need to have solid respect for them. But these kids' reaction to dogs was over-the-top fear. They would actually provoke the dogs—poking them with sticks, throwing things at them—out of fear. And they had no idea how helpful and loyal a dog could be. So we taught them to be smart about dogs—not overly friendly, but unafraid and respectful.

One girl, who was about ten years old, said, "It's easy to see that *this* dog perceives enough to be trained, but we are surrounded by dogs from the streets." I explained that Pumba had come from the streets and that street dogs were the best dogs because they needed a home so desperately and would be loyal to the person who provided one. The children had never heard such an idea. Dogs were just dangerous. Best to just throw rocks at them or hit them with sticks. Although they remained unconvinced, at least we gave the kids some safety information—and maybe even protected a few dogs.

The curriculum for the little kids was pretty simple. Often I brought them pages out of donated American coloring books. Many times, those experiences were the children's first time using crayons or pencils. We also made sure kids got to see and use scissors, also usually for the first time. (Mozambicans, even the children, use razor blades to cut things; a lot of men wear a razor blade on a chain around their neck for this purpose.)

I soon discovered that the students, regardless of their task, took their work very seriously. I would see young girls with babies tied to their backs, coloring intently. These kids would walk for miles, even if they had a child to carry, because today a Muzungu in town had brought some kind of magic thing that they could color with or because today there was a Muzungu in town and she might take their picture. It was the same desperation I had first seen at the Mozambican border. It was the sense that, always, there would be only one chance.

# 22

With my work taking so much of my time, I did not have time to play hostess at the Pink Papaya anymore, so I had to find a new home. I was also on the hunt for a property where I could run my own program to test out different styles of teaching safety in Chimoio and make safety manuals and training programs, without dealing with the complications of outside teachers and regulos.

Often during sundowner rounds with Helen, I heard the stories from Zimbabweans about the opulent homes in the suburban zone of SOALPO (an acronym that stood for a Portuguese phrase, meaning roughly, "Cotton Producers' Society"). I recognized the word SOALPO from the first night I had ridden into Chimoio. Now I knew that SOALPO was also known as Textáfrica and that company had been a huge textiles manufacturer. The tract of land owned by the company had essentially contained a small town—a church, a hospital, a preschool, a zoo, a bullfighting ring, two swimming pools, tennis courts, and an airstrip. But that was during the opulent days, before the wars. Since then, in Chimoio alone, the list of Textáfrica employees had been cut from over 3,000 people holding all types of manufacturing, administration, and community jobs to only a handful of guards, kept to watch over the virtually empty plant and surrounding corporate housing.

After it became clear that I didn't have time to work for her anymore, Helen Large told me there were some houses available for rent on the old Textáfrica property. Her friend Mandy Retzlaff, who ran a horse rescue with her husband, was living in one of them.

My mouth dropped open the first time I pulled into the yard of the available rental house Helen had mentioned. The house was blanketed in bougainvillea. The windows were adorned in ornate metal bars, and a sweeping veranda wrapped the house. On the right side, a big avocado tree grew near the front of the property. Behind that, there was a large garden.

The home had three bedrooms, a kitchen and pantry, an office, and a large living room/dining area. There was a two-car garage, two dog houses in fenced kennels, a duck pond and covered aviary, four little adjoining storage rooms, a fully cemented driveway, and an indoor animal area that was full of pigeons and turtles. *Who had lived here?* For $350 per month, I decided it didn't matter. I signed the lease, entitling me to all.

It took a while to fully appreciate the full bounty of that garden. There was every plant imaginable: Litchis, loquats, sun fruit, piri-piri (hot chili peppers), avocados the size of Nerf footballs, mangos, even some kind of endangered prehistoric plant called a cycad. Best of all, there was a magic vine right outside my bedroom. Magic vines are lush and have beautiful red flowers that turn snow white in the night. To me, they were angels watching over my dreams.

Living at Textáfrica was a dream for me. I quickly put some textured paint on the walls to brighten the dingy white, and I replaced the red linoleum tile in the hallway with light gray. The rest of the house was pristine. Best of all, I finally had running water, though it was the color of tea during the rainy season. It was also cold, except for in the shower, where I had a "steamy." Hardware stores sold them for about $25, and they acted as an on-demand hot water heater. My friend Steve, who was an electrician, had installed this one. "Be careful of this, Amy. These things are killers!" His Zimbabwean accent made it come out more like *Keelers.* He always spoke with such drama. "I'm not kidding, Amy. If you don't ground those properly, they'll electrocute you!"

The overseer of my rental, Angelo Gerónimo, had found me two guards to watch the property: Ernesto and Alface. Ernesto seemed to be very happy with the change. He was happy, charming—even flirtatious. But Alface was glum, the picture of abject disappointment. Over time I figured that Ernesto had seen an "opportunity" with this Muzungu, whereas Alface had likely been thinking that Muzungus are unpredictable and that his job would be as well. But they were both good guards.

Alface took his job very seriously. I never found him sleeping or otherwise neglecting his duties. As much as he seemed distressed about working for me, he had an incredible work ethic. Ultimately, Alface worked for me twelve hours a day for six years, without taking so much as an hour off.

Now, Ernesto, charming and a bit sneaky, was another story. I would sometimes find him checking the grill after dinner to see if I missed any morsels. I once found him sleeping under the windows on the veranda. Then I started watching, and napping on the job turned out to be a bit of a habit.

I suppose he thought, "Everyone knows Alface guards here, so nobody will try to break in. Or he might have thought by sleeping under the windows, he would hear if someone tried to break in. Either way, I was unimpressed. So one night I crouched under the windows in my living room and began to make ghostly noises, "Wooooooooooo – woooaaaaaa – wooooooo."

I had positioned myself so he couldn't see me but I could peek out and see him. He had been sleeping with his shirt pulled over his head in an attempt to ward off mosquitoes. He jumped with a start and ran to the other side of the patio, trying to pull his shirt off his face so he could see. Luckily he got the shirt off before he fell down the stairs. His face was fraught with fear. I had to cover my mouth to keep from laughing. I checked the next few nights, and he was always on guard, sitting or walking about the property. Good! Or as the Zimbabweans would say, "Sorted!"

I told Angelo that I was looking for a building and property where I could create a new program. So he took me around the campus to see if one of the Textáfrica buildings would work. As we drove around, I knew right away when I saw the one. I pointed. "I want that one."

"That one?" he seemed surprised. Evidently nobody ever wanted *that one*, or perhaps I had picked the dirty table in the restaurant—and *that one* would mean some extra work for him.

"Give me a day or two, and I will see if this is possible."

I intended to use the new space for creating and testing programs that would be under my own control. I could make materials to distribute to others, basing the videos and manuals on our interactive experience. I wanted to focus on creating the training programs, and I would use the Textáfrica building for R&D to determine whether my ideas worked. I believed that replicating our programs didn't have to cost much, and I knew that teaching costs almost nothing. I might not have all the skills necessary, but I could figure it out.

A few days later, we were back at the property, and this time I had Steve and Mandy with me. I figured he'd be a knowledgeable person to have with me when we went inside. It was in serious need of some exterior paint, but the roof seemed mostly intact, as did the windows and the bars that covered them. Angelo produced the silver skeleton keys and unlocked the first door.

"Whoa, would you get a look at this, China?" Steve said in his Zimbabwean accent. (He called everyone "China." It meant "my friend" in Steve-speak.) We stopped dead in our tracks. The building was a time capsule. It sat right here on the main road, yet it had apparently not been entered since September 17, 1994. That was the last date that Textáfrica had been open in Chimoio, or at least we assumed so, since it was the date written on the chalkboard in the office. Pencils, papers, cigarettes, photographs, and even money lay on the desks. It looked just as it must have looked at closing time on the final day of operation, more than ten years earlier. It was eerie, to say the least.

The building was perfect for my purposes. It had two offices, a lobby, three large classrooms, and a long skinny room with tons of windows that would be perfect for a library. The building even had a water fountain like those I'd grown up with in my elementary school in Minnesota. (The water fountain didn't work, of course, but it was there.) There was no electricity or running water, but that didn't matter. We didn't need electricity to teach safety and hand-sewing, and we didn't need it to use our new manual sewing machines.

A couple of days later, a friend of mine, who happened to be a seasoned Zimbabwean businesswoman with flawless Portuguese, offered to talk to the cranky landlord on my behalf. The two of them quickly made the arrangements for the rental—$550 per month for one year.

As far as I was concerned, that was way too much, and the discussion had not gone well. I think my friend and the landlord might have known each other from previous dealings, and I believe that she was trying to maintain her reputation for business by trying to benefit both the landlord and me. I felt I had gotten the short end of the stick.

"I have to go back to try to get a better deal," I told her. "I can't rent that building at $550 a month for a year. It needs way too many renovations. I need it for less, and I need it for longer." I gathered my courage and went back.

I was nervous that I might not have enough Portuguese to negotiate a lease, but I was going to give it a try anyway. The landlord, Alfredo, was virtually unapproachable, and he sat back, frowning as he tried to understand. He smoked yet another cigarette, adding the butt to his already full ashtray. His demeanor made it clear that Textáfrica had turned into a bit of a headache for him. He was tired of it.

I explained that renovations could take the better part of a year. There was substantial rot in the north windows, and they would likely have to be removed. I would have to re-dig the septic and dig a well. I was not even certain we would find water on the property.

I don't know if he saw my point or wanted to get rid of me (probably a bit of both), but God was on my side. I walked out with a lease: $350 per month for three years. I left wondering exactly what had happened, and I think he did too.

# 23

—◦◦◦◦—

I had secured a location for my school; now I needed funding. I ended up developing a small grants proposal, which I submitted to the U.S. Embassy in Maputo. The application process was straightforward and a way for a small project to get funds. I created a budget and an activity outline with specific objectives for a one-year program. This was not the first time I'd applied for a grant, and it had gotten easier over time. The grant was approved for $16,000, which I thought was plenty to bring in some teachers and students and get started. At that time, I had no idea just how instrumental the embassy would become in my growth and progress. And in some ways, I would help them as well.

As I left the embassy one afternoon, a guard stopped me. "What about this HIV thing? How do you get it? Can I get it from sweat on a shirt?"

"No. Haven't you taken any HIV classes?"

"Sure. But all they do is tell us not to have sex or to have sex only when using a condom." He chuckled self-consciously.

I wasn't too surprised. I had heard about this common but ineffective training. In an effort to be politically correct, many aid organizations weren't speaking openly about the facts of HIV. They were just saying over and over again, "Use a condom." But Mozambicans do not, by and large, trust Americans, especially given the prevalent rumor that Americans were putting HIV in condoms. (HIV is said to be the powder inside.) Who were these white people coming along and telling them what to do in their sex lives? They needed to know that the object of using a condom is to keep body fluids separate because the HIV virus travels in body fluids. When they have that information, they can make their own choice.

"Use a condom" was not particularly effective advice if the person did not understand *why*. The motivation was not there without understanding.

But it seemed like an embassy guard should have good information. After all, employers in Mozambique are required to provide HIV education to their employees every year. I related the conversation to a man in charge of the small grants being distributed through the embassy. He said he wasn't surprised.

"The guards are contract workers, so we aren't the ones required to provide their HIV education. That falls on their employers. They probably don't know too much about it."

"Well, do you think they know first aid?"

"Probably not."

"Really? These are the people who protect your life. Wouldn't it be better if they knew first aid in the case of an emergency? What if this place were blown up? Wouldn't you feel safer with them guarding you if they knew first aid? And wouldn't you want them to know how to prevent transmission of the disease if something like that happened?"

"Well, they work for another company, so their HIV training is not our responsibility."

I let him off the hook. I knew he probably agreed with me, and it wasn't in his hands to make policy anyway. I offered to come back and teach the class for free, but it never seemed to work out. Still, the guards continued to ask me questions with every visit.

Even though I had not wanted to focus on the HIV education effort, once I came to understand just how ineffective a lot of the available classes were—with little effort to accommodate cultural and language issues—I became more engaged with the problem and, I hoped, its solution. I vaguely recalled an automatic writing message I had taken down in 2002 or 2003 that suggested I would do this work, but I didn't have my journals with me to confirm.

Daniel had a friend named Walter who worked with ECMEP*, the company that oversaw the road workers. He contacted me to see if TIOS could do the annual required HIV training for his employees. I thought this would be the perfect opportunity for completing our curriculum, so we took the contract. A translator and I headed off into the bush.

Over the course of six months, we did twenty classes for the road workers, traveling up to six hours to teach a class. I wore dresses or skirts to teach these classes. Mozambicans consider seriousness to be indispensable, especially for people in power. So I dressed according to their expectations for a woman in my position. (Peace Corps volunteers often dressed more casually and were regarded less respectfully as a result.) Because I dressed professionally, people perceived me as serious, and they always gave me a chance.

After only one class with the road workers, I knew that posters showing intimate body parts were never going to work with the Mozambicans. They recoiled from graphic images of penises every bit as much as Grandma Clara might have.

So we had to think of another way. I remembered the anatomical dolls I had seen during my training in the States. They had been used for years to help children talk about sexual abuse, and I thought they might work here, where even adults struggled to talk about sex. I decided I needed to make some dolls.

I mentioned the idea to Yuri, who was helping me teach HIV classes. His mother, Elise, led a project teaching embroidery to local girls, and Yuri said she would be happy to help. I had one sewing machine, some fabric, and some thread when Elise showed up at my house. She had her friend Berta in tow. Together, the three of us began to sew dolls.

---

* *Construção e Manutenção de Estradas e Pontes* (Construction and Maintenance of Roads and Bridges)

Those first dolls needed some refinement. We hadn't yet figured out how to make hair, the shoulders were too square—like Herman Munster's—and they had crab-like claws where their hands should have been. They worked anyway! Our dolls were like pound puppies—so ugly they were cute.

I thought back to the professional $200 dolls that Cathy bought and decided we had done pretty well. Ours were much homelier; there was no denying that. But something about them was clearly Mozambican. Most people thought they were humorous, which worked for us. We used finger cots (like food-service workers use to cover a bandage) as condoms for the dolls. The finger cots came rolled like a real condom so they worked well for demonstration. They came in boxed packages of small, medium, and large, but our dolls never needed the small ones!

Soon Elise was taking her work home. She reveled as she told us dramatic stories of her nighttime work sessions. She would work well after her husband went to bed. Once he fell asleep, she would peek under the covers to compare her design to the "real deal." Then she would go back to sewing.

I wanted to close my eyes every time she pulled a doll out of a bag to proudly show the replica of her husband. But I would merely (and quickly) excuse myself to "go check something."

The dolls' private parts continued to get bigger. This was a good thing for doing a demonstration in front of a group. The problem was that I could only get the mixed-size boxes of finger cots. I was buying several boxes to get enough large condoms for our dolls. Then the penises got even too big for the large size, and since I couldn't just run to America to get XLs, I had to issue a "penis recall." Several of the male dolls had some pretty painful surgery that day.

The dolls worked like a charm. Instead of silencing people the way the posters had, the dolls improved interaction. Participants razzed and ribbed each other. In my experience, everybody loves to laugh (especially about sex), so humor became one of our most important tools.

Over the course of time, I had a number of different translators go with me to do the training. Translators' availability was unsteady, so I kept a list in my cell phone. At the road-worker sessions in the bush, we would often find that more than half of the group didn't even speak Portuguese, so my translator would translate English into Portuguese, and a local translator would translate that into a local dialect.

Still, HIV has a very specific vocabulary, and translating it was difficult because some words don't have a direct translation into Portuguese. For example, in Chimoio, the dialect word for anal sex translates to a word that means something like picking up a coin you've dropped. I could not imagine how other organizations were teaching the information without dolls to do the demonstrations. My Portuguese was just strong enough to follow the translation and make sure the information was relayed correctly.

We used the dolls to fill in the gaps. Instead of struggling for a polite word to reference oral sex or pulling out a poster or making a lewd gesture, we could simply hold the dolls up, without taking their clothes off, to show what we were saying. It was very effective. Of course, we did remove the clothes to demonstrate condom use.

One day, we were teaching in the bush at LorFor, a rural sawmill town. We started with the usual twenty-five or thirty employees required to take the course. Most of them had large families and many had more than one wife. Though their income was meager, their jobs likely provided enough cash to trade for an occasional "favor," and many of them got HIV in the bargain. They would then give the virus to their wives, and it was only a matter of time and a couple malarial mosquitoes before their kids were orphans.

The class that day at LorFor, like every class, began with a game of "Chinese Whispers." In the United States we call it the "telephone game." A message is whispered to the first person who whispers it to the second and so on until the message makes it to the last person. Then the message told to the first person is compared with what the last person heard. The two messages are always very different.

This game served the same purpose in Mozambique as it serves in U.S. elementary schools: It shows that when messages are passed around, they get changed, often in important ways. The game motivated the participants to sit down and pay attention before we got to critical information.

Then we played "The Four Consequences of Unprotected Sex." We posed the question directly: "What are the four possible outcomes of having unprotected sex?"

"Number one?"

Somebody would call out, "Pregnancy."

"Yep, everybody knows that one."

"Number two?"

"STDs."

"Yep. Bet nobody here's had one of those." (Chuckles here and there.)

By this time in the class, if we had not heard any laughter, we knew we weren't getting through. We needed to switch to a different language and/or a different translator. We would often test three languages before getting to the one that reached the majority of the group.

"Number three?"

"HIV?"

"Yep—the reason we're here talking today."

"And number four?"

Silence. This one stumped them.

"Number four?" Nobody could come up with it.

"Number four is satisfaction, guys—or at least we all hope it was satisfying."

"Then, when we wake up in the morning what are we thinking? Yah—'Satisfaction, nice.' But what about the other three consequences? Couldn't we have satisfaction *and* be pregnant *and* have an STD *and* have HIV—all four at the same time? Yes! And we would have no way of knowing. We would have no idea when we got up the next day that we were anything other than satisfied."

We did everything possible to improve our communication. First, we tried to make sure that we knew which local language we needed for communication. Then we made sure we were getting an interactive response. We also related the new HIV information to things the people already knew and really understood. People everywhere understand pregnancy. The association of new information with familiar facts would lock the information in their minds.

As time passed, a strange thing happened. Out there in the bush, the groups began to grow. People saw desperately needed information being taught in a way they could understand, and they wanted that information. Sometimes aid workers—even directors—complained that Mozambicans don't care. They say Mozambicans don't listen anyway, so nobody's training can work. But that was never my experience.

Instead of wondering whether the Mozambicans cared, we focused on showing them we cared, that we had their interest in mind. They saw that. We kept trying until we found a way for each group to understand what we were saying, and they saw that too. I also think they appreciated that we weren't there in a $60,000 Land Rover handing out biscuits.

At the end of our HIV classes, we taught first aid to give participants another viable tool to protect themselves and their coworkers and loved ones. Last, we taught an income-generating skill. Sometimes we taught how to reuse water so they didn't have to carry as much—but no matter what, we always taught some information that would improve the lives of participants.

We were doing pretty well. For example, by the time that ninety-minute class was done in LorFor, more than seventy-five people had gathered along the highway.

# 24

Early in 2006, a donor introduced me to Church World Service and their programs in Mozambique, including PEDRA*, which focuses on girls' empowerment, education, and skills training. One day while running errands in Maputo, I stopped in to meet them and explore the possibility of working together. The directors were a Canadian couple, Karen and Bill Butts.

I decided to come clean from the start. "Look. I have to tell you I'm not very experienced or even educated. But I've got a great program for teaching HIV prevention using anatomical dolls."

There was no missing the delight on the directors' faces as I pulled out one of the ugliest dolls ever created.

"What they lack in style, the make up for in usefulness," I said, returning their smiles. "We use them to bypass language barriers in many different kinds of classes: HIV prevention, especially condom use; accident prevention; first aid; mouth-to-mouth. All kinds of things."

They took a closer look. "These dolls are amazing, Amy," Karen said. "How have things been going during your start-up?"

"We've had our challenges. A teacher bailed out of my first project, a preschool in Mudzingadze, and it collapsed. Our second project—an orphan resource center in Macate—sometimes does great, but I think it may be suffering low-grade corruption. I'm waiting for the metaphorical roof to collapse at any moment."

The director opened a cupboard door and pulled out a box that held a number of HIV prevention T-shirts. The shirts

---

\* *Programa de Educação da Rapariga* (Program for Girls' Education and Protection)

reflected a common misunderstanding. They said, "Be positive and live free," implying that if you were HIV-positive, you could live free. Clearly, that was not the message they'd had in mind.

"Amy, we spent $4,000 on these T-shirts, and we can't even wear them to clean the house. I only keep the box to remind me to double- and triple-check things before they are done. We laugh about it now, but at the time it was pretty traumatic for everyone. So I'm not surprised you've made mistakes; we all have. Mozambique has a steep learning curve." I was grateful for her graciousness.

Aside from the regrettable error with the T-shirts, Karen's PEDRA projects struck me as very professionally organized. Karen and Bill were teaching girls about hygiene, sanitation, and sexual safety, along with small crafts that could conceivably become money makers. They had a school scholarship program that required the girls to complete interviews with adult leaders. The directors seemed excited for me to teach the girls about first aid and soap making, and I was excited to learn more about the structure of their program.

I knew that our anatomical dolls were a large part of our success with the HIV classes. They were also attracting the attention of powerful donors and other aid organizations. I saw potential to develop the dolls into a commercial concern that would fund the projects well into the future and provide jobs and income for our older female students.

The $200 anatomical dolls had been outside my price range, but now I decided the time had come to order one set to see how they compared to the dolls we were creating. Although Elise and Berta were doing a great job with the dolls, I wanted them to see what the commercial dolls looked like. If we could improve our design, we could sell the dolls to other agencies that were delivering HIV/AIDS information, thus generating income for our program while helping our girls to develop sewing skills.

Normally, only boys are taught to really sew in Mozambique because only men are tailors. However, dolls were considered children's toys, so women could make them without anybody saying anything. Little could any Mozambican imagine that our girls would generate more than $10,000 per year sewing those dolls, funding self-sustainable projects and earning income for themselves.

When the commercial dolls arrived, we compared them to those we had created. Ours were definitely more generously endowed than the American dolls, which were created mostly for use by children. Also, the American dolls had rather cute, cartoonish faces, whereas ours looked more like actual Mozambican people, right down to the clothing. So in most ways, the details of our dolls were different from the American dolls, and that suited me fine. I didn't want to be copying anyone else's work; I just wanted to show my sewers what a commercial cloth doll actually looked like.

When the renovations at the TIOS School in Textáfrica were completed, I needed to hire somebody to oversee the sewing and to start up our girls' projects. My time was spent in the office—coordinating documents, accounts, and paperwork. Keep in mind, I quit my second semester of college after the school counselor informed me that I had tested with the lowest math interest she had ever seen. Though I later developed pretty good math skills as a Cat adjuster, I never did develop a great love for spending a day at the computer doing accounts. Still, that's how I spent the majority of my time—administrating the program.

Berta was the easy choice to oversee the girls' work. She was very focused, serious, and skilled. She taught the girls how to sew, and she loved them. Her face would beam with pride when she worked with the girls. Berta learned and taught soap making, baking, proper hygiene and sanitation, and fine craft skills including electronic embroidery. She loved to bake banana bread, and she reveled in being the one Mozambican in Chimoio who knew how to do it. (In a country that had an abundance of bananas, it seemed nobody had seen banana bread or cake.)

At the same time, Berta was in school at night. This was very common in Mozambique—adults trying to finish their education with evening classes. Eventually, Berta attained a ninth- or tenth-grade education, far beyond the level reached by most Mozambican women. She is still one of the most hardworking people I've known. Berta always had a willingness to learn and to teach and to do whatever needed to be done. By the end of our time together, she had learned to use the computer, keep track of the accounts, and make payments. In retrospect, I should have trained Berta to be the director of the programs. I should have started that training in 2006, from the very start.

# 25

The director of the Labor Department had asked if he could come by on Saturday to see our dolls and our project. We had just finalized all of our documents in the city and were finally officially operating the TIOS School, and I could not have been happier. I knew the director had a full week, and it didn't seem unreasonable that he would ask to stop in on the weekend. Alface seemed dubious, but the director was coming at nine in the morning. What could possibly go wrong?

Well, when he first arrived, I could smell that he had been drinking, but I couldn't tell how drunk he was. Alface stayed close. I can see now that he recognized the man as trouble. I took the director through the building. He was in a surly mood and looked down his nose at everything. My anxiety was rising, and my heart was beating faster. I should have had him come on a day when Berta was there. She was the epitome of professionalism, and she could have handled this guy. I was very glad that Alface was standing by.

When I showed the dolls to the director, he said, "These dolls are ugly." There was really no denying that, but they were effective.

At that point, I had shown him everything. Suddenly he approached me in my office and took my hand, pulling me to him. I had no interest beyond business where this man was concerned, and not only because of the HIV threat. In a two-second prayer to God, I pulled away from him rather sharply. Then he shoved me up against the blackboard. There was no mystery where he was heading.

"Look, sir," I said, "You are a Director. I am a Director. There is no place for us to cross this line. It will only end badly for both of us." I'm sure God gave me the threatening presence necessary for my words to sink in. He grumbled at me, but I could see my words had hit home. He had just put himself in jeopardy. What if I turned him in? What if I reported him to the governor? He turned on his heel and stomped out of my office, clearly sore that he was not getting what he came for.

I had to sit down after he left. My legs were trembling uncontrollably, from a different kind of parasite this time. I was not easily rattled, but this man had a lot of power. Desperate to speak to someone about the experience, I gathered the pluck to phone Daniel in Quelimane.

"Daniel? Uh, I just had a situation with the director of the Labor Department." I tried to explain to him how this had happened, but my words fell short.

"Amy, if you want to have sex with this man, uh, it is okay. But keep in mind that these people can be a little bit dangerous."

*Hell, no! I didn't want to have sex with this man. Did Daniel seriously think I was calling to get permission to have sex with this guy?*

"No, Daniel. That's not what I'm saying at all. I'm scared this man will come shut us down because I refused to have sex with him. Is there anything I can do?"

"Well, you could talk to my brother Santos to make sure that your documents are in order. If your documents are right, he can do nothing to you. As you told him, you are both directors. And you are American, with diplomatic connections. He should not threaten you. Directors have a duty to maintain some level of professionalism. He should not have approached you the way he did."

I appreciated the reassurance, but I continued to live in fear, and the director and I had a tenuous relationship for all of my years in Mozambique.

I did talk to Daniel's brother Santos about the experience with the director. He listened to me carefully, getting every last detail before speaking. Then he assured me that my documents were in order and that the labor director posed no threat to me. To be absolutely certain, he called his older sister, who was very high up in the Finance Department. They agreed my documents were set up correctly and that the director could not touch me, politically at least.

Before then, I had not known that Daniel's siblings held such powerful positions. In this and many ways, it was clear the whole family was educated and savvy. Of the eleven siblings, not one had died of or contracted HIV, and they were all progressing in their careers, even Geoff, who was still in high school.

Not long after the run-in with the labor director, I had an opportunity to see Daniel. I went to Quelimane, where I had first met him and where he lived and worked. He got us a small room, where we met. He couldn't seem to sit still, and his eyes could not meet mine. He was in a hurry, and we made love quickly, desperately, and furiously—like everything depended on it, like time was running out.

Soon after, Daniel said he had to do some work and offered to drop me somewhere so I could have dinner. *Really? Not even dinner together?* He drove me to a street-side café about a mile from the bus station, saying he would be back in forty-five minutes. I saw his truck drive back and forth a few times and assumed he was running errands for work. I was annoyed. I would rather have ridden around with him in the truck than sit at a café alone. Also, I had paid for my own ticket, and the trip up to Quelimane had been downright harrowing—an uncomfortable bus ride, a bus breakdown, and several miles riding in the cab of a semi-truck, which Daniel had warned me was very dangerous.

I hadn't gone through all of that to sit alone at a café. But I knew that Daniel's work was very important to him, and I respected that. I picked up my cell phone. He was already twenty minutes late, and it was getting dark. I sent him a text to ask if I should walk to the bus station. He said that I should wait for him. I waited another fifteen minutes. Still he didn't come. I knew the road to the bus stop was dangerous, especially at night, and I wasn't going to sit there until the restaurant closed and I was stuck. So I began to walk. Minutes later, Daniel showed up out of nowhere.

153

When we got back to our room, Daniel said, "My uncle died and I need to move his body to Nampula."

"What? Now? A five-hour drive in the dark? You are the one who is always so adamant about the dangers of driving at night. You told me I was being foolish getting in that semi today, and I guess you were right. But now you're taking an even greater risk."

"I'm sorry, Amy." He put a bus ticket in my hand, and then he was gone.

Not long after Daniel left, I realized—*Oh, good Lord*—I was in a house full of men I did not know. I had no clear idea where I was—other than near the bus station for my 3AM walk in the dark. I tiptoed into the hall to use the bathroom and spent some very nervous minutes behind that unlockable door. Then I lay down for a while, but I did not get any rest. I felt foolish, like I had spent my time and my money coming to see a man who was not particularly interested. I flashed back to memories of chasing after my brother as a kid. I never caught him. Why did I keep chasing?

But abandoned wasn't the only thing I felt. I had great compassion for Daniel. Mozambique was his home, and low life expectancy and high child mortality were not just numbers to him. They affected his family. Maybe, just like he said, his uncle had died, and maybe that was part of a steady stream of death in his life, like the steady stream of funeral processions heading to Chimoio's cemetery.

# 26

One of my earliest and deepest connections in Mozambique was formed with Vasco Galante. We met because we were both volunteers with the same organization. He was from Portugal and came to Mozambique with the same organization I had come with, although later. We ended up developing similar goals for our work in Mozambique, and over time we developed a friendship that was very important to me.

We helped each other as much as we could. Once he sent his son to help me with a project, and I appreciated that both of them were willing to help. After that, his friend Christina had come from Portugal. He brought her to meet me, and she fell immediately in love with the children in Macate. I will admit that I was a bit jealous because she had the freedom to just love the children during her time in Mozambique; she didn't run a mission to help them stay alive. She was also young, pretty, wealthy, and charming. (Not that any of that bothered me!) The cherry on top was that Portuguese was her first language.

She was not an easy volunteer for me. I was already having plenty of communication issues with children and adults, and it was difficult to be around her while she casually chatted with everybody from her very first day. Never mind if the people couldn't understand what she said (because *their* Portuguese was so bad). She understood their confusion and repeated herself until her meaning was clear.

A Brazilian friend once joked with me that the reason his country was relatively undeveloped was because the people there spent their entire lives trying to learn Portuguese, their native language. That may have been a joke, but it sounded reasonable to me. I often heard Vasco and his son debate, sometimes to the point of arguing, just exactly how something should be said. If those two very educated native speakers could argue about how to say something in their own language, how did I ever stand a chance?

I could not communicate with Christina. She used a Portuguese conjugation I had never heard—one intended for cute little children. I had never been taught or introduced to it because the organization that trained me didn't want their volunteers to make a mistake and call a statesman or official a cute little child. We had been taught only one conjugation (the one for mid-level officials) out of about sixteen that are possible in Portuguese. *One* had been enough of a struggle for me!

Christine would chatter away in Portuguese, at a speed I could never follow, and my irritation over it added to my overall frustration. Portuguese was wearing me down on every front. Within a week of learning how to say something new, somebody would tell me, "You can't say it that way, Amy."

I had been an avid communicator my entire life. Mom had once told me I didn't really have a first word; I had a first sentence. Being unable to communicate in Mozambique was like a personal purgatory.

One day we were in the car when Christina said something starting with the dreaded conjugation. My mind raced, trying to figure out what she was saying. She repeated it again—in an overly soothing voice that came across as condescending. *Really, God? You have got to be kidding me.*

From the bottom of my belly, a scream rose to and through my lips… "I hate Portuguese!"

Poor Christina, who was there out of a desire to help, could not have imagined I would respond in such a childish and irrational manner.

She said something back like, *"Não gosta Portuguese, Amy?"* (You don't like Portuguese, Amy?)

I was over the top with stress, in particular with the language. Even with such an educated and accomplished conversation partner as Christina, I couldn't communicate. And of course there was no way I could help her understand that, either.

To her credit, Christina never criticized me for my rude outburst. Her bond with the Mozambicans continued to improve, and I was ashamed of myself for acting so childishly.

When I think about all of the ways my bad Portuguese got in my way, one story springs to mind. I'd had a long line of translators, some of whom were very distinguished. (One man who translated for me had translated for Jimmy Carter.) Most of them did a good job, but when I wrote to officials, I often asked Vasco to help me make sure I was getting the message right. Not long before this story took place, he had taken a position at Gorongosa National Park, which had been keeping him very busy. I didn't want to bother him with a short letter to the Portuguese ambassador, so I hired a translator who was well recommended by the Institute of Languages.

We always struggled to keep translators and teachers with decent English skills because of the dramatic split in Mozambique between the minimum wage (which is what Mozambicans receive) and the wages received by employees of NGOs. For laborers like road workers and guards, minimum wage was the U.S. equivalent of $100 per month for six days of work per week, and people in government jobs did not make much more than that. Compare those salaries with an NGO secretary who might make $1,000 per month or an NGO director who could easily make $2,000 per month hired in-country, or even double that if hired into Mozambique from another country.

Often translators started with us to get NGO experience, but they would usually transfer to an aid organization with proper salaries as soon as they had the chance.

I had a plan to go to Maputo, where the ambassador's office was located. The main reason for my trip was meeting with the Christian Council to demonstrate the effectiveness of our dolls, but I was hoping I could see the ambassador during the same trip. I was excited to show him the dolls and tell him about the programs we were creating.

I only had a few days before my flight, and I wanted to get the letter written and sent, so the translator came to my house in Textáfrica to take down the letter and type it up for me. Once he finished the translation, I read it, signed it, scanned it into the computer, and sent it off.

I didn't have to wait long for a response. Vasco called me the next day. "Amy, I heard from the Portuguese Ambassador."

"Oh, yeah?" I said, excited for news.

"Yes, Amy. He wants to know if you are crazy, if you are a crazy woman who has escaped from some asylum or someplace like that."

*What had gone wrong?* I could barely breathe. I kept my voice low. "Why? Vasco?"

"Amy, I've told you a hundred times you cannot use those computer translators. They don't work for Portuguese."

"I didn't use the computer, Vasco. I used a translator from the Institute of Languages. What went wrong?"

"Well, basically, your letter says you are making dolls—sex dolls. It says that you have orphan girls making these sex toys and that you would like to show them to the Ambassador to see if he is interested."

"Oh come on, Vasco. It didn't say anything like that." I had the letter in front of me. "Wait a minute. We said, *bonecas anatómicas,* anatomical dolls. That's what we have been saying since the very beginning. Even you have used that phrase."

"It's the context, Amy. You used a casual conjugation at the beginning. Your letter started like "Hi, Honey—I've got these dollies for you!"

I was horrified. Vasco was kind of laughing at me, but I could tell I had made a very big faux pas—for myself, for my program, even for Vasco. Vasco had smoothed it over with the Ambassador, explaining that I had used a computer translator to do the letter, not realizing how it would impact the tone of the message. Nevertheless (and maybe this goes without saying), the ambassador declined the visit. My Portuguese still had a ways to go!

# 27

We eventually created three PEDRA clubs for the girls in the Chimoio area. One was in Chissassa, a tiny village in the bush. There was no real town there, just a school that seemed to have been plopped down on the side of the road. But hundreds and hundreds of children attended that school. Pazit had told me that the word *chissassa* means "the bonding time." The word refers to the first week after the birth of a child, when a mother stays with her baby and no visitors are allowed. It is a time for mother and child to get to know each other.

I had vowed in 2004, when Pazit had taken me to Chissassa, that I would return one day and make a project there. (I often kicked myself for creating my first orphan center in Macate rather than Chissassa.) So I was excited to bring a PEDRA project there, with funding from Church World Service. Berta facilitated the project and the classes, and it was clear from Berta's beaming face and stories that Chissassa had been a perfect choice for the girls' club. The classroom, Berta told me, was often full to overflowing, with girls literally lined up at the windows wanting to join the activities.

We created one PEDRA club at the TIOS School, and one in the nearby *bairro,* or neighborhood, of Nyamaunya. Our programs mainly focused on health safety products, like anti-bacterial soaps, potholders to prevent burns, and cup covers to keep bugs out of drinks. We taught the girls hygiene, sanitation, early childcare, basic gender empowerment, and all the accident prevention and safety classes.

I prepared myself for what would be my first PEDRA visit to Quelimane, where I would teach first aid, accident prevention, and HIV prevention using the dolls. Karen, the director in Quelimane, found many uses for the dolls—including using them for theatre to prepare the girls for their scholarship interviews.

"Amy, you wouldn't believe it. Before the dolls, we couldn't get the girls to talk! They needed to get through these interviews, and they wouldn't say a word. We were starting to get worried that none of them were going to get scholarships to go on to school. Then we brought out the dolls and within half an hour, we couldn't get them to shut up! They were a huge success, Amy! Who could have ever guessed?"

I had a meeting in Quelimane to meet with Karen and Bill to talk about the programs. I was also excited to have the opportunity to see Daniel. I phoned him to tell him the good news: Finally I would be working in Quelimane.

"Ah, Amy. That is good news. But I am sorry. I have some not-so-good news. The WFP is moving me up to Nacala" (a city on the Indian Ocean north of Quelimane). Instead of it being easier and cheaper to see Daniel, it would be more difficult and more expensive.

The word *Nacala*, which has such a beautiful sound, means "Here I stay." For me, though, it meant Daniel was going away. For me, the word *nacala* meant "loneliness."

# 28

One thing I can say about aid work is that it is rarely boring. Ever since my first taste of the international community, so long ago in training, I've had very, very interesting people in my life. I've met people from all around the globe and people from all walks of life.

At a fundraiser in the States, I had been introduced to a private (and for the sake of his privacy, nameless) donor with an interesting approach to aid projects. His personal mission was to fund small projects around the globe. He would hear about a project and confirm it was run by a trustworthy organization. Then he would raise money for a specific material or financial donation, and travel to the location to see that the donation was put to good use. In other words, he took the funds and donations he collected directly to the programs to make sure they were used as intended.

Since meeting, we had been emailing about which of my projects he might help with. After kicking around a few ideas, we decided to build a brick bread oven. My thinking was that we could stop buying bread in town and instead make bread at the center. We would save money, the girls would learn how to bake bread in a homemade oven, and we could sell surplus in the community.

The donor was excited to be part of a project that would give the kids a vocational skill for the future as well as make money to help the program be self-sustaining. It was an approach he continued after our project.

I headed to Beira to meet the donor, who was traveling with his nephew, a student at Stanford. It was a rainy, gray, and fairly cool day, and my car had a problem. Something was making a horrendous racket the three hours back to Chimoio. The angels must have been watching over us that entire trip to get us back in one piece.

The next day, the donor and his nephew set the oven's first bricks. The oven was built from all local materials. It was about five feet tall, four feet wide, and five feet deep. It had a simple steel door like you would find on a wood-burning stove.

The donor also brought toothbrushes and toothpaste for the kids. The kids loved it. I can still see those forty children brushing their teeth on my porch, swishing and seeing who could spit the farthest.

The donor came to me one morning during his stay and said, "You know, I can't believe how late I've been sleeping here. I never sleep past six."

I'd had a similar experience, and it had taken me awhile to figure it out. "It's because there are no birds here," I told him.

"What? Wow—I hadn't noticed it. Where are they?"

"I don't know. There have never been birds here during my time, just those big white and black crows. My theory is that the birds were either killed for food during the wars or they left because of the shooting and artillery. Now there is not much habitat, so they still haven't returned, even though the war has been over for ten years."

That story brings me to another great character (and friend) in Mozambique, Allan Schwarz, who was somewhat of a celebrity. He had been a professor of design at MIT and college mates with John Kerry. He had had once dated the lead actress from *The Gods Must Be Crazy*, who was very famous in Africa. Now Allan lived in a tent in the bush, raising trees to mitigate the deforestation in Mozambique. He was creating habitat, adding oxygen to the atmosphere, and providing wood for cooking fires.

A year or so after my conversation with the donor about the birds, I heard one singing. Then a month or so later, with great excitement, I ran outside because I thought I heard two birds fighting. There they were, a couple of robins squabbling over a bit of food. I was overjoyed, and I gave Allan credit for the birds' return.

Allan knew a little about the projects I'd been building and contacted me to ask if I'd teach the required HIV prevention class to his workers in Maffambisse, a village just past Lamego on the road to Beira. The teaching needed to last a day and a half, and he had budgeted $1,200 to pay for the training.

It certainly sounded good to me! I headed over so that we could talk about the class. I adored spending time with Allan. We discussed the details of the class over dinner in Chimoio, and a great conversation over a glass of red wine was music to my soul.

I asked Allan, "Do you want me to teach your guys about HIV or do you want them to *learn* about HIV?"

His response was crisper than I had expected. "Look, Amy. You're cute, your dolls are cute, but come teach your class, take your check, and go home. I have had every aid organization here to teach HIV prevention, and nothing has changed.

"My organization gets a lot of things done. We plant 60,000 indigenous trees a year. We are turning a profit. We make beautiful jewelry, tables—all kinds of wonderful things. But nothing we have tried has made a difference in reducing HIV rates among our workers. Sixty of our seventy employees died from HIV in just six years."

He proceeded to name the aid agencies that had been to his place to teach, and the list was impressive. Still his people were dying left and right of HIV. I understood his opinion that nothing could affect rates of HIV; I had run into it many times. But I knew our approach worked. I had seen the light bulb come on for people who attended our classes. You could see that people really got it—we were talking about *them*. They might already have HIV.

We taught the classes at Allan's project in Maffambisse. We used a local Portuguese dialect and English when it was requested by a couple of workers from Zimbabwe. We began our first class, as always, with the telephone game… and so it went.

At some point in each class, I asked an audience member to tell me the number of sexual partners the average person in their local community would have in a week. Then I drew a chart on the blackboard showing how one couple having unprotected sex at that rate could lead to a huge number of infections before the first couple could even get an accurate HIV test result. At that point, people always started to squirm, which told me we'd gotten a gut reaction. By supplying the first numbers, the locals were building the information for themselves and would have ownership over their new knowledge (as opposed to another Muzungu just telling them how it is).

In addition to the HIV information, we taught Allan's employees how to make a clay-pot beehive for producing honey and a backyard fish tank to use for raising fish. These income-generation projects gave people a viable and valuable tool, and it showed them that I was interested in their well-being, not just making money for my organization.

At the end of the class, Allan thanked me and of course paid me, but I could see he was not convinced. After more than five years of one ineffective HIV prevention class after another, his expectations stayed low.

A year later, Allan apologized for his skepticism and became one of our most vocal advocates. His men started using condoms; he could tell because the free condoms in his office needed to be replaced more often. Then unintended pregnancy virtually became a thing of the past among his workers and their women. Before our training, his men often bemoaned, "Oh, no! I got a girl pregnant!" But that didn't happen anymore.

Allan was not my only friend involved in the rehabilitation of Mozambique's natural resources. Vasco had moved on to become the Communications Manager at Gorongosa National Park. He was working with a man named Greg Carr. Greg, who was from Idaho, had been the inventor of voicemail and now was using some of his funds to help restock Gorongosa Park with the game that had been wiped out during the wars.

Prior to the wars, Mozambique had the largest wildlife herds in the world. As the war raged on, food became scarcer, and the military units moved into the game parks so they could have a food supply. Between 1976 and 1994, the wildlife populations were decimated. The lion population alone had decreased from 500 to 6.

Vasco asked us to teach an HIV training course to the workers at Gorongosa Park. So Yuri, Vic, and I traveled to the park to teach the class. As Greg was away, I slept in his tent. But the word *tent* hardly does the structure justice. It was about ten by twenty feet, with a built-on bathroom at the back that even had a toilet, sink, and shower.

I woke the next day to a terrible racket on the roof. It turned out to be baboons playing in the morning sunlight. Thankfully, by the time I was up and ready to join the rest of the group, the animals had moved off into the distance. I was very happy they had left. Baboons are very dangerous, and when they come around people they often need to be tranquilized and relocated or shot.

After we taught our class, Vasco treated us to a safari. Nothing compares to the first time you see an elephant in the wild! They move with unimaginable grace. A herd of forty elephants can be with you one minute and slide into the grass and disappear the next. As we approached the lions, our guide assured us they posed no danger. Evidently, once they've eaten, they won't attack for twenty-four hours unless they are provoked.

The animals were not yet accustomed to humans driving through the park, and Vasco explained that was part of the reason for driving around like we did—to acclimate the animals to the presence of people. When we were charged by a young bull elephant, I could see that they had a little ways to go with this effort. I thought of a woman who had been killed by a water buffalo on her honeymoon. That thought made me a bit nervous. I had a mission to complete.

# 29

My second fundraising trip to the States, in the summer of 2006, was going to be a whirlwind tour. This time I had gotten a lift to Beira to catch the flight to South Africa. I didn't particularly like to fly out of Beira because that airport had low weight limits for luggage. This was not too much of an issue on the way out of the country, but on the way back, I could bring my 210 pounds of tourist bags plus my two carry-ons only as far as Johannesburg. From there, if I was flying into Beira, I would have to ship all but seventy pounds to Chimoio at a great cost.

When we stopped to refuel in Dakkar, a couple armed men came onto the plane to do a search. Well, sort of a search—they made everyone get up (never mind that it was one in the morning) and then they took a look under some people's pillow-backs and flipped through some of the magazines from the pockets of the seats. Then they announced that we needed to get our bags from the overhead compartment so they could be searched. If we refused, they said they would arrest us and confiscate our possessions. So we all took our bags down, and the guards searched a few of them.

Speaking of arrested, I glanced out the window and saw a couple of jeeps with machine guns fixed on the back that were circling the plane. *You've got to be kidding.*

When the guards left, I gestured to the action on the ground outside the plane and asked the person next to me, "What's with the guns?"

"Oh. That's standard here," he said in a South African accent. "There's trouble with the locals climbing up into the wheel wells of the plane. Of course they freeze to death as the plane flies over the Atlantic, and when the landing gear drops, the dead body falls out."

"No way."

"Yeh. It's true. I've seen it on the news a number of times. It causes bad publicity, so now they drive around with guns threatening to kill anyone who tries to stow away. Poor bastards. Imagine how bad their lives must be that they are willing to risk killing themselves trying to escape."

As soon as the search was over, I pulled out my computer so I could get a little practice with PowerPoint. I was going to visit my hometown to see Mom and Dad and to make presentations at a Rotary Club and at the American Legion. The presentations were going to be my first experience using PowerPoint. It had taken me a week to figure out the transitions between slides and to choose which pictures to show. I chewed my lip nervously as I thought of everything that could go wrong.

Yet the trip went well. I managed to raise a few thousand dollars to cover rent and fuel and other things that were not funded by our grants. One donor very generously agreed to donate an annual salary or stipend for me—$1,000 per month—and because I was maintaining residency outside of the States, I didn't have to pay taxes, which meant $1,000 gross was also $1,000 net. That amount would pretty much cover my personal expenses—rent, fuel, groceries, and so forth.

I was satisfied with the trip, but afterward I needed some time off. The fundraising trips were wonderful and productive, but they were also exhausting. In additional to all of the speaking engagements, which by their nature were taxing for an introvert, staying in people's homes meant I could not sleep in or go to bed early. I longed for a hotel room on the trips for a minute of privacy, a chance to let down my guard. But I continued to operate on a shoestring and commit the funds to the children I was trying to help. Usually lost sleep was a fairly small thing, but when my sleep deficit got to be too much, it started feeling pretty huge.

At the end of the trip I decided to fly to Nacala to visit Daniel before returning to the projects. Daniel picked me up at the airport in Nampula. We planned to wait until the next day to travel the few hours to Nacala because it was already getting dark when my plane landed. We pulled up in front of the Masque Hotel and went into the lobby. The wood paneling on the walls was indigenous cherry, with a beautiful red sheen and a sturdy feel. The clerk took our information and led us up the stairs.

I had been questioning whether I should see Daniel again. Things had been strained the last couple of years. Yet there was always something about him… I always felt that he was supposed to be in my life. In addition to our one-to-one connection, there were too many signs to ignore: he shared a name with my birthmother and a birthdate with my late husband. I had also recently received an automatic writing message that indicated there was some reason we were to stay together, though the message was confounding and vague.

The situation was difficult at best. The mother of his kids was back in his home, and even though he kept insisting he loved me and they weren't really together, I wasn't completely blind—just blind enough to keep coming back and to keep bringing him American clothing and a used computer. There was something about Daniel…

As we started up the stairs, I contemplated how this night might go and whether the decision to come visit him had been the right one. I looked back at him over my shoulder. The staircase was narrow and steep and seemed to go on and on without any place to turn.

After about a flight and a half, we reached the landing. The hallway was as narrow as the staircase, with windows above for ventilation. We stepped through a doorway to the right and there was a landing that resembled a loading dock. I gasped and stopped dead in my tracks. The landing had no railing. There were steps going down each direction from the stairs to the landing below. It was as if they had joined two buildings that didn't line up. Or maybe the enclosed space between the buildings had been created to provide a place to hide—for frightened citizens during the wars or for naughty officials who came to this house to visit with their mistresses.

The thing that stopped me dead was that I had seen these stairs before. They were the same stairs I had seen during my recurrent childhood vision. Every detail matched up. There was no mistaking these were the stairs from the vision I'd repeatedly seen as a five-year-old little girl in Minnesota.

When my eyes met Daniel's, he said, "What's wrong, Amy?"

"Nothing," I said softly. I really had no way to explain. The front-desk clerk led us down the stairs to our room.

Daniel asked, "Is it okay, Amy? We can go somewhere else if you don't like it."

"It's okay, Daniel." I handed the tip to the attendant, closed the door, and set down my bags.

Daniel was already wearing the Colorado Rockies shirt I had brought back from the States. He loved the goodies I unpacked for him and his son after my trips. He loved that I knew him well enough to pick the perfect things in the perfect size

I had a head full of doubts. I remembered how, long ago, he had not told me I was beautiful, but that "all women could be beautiful."

*What was it he saw in me? Why see me if it could only be once or twice a year? Why not just walk away?*

Whatever thimble of confidence I had felt at the beginning of our relationship had long since disappeared. I wondered if the gifts from the United States were the only reason he kept meeting up with me.

# 30

One day, the kids in Macate presented me with an Amy doll. It was twenty-four inches tall and looked Chinese. They even made me a Chinese man doll to be my partner. They saw me as Chinese because of my half-moon eyes, which have a tendency to disappear when I smile, especially when I'm carrying extra weight like I was then.

I wasn't sure how to feel about the doll. I was proud of them, for sure. But I also felt like I'd gotten my own action figure like, say, Harrison Ford when he first saw the Han Solo doll. *Is this how I come across?*

The man doll also made me uneasy. It echoed what I heard regularly from Mozambicans—that I needed a man, that I needed children. The attitude is that if you do not have children, you have nothing. "Oh, you don't have children. You are a *different* woman." Still, I was very touched and laughed with surprise at the gift. It was the right response for the Mozambicans. They would have been offended or even startled and disappointed if I had become sentimental and teary-eyed.

I played with the dolls and the kids. The kids were thrilled that I liked my doll. And I was thrilled for their happiness. Beyond that, I respected them. I respected their struggle. I would not be there years from now to watch them grow up; the best I could give them was the skills to stay alive long enough to get to their own future, whatever it would be. That is how I bonded with them. I was not like a Disneyland parent, trying to win a popularity contest. I was more like a practical parent—brush your teeth, eat your vegetables, and get to bed on time.

When I was alone later that evening, I got to thinking about Macate and my kids and my work in a larger sense. People who have never done aid work tend to relate to some aspects of it more than others. Most people fix their minds on the children, just as I had. And they wonder how a person with normal American experiences and sensibilities can handle seeing little children suffer the way they often do in developing countries.

I understand all of that, and I admit that sometimes the kids' suffering and the suffering of people close to me was very painful. For the most part, though, I had a broader—much broader—perspective on these things.

Right before I left my position at Cat, my birthmother died of chronic obstructive pulmonary disease (COPD). Before she died, we shared long conversations about "the other side" and what she would find there. When I left her for the last time, I felt she was peacefully on her way.

About the time I was filing bankruptcy, one of my birthmother's friends sent me some snapshots of her with a note that read, "It's hard to believe Annie has been gone a whole year."

"Wow," I said aloud. "Have you been gone a year already?"

Then, for the second time in my life, I physically heard a voice from beyond. Just as clearly as if she were standing in my kitchen, I heard my birthmother say, "Gone? I'm not gone. I'm in your hutch over there."

I laughed out loud (her ashes were in the hutch) and said, "Where have you been? I thought I would have heard from you before this."

Then (this time in my mind, rather than aloud), I heard her say, "I've been busy."

I was dumbstruck. *Busy? What's busy in heaven?*

Then "the review" began. It was as if my living room transformed into a holographic IMAX theater. My furnishings disappeared into a warm grey fog—formless and gentle, yet "thick." The room expanded.

I was wide awake, but in some ways the experience was like a dream.

I could feel my presence, my essence, my very existence. But I had no sense of my body. I was free from all labels, all gender, all form and identity. I knew I had been this entity for

171

all ages and would continue to be for all ages. At the same time, I could feel the presence and existence of many others in this same grayish-cloud space.

I knew that the spectacle before me was for my sake, yet it was not about me. It was as though this experience was a giant example created for me, like Ebenezer Scrooge's "Christmas Future."

In the center of this dimension was a light—a brighter area that felt like the master presence, for lack of a better description. It had a lighter and higher energy than the surrounding beings. It seemed as if that light was the one directing the events I was witnessing (or perhaps acting as a projector). Calmly, I watched the review, which had the look of IMAX 3D. The spectacle before me encompassed an entire lifetime (of somebody I did not know). I could somehow review two completely different aspects of life at the same time.

One review was the full extent of every action a person had taken in life (including thoughts and intentions) as well as what happened as a result. One day the person put money in the Ronald McDonald box. The money was collected, deposited in the bank, and so forth. And because of that money, a child receiving cancer treatment had his parents nearby. You got to see how important it was for the parents to be there and that the child was saved and then went on to save others.

I saw the full extent of every single thought, intent, and action for generations. I saw how every single action a person takes will be replayed in its entirety through several generations, during the review that follows death.

Like a dream that seems to work in compressed time, this review took only about twenty minutes, though it followed every decision in a person's entire life from beginning to end. It was like being shown life in a different language, the language of feeling. I saw how the person had felt prior to making decisions and taking actions. I saw how others felt as a result. I saw what impact people felt from those decisions and actions.

Not all of the actions in a lifetime are positive, of course. I was also shown how one day a person might yell at a clerk in a store. Then, in frustration, that person went home and beat their child, who years later beat their child, who years later beat their child—until finally, three generations later, that child broke the cycle by creating a motivational program that helped people who had suffered child abuse.

But the review did not lay blame at the grouchy customer's feet. It did not imply that yelling at a clerk was the cause of generations of abuse. In fact, I also saw how yelling at a store clerk could have a very different outcome. In another version, the clerk quit her job and started a new career that changed the world.

When actions of love or compassion were taken and then reviewed, the entire universe (all the essences that were in this dimension) went "Oooohh" or "Yay!" This was not audible, but a surging of the collective consciousness rising with an individual whenever he or she chose love, support, and helpful action. Equally, every time the person chose something self-defeating, hateful, fearful, or anguished, the entire room deflated with the feeling of "OHHHHHH" or "Oh, shoot." If you've ever been to a melodrama, it was something like that, only without the sound.

The second of the two simultaneous reviews showed every single gift that had been missed. The person was shown walking down the street and crying hysterically because there was no money to pay the gas bill and the kids were going to freeze. Then, because of being distraught, the person stepped on a $100 bill without ever seeing it. There were countless missed gifts and support along the pathway of life—people who were about to call or send money or say something encouraging. But dark moods, sadness, lack of faith, fear, and so on cut off those possibilities or somehow pushed them away. The very thing that had been needed was right there the whole time but went unseen because of sorrow, anger, or a sense of victimization.

I often wanted to explain this experience to the people in Mozambique. I had the sense that perhaps this was the one and only thing I had really come to teach—that perhaps this was the information I was meant to share with the children of darkness and the people who were taking care of them. But how could I explain such things—especially when I was struggling to communicate even basic ideas?

Nevertheless, the experience had given me perspective on the difficult problems that I witnessed and tried to mitigate in Mozambique. It helped me keep going.

But then the day came that the difficulties hit far too close to home. My old friend Manuel, the taxi driver who had been such a wonderful collaborator and source of insight in my early days in Chimoio, came to visit me. He sat in my living room, with tears welling in his eyes as he told me this story.

He had been at the airport picking up a passenger, when he received a call from his wife saying he must come home. His son, Psalm, was dead.

"Dead?" Manuel had said. "How is he dead? I just had breakfast with him two hours ago!"

"Come home. Come home. Your son is dead!" she screamed into the phone.

Manuel said he had raced home through the bairro, arriving to find thirty people at his home, wailing and crying.

"Where is my son?" Manuel cried as he burst through the door.

"He's dead. He's dead."

"But, where is he?"

They pointed to the table.

Manuel went to the boy and carefully pulled back the fabric he had been wrapped in. He discovered that two-year-old Psalm, who had fallen into a well and either hit his head or taken water into his lungs, was unconscious but not dead. This meant that the boy had been struggling to breathe for the past thirty minutes, while wailing and crying drowned out the sound of his gurgling.

Manuel screamed, "He's not dead! We must get him to the hospital."

"He's dead! He's dead!" the family told him. "Let him go, or you will bring bad spirits to our home!"

Manuel tried in vain to convince his wife to go with him and then raced with Psalm the three miles to the hospital. As he drove, Manuel rubbed Psalm's chest and shook him, trying to help him breathe. Two blocks before they got to the hospital, the little boy died. There was nothing to be done. Manuel took his dead son back home and made a casket, as was customary in Mozambique.

Manuel did not have crucial knowledge that could have saved his son's life. I am ashamed to say that I had never taught Manuel CPR. Not only that, but during that three-mile drive, Manuel passed five to ten NGOs where somebody—a volunteer or management—would surely have known basic first aid and mouth-to-mouth and could have possibly saved Psalm's life.

On the face of it, those NGOs could have offered classes that would have taught people in Manuel's position to save the lives of their children. Perhaps those huge organizations were so top-heavy—with much of the staff attending to administrative tasks—that there was nothing left at the end of the day (no time, no manpower) to teach such life-saving skills. Perhaps they were teaching some of the skills, but if so, I heard nothing about it in the time I spent there.

I had spoken with Europeans who told me that all across that continent, people had to have basic first-aid training in order to get a driver's license. And people in the United States get first-aid training from a variety of sources; most of us know at least the basics. But not in Mozambique. In Mozambique, most people were helpless to save their loved ones and often blamed accidents and deaths on evil spirits or "God's will" to assuage any sense of guilt that would have plagued them if they had known the accident or death was preventable.

At times like this, the review did little to ease my pain and frustration. Years passed before I could even tell the story of

Psalm's death without crying. I had always known Manuel to be a good man who deeply loved his family. The situation was heartbreaking, too horrible to comprehend, and entirely too common in Chimoio. More than ever, I was consumed with a fire to continue my work teaching survival skills and first aid so senseless deaths could be prevented.

I had decided after some of the corruption issues in Macate to focus on teaching children. Even in America, safety campaigns start with the children because they naturally will teach their friends, siblings, and parents. The same is true in Mozambique; the children teach up and out, spreading the information. In addition, Mozambican parents were too busy just feeding their children to teach them safety. I would make sure the kids got the training they needed to protect themselves.

I considered Psalm to be my first casualty. I had failed him and Manuel both. I knew how untrained the medical personnel at the hospital were—and in any case, it was unlikely that they would ever consider giving mouth-to-mouth resuscitation because of rumors that HIV could be transmitted in saliva.

The theory that I was holding close to my heart was that by teaching Mozambican children about health safety and accident prevention from the youngest age, great improvement could be achieved in forty years, just two generations in Mozambique. I kept remembering that Castro had virtually eliminated illiteracy in Cuba in a very short time frame, and I set my bar high, hoping to spread this educational information at a similar rate.

Even with the knowledge provided by the review, I still got caught up in the events at hand—the sadness, fear, frustration, stress, and just plain anger about corruption and death and so many other things. Then I would try to pull back and remember the larger perspective. Some days I did better than others.

# 31

My friendship with the Zimbabwean farmers meant that they knew my struggles and my goals. They believed in my work, and having been through so much themselves, they were compassionate people. They wanted to do what they could to help. About this time, some of them collected seven garbage bags full of clothes to donate to our orphan center in Macate.

I thought of distributing all of the clothes directly to the children, but I saw that the donation would have a more far-reaching effect if it could be used to generate income.

First, we went ahead and distributed a few of the children's clothes as Christmas gifts. Then we made an inventory of the rest. Next, I met with Sr. Chimoio at the Development Center, and we made an agreement regarding who would handle the clothing sales.

Over the following few weeks, it became clear that the clothes were being sold but the money wasn't making it to the children. We had about one-tenth of the money we should have had. The rest was just gone. Sr. Chimoio could provide no answers. The simple questions, "Who was handling the money?" and "Who was keeping track of the clothes?" went unanswered. The stories I got varied wildly from one to another.

Then things at Macate got even worse. Classes were not being held regularly. Sometimes kids would tell me that they hadn't been there since the week before. Apparently the Development Committee was telling the kids to go home because the adults were having meetings. Some of those children were walking miles with babies on their backs, and the administration in Macate was telling them to turn around and go back home.

For once, even my own self-blaming tendencies couldn't cover the "wrongness" of what they were doing with CNCS's money, my program, and my kids! My initial suspicions—that sharing the space would be easier said than done—were confirmed.

I thought of Mom, who often said, "I knew it!" in moments like these. I heard it so often from her that you would think her great karmic lesson for this lifetime was to learn to trust her own intuition. Apparently, I needed to learn that lesson as well.

I had asked the committee in one of the first meetings (the one after which Manuel would not return) how they would have children in that building at the same time as adult meetings. I had been, as they say, pooh-poohed: "That will be no problem." This should have been my clue to simply walk away, but I missed it just as I had missed similar clues in Mudzingdaze. I couldn't leave Macate, though; I had a contract and a legal obligation to keep the project operating for a full year.

I made a few surprise visits to see when classes were and weren't taking place, with varied results. It was time to make critical changes in the way I was operating. I needed to find a teacher for Macate, somebody to essentially take care of the program so that I could become the ghost I had promised to be from the very start.

Before I could take that step, though, it was time for Macate's inauguration. Inaugurations are a special thing in Mozambique. They are pretty much a necessary part of operating there, like hiring guards. For an extroverted, sociable person, they would have been great; Helen, for example, would have reveled in them. But I am a bit more introverted when it comes to social gatherings with too many strangers, and I dreaded them every time. Even if I weren't wearing a too-tight silver-sequined dress, I always felt like a social clod at public gatherings. As a result, I had put off the Macate inauguration for as long as possible. Now it was time to face the music.

My translator-of-the-day was the one who raised the topic. Ugh.

"Inauguration, eh?" I asked.

"Yes, Amy, a special event for the community and for the children to celebrate their wonderful building, their wonderful programs, and all the great things they are doing. It's expected and it's very important you invite the correct people, that you don't forget anybody important."

A celebration like he described would be a beautiful thing for the kids. I'd love to give them a special day, even if some of the adults were taking advantage of the situation, skimming money when the opportunity presented itself. But the correct people? Ugh. It reminded me of the day we needed "special hands" to paint the floors. How I hated this part of the work.

"Okay. So we didn't budget for an inauguration since I didn't realize it in the beginning. We'll have to figure out the food and the activities on a pretty tight budget."

The Development Committee did most of the planning. They figured out how to make a meal of rice (lots of rice per person), along with a dish of tomatoes, onion, peppers, and chicken bits.

Eventually—nearly a year and a half after my first visit to the Development Committee building—we finally inaugurated the Macate orphan school. The building was packed. I parked out front and brought in the dolls and the last of the materials for the big day. I wore a puffy-sleeved, polka-dot, turquoise blouse under an ankle-length black dress, a bit like Snow White.

The children were excited to show the fabric painting they had learned under the direction of Shirley Buckley, an incredible Zimbabwean artist who donated her time and her materials to teach this skill. Shirley would create Zimbabwean designs on fabric, and the children would fill them in. Some of the kids' work was outside the lines, but I thought every piece was beautiful. In fact, every single thing the kids made and presented that day was beautiful to me because each craft represented a skill the children had not known before I came to Mozambique. The girls presented their crocheted and knitted items, created using skills Christina had taught them.

All of the items were priced, showing the girls' new business skills.

After the children presented their work, we showed a short HIV prevention video on the television and VCR. These videos were produced and provided by CNCS, and we were required by our grant to show them to the adults who attended events at the orphan center. The audience watched politely, though there was no discussion after the viewing and very little applause.

In front of the group sat the local regulo in full military dress, Sr. Chimoio, the Vice President of the Development Committee, and Edalina, as well as me and my translator of the day. I presented the dolls and did some first aid demonstrations. All-in-all we must have had about 100 people squeezed into that small space. The kids made colored paper hats and pinwheels during the inauguration.

As I looked around the room at the children and guests, I thought of the poem I'd written and the review I'd been shown. I would be leaving soon. Would the skills the children had learned impact their lives? Would they impact the lives of their children and grandchildren? I would know the answer one day, when I was shown my own review.

I sighed as I thought of how somebody more organized, trained, educated, and fluent in Portuguese might have had a better result.

My translator touched my arm. "Amy?"

"Oh, sorry? Yes, let's go eat. Have I thanked everyone well enough?"

"Yes, Amy. You said everything. It is time to eat."

I was glad to be released from the social obligation I had put off for nearly a year. Yet I have to admit that, despite all of my mental wandering during the meeting, I beamed from ear to ear as people came up to thank me for what I had brought to their community. I knew it was very likely that within a year or so the program would be gone or be much, much smaller. Then it would wait for the next Muzungu to come inject some new inspiration (and money) into the project. The thing I knew for sure in that moment was that it would not be me. I had done nearly all I could for that orphan center. It was time for me to move on.

As I drove back to Chimoio after the inauguration, I recounted my steps on this mission. I had left America with the mistaken idea that there was just one Goliath waiting for me in Mozambique, but Goliath had many faces here. Ruefully I remembered how Jorge had told me about a community that had burned down another community's preschool. The school had been a wonderful donation by a group of well-meaning young volunteers. It had been operating for a couple of years and had wonderful classes and porridge for the kids each morning. Still some scuttlebutt had gotten started, and people had become jealous and indignant that the preschool hadn't been placed in their town. So they burned it down. Apparently one of Goliath's faces was jealousy.

The man I found to teach in Macate came to me from the Development Committee and had taught preschool before. I believe he was a trained teacher who couldn't garner one of the few teaching positions in Macate. He was happy enough to receive the salary I was paying him to make sure the safety and survival skills were being effectively taught. I knew it was a double-edged sword to choose someone involved with the Committee, but I was just going to have to trust God.

Things seemed to be on track, but I kept flashing back to the enthusiastic teacher in Mudzingadze who had assured me he would do a great job and stay for three years. His resignation, which came within a year of getting up and running, had virtually shut down that project. Nevertheless, the Macate teacher started off pretty strong. He was paid minimum wage, and he liked dressing professionally and teaching the children.

About once every other week, he traveled to my house to turn in the curriculum and to report about the children's activities. Usually the meetings were fairly pleasant and we got a lot accomplished. Then one day, after arriving on the chapa as usual, the teacher began to talk about the needs of the school, how the children were suffering without a snack (which had ceased to be my fault, given the clothing debacle), and how he was suffering without adequate pay.

As he went on about the challenges he was facing trying to teach in Macate, my mind again raced for a response. He was being rude and disrespectful. He received a salary as high as that received by the director of the Development Committee—and the teacher wasn't working anything close to full-time. He worked himself into a lather and slammed his Coke bottle on my desk while trying to make his point. My guard, Alface, paced outside my window. Things were getting a bit frightening. *Come on, God, I need a hint!*

It was time to try some humor. "Really? Is there some school in Macate offering children hot lunches for coming to school? I'd like to sign up so I can get lunch there, and you should probably sign up too." A sheepish grin flashed across his face.

I went on. "You know, even in America, the children bring their food to school or pay to get food from the school. Also, you receive the legal minimum wage for a full-time job, and you are not working full-time. Were you receiving more money someplace else before I came into your life?"

"Well, no." He looked down for a moment before meeting my eyes. "Edalina said that if I came to you angry and told you everything that was wrong, I could get more money."

The Macate teacher was not the first to come to me with corrupt intentions, and I was no longer a pushover. He went back to Macate empty-handed.

After the teacher left, I had the opportunity to discuss the encounter with my translator Yunas, a white Mozambican who had been deported to Portugal during the war. Over time Yunas had shared some of his perspectives on life, and I had come to trust him. He often spoke of what an odd and terrible situation it had been to be thrown out of his own country, labeled "not Mozambican," and deported to a country he had never set foot in, which was then said to be his true home. Yunas was not only a translator. He was also a fine writer, a journalist who portrayed stories of everyday life and stories of torment.

After the teacher left, Yunas looked at me thoughtfully. Unlike Manuel who refused to discuss what, exactly, Edalina had said in the meeting that had disturbed him, Yunas was going to give me all the unpleasant details, the things he had not translated during the conversation. "He said that they saw you coming. When you first arrived with that Israeli girl, they saw that they might be able to take you in." His voice was gentle and wise, and he looked off into the distance as he went on.

"They sort of felt out your weaknesses as they watched you teetering, testing your parameters, getting your bearings. They saw your weakness for children and your weakness with the language, and they began planning how they could get what they wanted and needed from you."

I was nauseous thinking that these were the kind of things Manuel had kept from me. *How much of this had he known? What had made him decide not to share it with me?*

"All they had to do was gather up some kids for you to be taken in by. It's sometimes how they do things here. When that was done, they began to push harder. They got their building. They got their television."

The smoke from his cigarette seemed to disappear, almost as if it had never existed. Yet it was still there, dispersing, making everything dirty. In Mozambique, corruption was like that—now you see it. . . now you don't. But it's still there.

After talking with Yunas, I could see that adults were happy to use their kids to get what they wanted. "Oh, look at our poor children. You must help them by fixing this building. You must help them by bringing a snack to *my house*... and I will feed them for you." *Yeah, right.*

# 32

Mozambique was different from any other place I had known; it was a place governed by survival. As in the early years of America, being alone often meant death; it was like that in Mozambique. Your very livelihood was determined by the strength of your relationships with the people in your community. How you lived as a foreigner was watched and evaluated by everyone because it was different. If you stayed there long enough, relationships evolved the way they do elsewhere. Work relationships spilled over into personal friendships, and friendships often took on a nuance of family.

One of the Japanese volunteers, Satoko, had moved into the house next door to me. We had quite a little community out there, with parties every couple of weeks, and many nights we shared dinner at each other's houses. It was my home away from home. The tightly grouped social scene was very similar to what I'd grown up with on the farm. After difficult days in Macate or in the bush doing HIV training, I had a haven waiting for me at the end of the day.

One evening, several of the volunteers from Japan put together a grand display of wonderful Japanese delicacies, including tiny hand-carved tomatoes. I watched in amazement as they brought out dish after dish that looked like it had been prepared at a Japanese country club. We dined and laughed and had a wonderful evening.

Even here, everyone knew the Japanese as being very disciplined. They did great work in Chimoio, each volunteer being placed in a different project. One of the Japanese volunteers, Hajime, came to our school a number of times and taught the kids to do origami and then put on drumming and dance presentations. Satoko asked if she could present our dolls and HIV training method in Zimbabwe at a conference for Japan's version of Peace Corps (JICA[*]). I was honored. Of course I said yes!

Soon it was time for me to have a party at my Textáfrica house. I had never thrown a party with so many people, and it was kind of fun. It was going to be a South African *Braai* (barbecue). I knew I wouldn't need to do much. Braais are like potlucks: you invite everybody to bring their own meat, drink, chair, and silverware. The host provides the location and cooking fire. Someone would ring you up and say, "We're having a braai. Come on over at four to join us."

Funny enough, the Dutch called a potluck "eating American," and I explained to them that Americans call it "going Dutch" when two people go out as a couple but pay separately.

Helen brought a couple of Dutch guests, John and Tjitske. The two of them were planning to take a contract in Chimoio to work on problems with the city water supply. Soon we became very good friends.

My guests brought their meat, flatware, some drinks, and chairs, while I provided a few side dishes, as I would have in the States. Many of my guests had never seen a watermelon boat, and it was fun to make. I had an extra case or two of beer and soda on hand. Coca-Cola had a bottling plant in Chimoio; the locals bought their soda in glass bottles that had to be returned when empty. If you stopped at a gas station to buy a Coke, you had to have an empty bottle to exchange or you had to drink it there.

Four people in our group had January birthdays, which is what prompted the party. The music blared from a friend's car stereo, and I had a mirrored ball on my veranda. The local children all danced outside the gates of my driveway. Like most African parties, it went on until about four in the morning— people from America, Zimbabwe, South Africa, Netherlands, England, Japan, Czech Republic, and Australia all laughing,

---

[*] Japan International Cooperation Agency

dancing, and drinking together. Life in Mozambique was getting to be fun.

On the other hand, bonding with locals in a country with a life expectancy as low as Mozambique's had a dark and painful side. Less than a year after Manuel's son died, a tattered man had come to my house to tell me that Manuel was in the hospital. He said that our friend was dying, and I needed to come quickly. I changed clothes and ran to the hospital.

It had been a while since Manuel and I'd had a chance to talk. I would sometimes see him carrying passengers through town, and we would cheerfully wave. But I missed our conversations about life in Mozambique and how best to empower the children. I had been meaning to call him to see how things were going.

The smell of the hospital, which was the smell of death, always shocked me. Every cell in my body screamed, "Get out! Get out now!" It was more of a morgue than a hospital—plain and simple, people went there to die. My heart already ached for Manuel.

I walked past rubber gloves hanging on a clothesline, still dripping from being washed so they could be reused. The sight no longer shocked me. At least they were trying to sanitize the gloves. I held my breath as I walked in the main entrance and asked for Manuel's room. I walked up to the second story to find him, passing room after room. Cheap blue mosquito nets covered the beds. I wondered (as I had before) at the absurdity of holding visiting hours from 4 to 6PM, prime malaria-mosquito hours. In Mozambique, you never see a mosquito until 3:30 in the afternoon, but then they start biting and don't stop until morning. How could the hospital administration not consider this factor when establishing visiting hours—especially when so many patients were in the hospital with malaria?

Malaria is caused by the anopheles mosquito. If the anopheles bites someone with malaria, it transmits the illness to the next person it bites. If that person didn't have malaria before the bite, they would within a couple of weeks. And if they were infected with HIV, they would most likely be dead not long after contracting malaria.

I came to the room where I had been told I would find Manuel. Under the blue mosquito net, there was a tiny form of a man. Other than the patient, there were five or six people in the room. One bored-looking woman was texting away on her cell phone. Her expression seemed to say, "How much longer until you die so I can go home?"

This patient was certainly not Manuel, so I continued down the corridor. I asked another nurse. Nobody could tell me where to find him, and I was not sure who I could call to ask. As I headed back to my car, I prayed he had not already died. When I reached the parking lot, a man stopped me and pointed to the second floor window, where a man was beckoning to me. I hurried back, and he met me to walk me down the same corridor to the same door, where the same bored woman continued her texting. A minister was giving the patient final rites.

*My God, how can this be Manuel?* The man I had known weighed 180 or 190 pounds. The man in the bed weighed less than 100 pounds. But of course it was my friend, and though he was nearly too tired to speak, he gestured to me to come talk with him. He said he had waited for me. We spoke of trying to save the children and how we wanted to make an impact on behalf of his son, Psalm. I told him he had to get out of there, that those people were going to pray him right into the grave. He smiled.

Manuel died that evening, and that was the first time I lost a real friend to the lethal combination of HIV and malaria. I was heartbroken.

The next day Manuel's wife was seen riding all over town in her inherited taxis. She was apparently oblivious to the fact that she was infected with HIV and would likely die during her next bout of malaria, with her life ending in the same hospital where her husband had died. Or maybe she did know; maybe she knew all of that and wanted, while she could, to enjoy herself.

# 33

Sheila was a twenty-something Zimbabwean who came to work at the school as a secretary and bookkeeper. I had immediately recognized her potential. Because she spoke fluent English, there was no language barrier between us. She was fantastic. She could communicate with me and with the children and with officials. She did a great job with the paperwork, and was especially helpful with quarterly reports, which we had a reputation for doing right.

I could talk at length with Sheila about project ideas and new classes. She had a little girl herself, and that fueled her interest in the safety of children. Sheila also helped teach computer classes to the girls, using computers donated by a businessman from Maputo. The computers were somewhat outdated and didn't have Microsoft Office, but they provided a first computer experience. Sheila did a wonderful job teaching that class, and the experience gave the girls confidence that one day they could have a real job—hopefully at an NGO in town because NGOs were by far the best employers in the area.

During the time that Sheila was with me, I met a woman from an organization called fhi360[*], which focuses on capacity training for small and large aid organizations. At that time, they were teaching bookkeeping and accounting, report development, and other important skills for project administration. To me, they were like a survival-skills training program for NGOs, and I was thrilled that fhi360 were offering capacity-building seminars for NGO employees.

I was excited for TIOS and for Sheila when we decided to send her to the fhi360 training, and she was excited to build her skills. She came back from their training bursting with the

[*] http://www.fhi360.org/

exciting things she had learned—how to use Microsoft Excel to track our payments and accounts and how to create a labor contract in alignment with regulations. These documents were critical to our survival and success.

Unfortunately, a very few days later she invited me into her office. She was quitting. Right then. No notice. Just tomorrow there would be no Sheila. She was taking a job at the International School—a wonderful step for her that would benefit her family greatly. But she was taking all of the wonderful training with her.

Forget my experience of the review. I lost it. "You can't just leave without giving two weeks' notice! We just paid for you to go to that training. We would have sent someone else if we'd known you were leaving."

I was suspicious that she had stayed on with us a few weeks longer than originally intended just to get the free training, and I was pissed off at her deception. "You have to give us notice! You have to give us opportunity to hire someone, and you should really pass along the information we just paid for you to learn!"

I was understandably upset that the training we had paid for was leaving our organization, but when it came to volume, Sheila got more than she deserved. She stayed calm in the face of it, though her eyes betrayed an intense anger. "You are supposed to pay me today."

I did pay her, and she left.

Everybody at the school was cowering in the wake of my outburst, and it wasn't the first time. When it came to my emotions, I was as fragile as Humpty Dumpty. Yuri used to tease, "The madder Amy gets, the funnier she gets." And it was true. My first defense was sarcasm, and then I would escalate into a full-blown smartass. Beyond that, either I'd go silent, or (as Sheila can vouch) I'd blow up. It took a long time for me to get to a blow up, but nonetheless, if someone pushed my buttons too long, too harshly, or at the wrong moment, a blow up was coming. By this time (March 2008), four years of operating in Mozambique had not done my patience any favors.

I don't think I would have freaked out at Sheila quite as badly if I had not been pulled tight with money worries. I had been in tears for days about how we were out of funds and how I was going to lose the schools and how I had let everyone down—my employees, my donors, my family, and mostly the Mozambican children.

I finally said, "Look, God—you sent me here, and if you want me to continue, we need money. If money comes, I will know that's your sign that you want me to continue. If no money comes, I will assume and trust that you have something else in mind. I will see that it's only my ego wanting me to continue here, not you." After that prayer, I pretty much let go of the worry.

Not long after that, I took a road trip with Helen Large to pick up a volunteer at the Harare airport. I was excited to spend the day with my friend. Our first order of business was to change some money so we could get groceries. I had a few bills in my bra, and I took that money out before we got to the corner where the money changers hung out. They were always a seedy bunch, and I wanted to make sure I did not "lose" any of the U.S. dollars that I would need for the hotel. These days Zimbabwean money had about the same value as toilet paper, except the money had a clearly stamped expiration date, after which it was completely useless.

I handed the man one thin hundred dollar bill, and he reached in his backpack and pulled out what I can only describe as a bail of money. It was the size of a computer modem and wrapped in plastic. Inside were rubber-banded stacks of Zimbabwean dollars—bearer bonds, actually. This "money" would expire on 12/31, so we'd better spend it.

The Zimbabwean money situation was an anomaly that is sure to be studied in economics classes through eternity. Inflation had risen so rapidly that restaurants and businesses had begun writing their prices with grease pencils or providing Excel worksheets to show their prices. It was funny to me, but

190

I only had to deal with it for one day. For the Zimbabweans, it had to be a complete nightmare. When my Zimbabwean friend Michele had told me her story of exile, she had chosen the perfect word, *untenable*, to describe the situation of business owners and farmers.

We got through the border at Machipanda without a hitch and were headed along the highway to Harare when we came to our first police stop. The policeman was on foot, which was common, and he waved our car to stop. Helen told me to just be quiet; she knew how to handle him.

The officer looked inside the car and asked, "Where are your men?" To which Helen promptly replied, "We have no men."

"Ah, do you have guns?"

"No, we have no guns."

"Okay. You can pass."

Honestly, we had a car full of Helen's signature pink luggage. Did they really think we had guns? And what was this, an honor system? "Give up your guns or pay the fine"?

Who would ever say, "Oh, yes, we have guns"? This scenario continued, almost verbatim, for the next three police stops. The questions were always the same: "Where are your men?" followed by "Do you have guns?" Helen explained to me that it was quite uncommon for two white women to be traveling across Zimbabwe without a man.

At the fourth stop the policeman asked, "Where are your men?" To which we replied we had none and the man said, "No men?"

"No," I said. "We have God."

"Oh. You have God. Okay, you can pass."

At the fifth and final stop, the policemen began with the required, "Where are your men?"

Helen responded, "We have no man. Would you like to be our man?"

He answered, "Me? Myself? No. I have no capacity to be your man. You can go."

Evidently he wasn't too concerned if we had guns or not at that point. We had sufficiently frightened him with the idea of having to deal with two white women on a personal basis.

As we pulled into the outskirts of Harare, we were ahead of schedule, even with the five police stops, so Helen asked if we could stop at the mall and use the Internet. I said sure. For me, Harare was a haven—ice cream, books, shops, English, hot water, toilets, complete bathrooms, coffee from beans rather than instant. Harare was a sheer delight.

We arrived at the Internet café, and Helen told me in her proper British accent that "the most extraordinary thing" had happened. She asked me if I remembered a man we had met named Simon.

I had to think a minute. "The guy who sat at the end of the table at Mario's Place the night we were with the Dutch men from Vitens*?"

"Yes, that's the one. Well, this is such a coincidence. I received an email from a different woman named Helen Large who is an Australian, teaching skiing in Japan. She had gotten an email from Simon because he was looking for you. The Australian Helen Large had never been in Mozambique so she went online looking for a Helen Large from Mozambique. She found me and forwarded me the email."

Helen emailed me the note from Simon, and I read his brief message saying that he had been impressed with my work and that he had some money he needed to donate and would I be interested to take it? He wanted to donate about $13,000 U.S.

Of course I wrote him back promptly and said yes. The money arrived within a month, and we were once again on our feet. The situation brought to mind the message I had received about finances but then doubted all through bankruptcy court and the end of my insurance job and even the day before I received the news of Simon's donation: *Do not fear. You are well guided and protected.*

---

* A Dutch aid organization concerned with safe drinking water.

I did not doubt the message anymore: God wanted me to continue a while longer.

This is the intuitive drawing by Deborah Hanna, showing the little girl was trying to get my attention.

One of the original TIOS anatomical dolls designed and sewn by our sewing girls (age 14- 19).

Children often carry babies on their backs, particularly in rural areas like Macate.

Manuel watches over the Macate kids during our early days.

Designing the first TIOS dolls in the back bedroom of my house at Textáfrica.

Two of my assistants use the first "ugly" dolls to teach HIV prevention, with great success.

Amy and Yuri evaluate as one of the road workers demonstrates the correct way to use a condom.

Our anatomical dolls turned out to be a very effective tool for teaching HIV prevention.

Nelson was a street kid who became a safety-school teacher at the TIOS school at Textáfrica. Here he is standing in front of a painting created by our volunteer, Pippa.

Volunteers from Belgium and Austria teaching self-defense to young ladies at the TIOS school at Textáfrica.

Yuri and David use the dolls to demonstrate how to use condoms at a training location in the bush.

Before the renovations were done at the farm, we began teaching safety school and girls' clubs there.

My house—first day on the farm: June 30, 2008.

Students walking home "safely" from the TIOS school at Textáfrica.

On cold, rainy days at the farm we brought the children into the storage room at the bakery where they would stay warm.

Celebrating "Children's Day" (June 1) at the TIOS school at Textáfrica. Some of the kids wear their TIOS T-shirts and bandanas to show off after they made the first safety video.

We had to go to Zimbabwe to get the rabbits for our animal safety and production class.

Halo Trust comes to the rescue to grid-out our farm during the de-mining training exercise that solved our trespassing problem.

Teaching the kids to cross the street safely.

This is a fairly common sight in Mozambique—entire families traveling on a single motorcycle. Practices likes this reinforced my determination to teach first aid and safety skills.

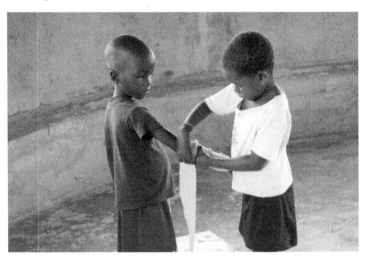

A girl practices bandaging another student on the farm.

A guest from the Pink Papaya, Ricky Monopoly, visited our school and taught our kids the famous Mali war dance, the Hakke.

The team bringing water to grandmothers in the community.

*Photo by Clay Hall*

The children learned how to safely get water
from a well and how to handle it safely.

Cabeça de Velho (the old man's head) is a well-known rock
formation in Chimoio.

The road-safety scene from our safety video.

Rehearsing the "falling into the well" scene for our safety video.
The video is available on YouTube and on the TIOS website.

# PART III:
# SURRENDER

# 34

⊃∘C∽⊃∘⊂

One evening, a South African friend of mine, Evan, and I met for a sundowner at Mario's place. Evan opened the conversation with, "Agh, this bloody Mozambleak! We did HIV tests on our workers and got the results today. You can't believe it! Eighty percent of our men are infected and 100% of our women. 100%! It will be a tragedy for so many families. And can you imagine what that is going to do to our training costs and productivity?"

The high numbers Evan was citing backed up the HIV rates we had been quoted in training nearly six years earlier (but that I had never seen in print on a single verifiable document). All the published reports stated something like a maximum of 30–40% HIV rates in Chimoio. Yet this employer had found 80–100% of his 300 employees to be infected.

"So much for anonymous testing," I said softly. But I understood the problem. Put a man in a uniform in Chimoio, and you're endangering his life. The uniform says he has a job, an income, and a payday; "professional girls" will be looking for him, as will local women in need of support.

But high rates of HIV infection tell only part of the story when it comes to death rates in Chimoio. People were dying left and right for many, many reasons.

My guard Ernesto's young child had died the year before, of undetermined causes. Many people speculated the death had something to do with the baby's mother, but nobody looked into the possibility. It was like that in Mozambique; sometimes children died under circumstances that would have prompted autopsy or investigation in other countries. There were no resources for that in Mozambique; the hospital didn't have money for latex gloves, let alone autopsies. Anyway, what would an autopsy prove? Dead was dead.

The roads in Mozambique are very dangerous, even during the day. One of the main hazards is semi-trucks. They have no reflectors, and they often stop on the road. At night they are basically invisible, but in the day—especially when in a car flying down the highway—they can be just as lethal. Cars can drive under them, killing or injuring the passengers before the drivers have time to stop. The rules of the road in Mozambique actually say that it is okay to drive at night, even if you don't have lights. The only caveat is that you have to use a flashlight and drive under twenty miles per hour.

In addition, most of the roads are in terrible shape; the road to Chimoio from Maputo, the one I had traveled early on in that purgatorial bus—the *perigoso* road—was representative of the level of disrepair to be found throughout the country.

The list goes on and on: the ten-year-old girl who died from cat-scratch fever, the Zimbabwean man who died on the coast and whose body was hidden in a freezer and taken home to Zimbabwe. My dear friend Manuel and his son, little Psalm.

The next morning after hearing about the HIV rates in Evan's company, I arrived at the TIOS School early. I liked to get my laptop up and running, and I liked to talk with the guards and set a positive tone for the day.

On this day, Ernesto stood in my office doorway looking a bit shy, like a child who has brought home a bad report card. He explained to me in his very rudimentary Portuguese that his seven-year-old son had fallen out of a tree over the weekend. I barely looked up from my laptop as I admonished, "Oh, Ernesto, I am always telling you to bring your children in here so they can learn how to avoid accidents like this. Did he break his arm?"

"No," he said. "He died. We buried him yesterday."

Now I looked up, ashamed of my comment and already angry anticipating the rest of the story, which I knew would be a tale of another life wasted.

"Did he break his neck?" I asked softly, fingering the scar on my chin that was the result of my own fall from a tree as a child.

Ernesto looked perplexed. "No. He didn't break anything. He just died."

Now my heart sank. I knew there were a few possibilities. He might have had internal injuries or a broken neck; in either of those scenarios, he actually might have been dead. Or maybe his heart had stopped, but nobody knew what to do to revive him. The most upsetting possibility was that he might have been merely unconscious, in which case the little boy had been buried alive.

Ernesto was sad, but he had a Mozambican perspective. As the expression goes, "Fazer o que?" I was coming to see the advantages of this concept. Death is still sad, but if it is God's will, nobody is blamed and nobody feels guilty; though painful, the experience is less emotionally complicated, less stressful.

Mozambicans don't handle stress well. They enjoy simple comforts and like to take it easy. They are happy, peaceful, and compassionate. They love to laugh, drink, dance, eat, rest, and make love. Most of all, though, they refuse to be stressed.

I did not share with Ernesto my fears about what might have happened to his son or my thinking that perhaps he could have been saved. It was too late now, so as they say, "Fazer o que?" It would help nothing and nobody for me to add to or complicate Ernesto's grief.

About six months later, I came to the school early one morning. My other guard, Alface, met me at the gate. His face was wracked with exhaustion, stress, and something more.

"Alface, what's wrong?"

"My son died."

The words hit me hard. What was he doing at the school if his son had died?

"I'm so sorry, Alface. Why didn't you go home?"

"My job is here."

"You could have sent someone to tell me. You could have left the school for a while to tell me. You could have just left Pumba guarding all night. When did you find out?"

"My wife came at 4:30 yesterday."

Just a half hour after I had left, he had received this terrible news, and he had sat there the entire night, not wanting to leave his post. Softly, I said, "You go home now and don't worry a bit. Take the time that you need."

Alface seemed to shrink from his normally six-foot frame as he pushed his bicycle out of the gate to go home and bury his son. We closed the school for the funeral so everyone could attend, but I didn't go. I felt like if I allowed a crack in the dam that was holding back my emotions, I might drown.

# 35

A friend and I were driving to his farm one evening when we saw a shooting star. It had no more than disappeared when a call came into my cell phone from a New York number. Curious, I picked up right away.

"This is Christy Zelling from CNN Heroes."

"Yes?" I said, not really understanding what was happening.

She went on. "I don't know if you are aware of it, but Maria Holt submitted you as a candidate for a Champion for Children CNN Heroes Award."

"Maria Holt?" It took me a minute to place her name. She was an acquaintance from Unity Church in the Rockies, and for the past four years, I'd only seen her on fundraising trips.

After I had oriented myself a bit, I said, "I'm sorry. What is CNN Heroes?"

"CNN Heroes is an annual television program in which CNN honors ordinary people who make extraordinary contributions to humanitarian aid. A panel of judges chose the top fifteen finalists, and you are on that list, Amy, as an ordinary person who helps children."

"I am?" Then she wanted to know if this was a good time to talk or if she should call back a different day. I was caught off guard and it was almost nine at night, but I told her this would be a good time to talk. Libor pulled in his driveway, and I motioned for him to go in for dinner while I chatted with her about our programs for kids.

I told her that I had designed a new way of teaching HIV prevention. We were receiving repeated reports that people were going to get their very first HIV test within a month or two of taking our class, and we estimated that 60% of our participants were going to take an HIV test after attending our class. In addition to the HIV component, I told her we had built a comprehensive program of survival skills for children and established a vocational skills training program for young girls by providing them with vocational skills to make health-safety products.

I don't mind admitting that I was pretty proud of that summary. It was not often that I put everything together in one place. When it was summarized like that I was a bit overwhelmed.

But then I gave her the downside. From the start I had been so busy building and implementing my programs that I had not had the time or taken the time to keep proper records. Anyway, it would only have been "trying." On the HIV side of things, accurate numbers were impossible, and the results for individuals were confidential.

"So I can't tout numbers," I told her. "I believe we are doing great work, and I see lives changing. But I only have anecdotal information." I certainly didn't want to get some award without telling her all the good, bad, and the ugly.

"I understand," she said. "And somebody from CNN will be in touch if you make the top ten list that viewers will choose from. Then you can let your supporters know so that they can vote for you."

"Okay. Well, thank you for calling."

"You're welcome, Amy. Thank you for the work you are doing, and good luck!"

After we got off the phone I wondered about my responses. Had I been too modest? Had I not been modest enough?

Libor and his family had already started dinner as I ran inside and excitedly told them the story of the phone call. One of Libor's favorite phrases was "Life is beautiful!" and tonight I had to agree with him.

The next morning, I called Mom. "Hey, Mom, do you know what CNN Heroes is?"

"Of course I do. It's a television program where they award people for humanitarian work."

"Oh, yeah? Well, they called me last night. I'm on a list of fifteen nominees. Today I have to sign a release so they can use my photo or story if I advance further in the selection process."

"Good for you, Amy!" That was a standard Momism, and I loved hearing it.

The CNN call was the first time I felt like there was something special about the job I was doing. It was the first time I was certain that my parents were proud of my efforts, and I knew that would be true whether or not I won the award.

December 7, the big day, came and went without a call. A few days later I got online to check out the winners and to confirm that my name was not among them. It wasn't. After exploring the work of the people on the list, I could hardly believe my name had been submitted among them. They had fed or saved tens of thousands of people. I never felt like I doing something that extraordinary. I was putting my hands where God told me to and trying to get the next thing done.

I wondered how things might be different if we had kept proper numbers. Could we have won CNN heroes? Would we have more funding? And if we had more funding and got bigger still, would that be a good thing?

I didn't have to wait long to find out. After the CNN Heroes call, I suddenly had volunteers coming from everywhere; apparently, merely being nominated for the award had raised our profile.

We were also getting more invitations to the U.S. Embassy. Our girls' clubs were getting busier and busier. We had a bio-sand filter project coming up and had scheduled the filming of an accident-prevention video for children.

I had been so anxious to get some help, but I was starting to see that I had taken on too many projects and too many volunteers. In many ways, we were like the organization that had brought me to Mozambique; I had not developed the personnel infrastructure to handle this volume of activity. I was really grateful when I got word that in a couple months we would be receiving our own Peace Corps volunteer from the States who would be a stable part of our project for a year.

Still, I needed a break, and I hoped my upcoming trip to the States would give me a chance to relax a bit and recharge my batteries before our new volunteer arrived.

# 36

——◦◦◦◦◦◦——

In June 2008, I headed back to the United States for a six-week fundraising trip. While I was gone, my friend Jenn kept an eye on things. Jenn was originally from Britain and had married a Zimbabwean. Together they had come to Mozambique, like so many others, after the farm takeovers in Zimbabwe. Now they owned a number of businesses in Chimoio.

Jenn was more than capable of running my school. She was a very accomplished woman, with a degree in math (which, as a Brit, she called "maths"). And she had always been a wonderful supporter and friend. So I left with confidence that all would be well and with relief that I would not have to worry.

In all this time, I still hadn't found a Mozambican director who was motivated by a personal commitment to help the people of Mozambique—at least not one that I could afford to hire on our budget. Berta was probably my most committed staff member, but I couldn't communicate with her. Besides, her hands-on work with the girls was indispensable.

I had recently hired David, a Mozambican, through one of the German development organizations, and he was showing strong promise. He was great at production and engineering, he had good English, and he was great with Excel. As a father, he seemed to really enjoy the kids and the school and the safety aspects of the program. Still, I was concerned about whether he would develop the savvy necessary to work with high-profile donors. Like me, when it came to professionalism, David was a bit rough around the edges.

A year before this trip to the States, I had moved my U.S. board of directors (and hence my annual meeting with them), from the Eastern United States back to Colorado Springs. The Springs was the home of Unity Church of the Rockies and still felt like home, even though I didn't have a house or apartment there.

On this trip, I stayed with Dave Bryan, one of my board members. My board members had been kind enough to take turns housing me on my fundraising trips, so I never paid hotel fees.

As I was walking toward the front doors of the Colorado Springs airport, having just picked up my luggage, I heard a laugh and looked up. Dave seemed to find it funny that I was stabbing at my cell phone with mittens on.

"Can I help you with that, Ma'am?" he asked.

"Yeah, I think I'm a little out of practice."

I had already felt worn out before leaving Mozambique; my head had been spinning for weeks with details I had to address before I left—details related to projects and volunteers and donors and radio interviews and media. So when I got to the Springs, I would've preferred at least four days soaking and relaxing at the hot springs before I had to face anyone. I felt I could barely find my personality. Who had I become? How had things gotten so out of hand?

But, as they say, there is no rest for the weary. As soon as I arrived in Colorado Springs, I had to schedule events, meet donors, and make public appearances until it was time to return to Mozambique. I couldn't seem to catch my breath.

Dave was an excellent networker and on this trip to the Springs (as on every trip), he had some potential supporters/donors lined up to meet me. As an introvert, I'd always found networking the most difficult part of my self-made job. I was challenged by the social interaction, even though I knew that in the long run it was good for me and my projects. I needed to gather my energy and brace myself so that I could be "on."

When I first got to Dave's, the emails and text messages from Jenn were cheerful and promising. She was organizing things at the school in a way that I never had. She had made a promotional CD of our work, including photos, and had sorted out our books and accounts. It was great to know somebody had it all under control.

After a couple of weeks, though, Jenn stopped responding to my text messages. Worried, I called Mandy who told me Jenn's son was sick—very sick—with malaria.

I couldn't imagine being the parent of a child growing up with malaria. The only thing consistent about the disease is that the symptoms come and go and vary in their nature. Symptoms of malaria can be similar to those of such diverse conditions as teething, the flu, menopause, stomachache, or mono. I was worried.

An NGO director, coincidentally named Amy, had died from malaria the year before. Healthy people routinely survive malaria, but in a person with a compromised immune system it could be fatal. Amy had left Mozambique for a family vacation in her husband's home country of Puerto Rico. Several days before leaving Mozambique, she had the flu, which probably weakened her immune system.

She left Mozambique without packing malaria medicine, and when she got to Puerto Rico, she was quite sick and went straight into the hospital. For whatever reason, they didn't diagnose the malaria for a couple of days. Then they didn't have the correct medicine. They sent to the States for it, but by the time it arrived Amy was already on life support. She died, leaving behind her husband and little girl.

That hectic trip to the States did not allow me the down time I'd been hoping for. As I headed to the airport in Colorado Springs, I relaxed enough to realize just how exhausted I was. I was tired emotionally, physically, and spiritually. Although it was uplifting for me to speak about my projects, I was always wiped out at the end of fundraising events.

Jenn's situation compounded my stress. Her text messages had grown increasingly distant and infrequent, and I had grown increasingly worried. Nobody I talked with in Chimoio could tell me how her son was doing or what was happening at school. As I settled into my seat on the plane, I tried to trust that God had the situation in hand.

The airlines I used offer a missionary rate that allows aid workers two carry-on bags and three seventy-pound international bags. It was always a lot to maneuver by myself. At best someone would drop me at the airport door, and I would get a cart and put my 250 pounds on it. At worst, I would become the star in some kind of twisted comedy, like Lucy and Ethel at the conveyor belt.

Once on a trip through O'Hare in Chicago, I found myself throwing my bags from the top of a staircase to the bottom and then asking God to keep an eye on them while I ran to find a cart. I had become one of those people they talk about over loudspeakers in airport terminals: "If you see unattended bags..."

During the trip, I had looked forward to seeing what Jenn had accomplished. I imagined that she had done some things better than I ever could have; after all, she was used to operating in Africa, and she was college educated. What I realized later, as part of a "dark night of the soul," is that even people like Jenn, a very capable and trusted friend, did not really share my mission.

One of the fundamental ideas of the Unity Church is Papa Charlie Fillmore's insight that we should each live our own true mission—"Doing that which is meant to be done by me." Taking care of her family and nursing that little boy through malaria—those were the things *meant to be done* by Jenn. Running my school was *meant to be done* by me.

When I arrived back to my home in Mozambique, I dropped my bags and took a seat. I needed a minute to exhale—and to notice and be thankful for the cool breeze and the wonderful, shading fruit trees outside my window. But it really was just a minute. Then I left for the school.

When I got there, I looked around. Things appeared to be in perfect order, but something felt out of place. Then I realized—my little dog had not come to greet me.

"Where's Pumba?" I asked Alface.

Looking down and shuffling his feet, he broke the news. *"Morreu."* Dead, but not just dead, killed. When someone or something dies from sickness the word is *faleceu.*

I kept my cool. "How?"

"He got out. And then yesterday he was hit by a car."

He had been alive the entire time I was gone until I was nearly home. The thought pained me. I would miss Pumba. He had always been my favorite over his brother, Bobo, who was a little too big and clumsy for my taste.

Daniel had taught me about the cultural pitfalls of expressing emotion publicly in Mozambique. To have expressed my sadness would have been shameful, and I knew it.

"Mm hmmm," was all I said with my lips pursed tightly.

Next I wandered from room to room, checking things over on my own because Jenn had not been able to meet me.

"And, where's David?"

"Oh, he's been fired," Berta said.

"Fired? What happened?"

"There was a theft, and David was asked to go out."

"Mm hmm," I said again. (Expressing anger was not allowed, either.) "And where's the computer that he had been using?"

"Stolen."

I calmly continued, "Where's my refrigerator?"

"Oh, was that *your* refrigerator?" Berta asked. "We thought it belonged to Textáfrica so we took it back."

"Where's the black laptop?"

"Oh, that's right! We had a black laptop, didn't we?"

"Well, yes. We did before I left anyway."

This question-and-answer scenario continued over the next week as I uncovered one small anomaly after another. Apparently, Jenn had discovered that a laptop had been stolen along with a few other things, and she had deduced that it was probably David, whom she had sent home until the truth could be determined. She then looked into it and determined that David had been responsible for the thefts.

223

But I doubted that David was at fault. My experience investigating insurance fraud and my knowledge of David and his character told me that a mistake had been made. But he was gone, and now that he had lost face and been fired there was no way to bring him back. I wondered who had really committed the theft and worried that they would strike again.

However, I did not have the time to worry for long. I had a school to run, and that meant that I needed to control the damage and get on with it. I knew that we would miss David— and that we would miss his welding and production experience during our upcoming clean water project, which would involve manufacturing, selling, and installing bio-sand filters.

They say good help is hard to find. My experience in Mozambique was that good help is hard to keep.

# 37

I often met Steve the electrician for a sundowner, and he had introduced me to his friend Monteiro, who was a high-up director with the electric company.

One day when the three of us were talking at Mario's place, Monteiro said he was thinking of selling his farm. "Why don't you buy it?" he asked me.

"I can't buy your farm, Monteiro!"

"I'll give you a good price."

Monteiro had watched me go through countless problems with the electricity at the school, and he reminded me of those struggles as part of his argument that I should buy his farm. He made some good points. I needed reliable electricity. For nearly two years after first starting work at the TIOS School in Textáfrica, we had worked with no electricity, which meant I had to do all the computer work at my house.

Even after we got electricity at the school, we would often hear a "pop," indicating a power surge which had likely taken out a computer or two. As a result, we were spending a lot of money on electric repairs and new computers, and that money could be put to better use. The main power supply that was feeding our school was unpredictable, and Steve had tried everything to rectify the problem. Even the engineers from the electric company said it would never be quite right. Something had to be done. Besides that, I knew our rent would go up the next year if we were even given the option to renew.

But I continued to protest. "I can't buy your farm! You've been to my school. You've seen how it is. We run on a small budget."

"Just come out and see the place. I'll make you a good price." And so, on my forty-third birthday in the summer of 2008, I went to see his farm.

He picked me up, and we drove out of town. Monteiro's property butted up against the backside of the Textáfrica property. The farm was approximately four miles from the TIOS school and just off the main road to Macate. As we approached the sign for the cemetery, we turned right, onto an overgrown path. We swished through the grass as we drove.

After about a mile on that tiny road, Monteiro turned left, and shortly thereafter we arrived. I remembered being impressed that, even with the swishing, the trip had not been nearly as rough as the trek to the preschool in Mudzingadze.

The property had been empty since the war years; Monteiro purchased it after the wars, but he had never occupied it. I was not too surprised to see that the house was stripped. All that remained was a cement shell with openings where windows had once been. The roof was long gone, and a papaya tree was growing in the back bedroom. The farm boasted shells of three out-buildings, and a water tank stand that had been lifted off of its foundation by termites. Termites were always a sign of water; it was a good thing. A single-car garage, with an opening for a picture-window that would overlook the property, remained in the back. And a round machessa, which I loved.

The farm was maybe half-a-mile long and somewhat funnel-shaped, with a small creek running along one side and the road on the other. These borders meant the property did not directly border the neighbors' properties, except for the East Indian-owned farm that bordered Monteiro's to the east.

Coconut trees framed the driveway, an abandoned orange grove was next to the house, and I spotted various other fruit trees here and there around the property. With just a little care, those trees would thrive, and there could be a productive farm here, and the improvements I could make would help me earn some equity as well as provide a great place for the kids.

On the back edge of the farm was an electrical transformer, which Monteiro said could provide enough electricity for a small town. He said that except for the East Indian-owned farm, which had already been tapped into the line, anybody else who wanted the electricity would have to buy it from me.

Two years prior (in 2006), I had applied for funds from the World Bank and had included a drawing of my vision. We didn't receive that funding, but that drawing (titled "TIOS 2008") had been pinned to the wall at the school since its creation. That drawing was a perfect match to Monteiro's farm! I felt as though I had been dropped into a scene from the movie *The Secret*. The closer I looked at the drawing, the stronger my impression became that I was supposed to buy this farm!

Monteiro gave me a good price—just $25,000 for this eleven- or twelve-acre property. In addition, before I took over, Monteiro would put in new floors, doors, windows, electrical conduit, basic plumbing fixtures, and roof.

But none of that fixed the fact that I didn't have $25,000. In fact, I didn't have even $1,000 in savings, since we often used my salary to pay for the needs of the projects. So even at a good price and with a good deal, buying the farm seemed impossible.

At the same time, I recognized that if I could figure out a way to get a loan and make payments from my salary, I could sell the farm when the time came for me to move back to the States. Any profit I could eke out of the deal would help me rent an apartment and make a down payment on a car. If I couldn't start putting some money away, I would never get out of Africa.

After almost a month of trying to secure a bank loan, things were becoming tense with Monteiro, and it looked as if the deal was going to fall through. The purchase had seemed so destined, but it wasn't coming together.

One night over dinner, I was discussing my dilemma with my Dutch friends, and one couple made me a wonderful offer. "We could lend you the money. If we lend it to you at 4%, we'll be making more than we make keeping the funds in our savings account. Would that be okay?"

Okay? My prayers were answered! The next day I went to my Mozambican lawyer, and he drew up the documents. It was, as they say, "sorted."

I called Daniel to tell him I was buying a farm. Most of the time since he had left Quelimane to work in Nacala, our connection was kept alive via texting and an occasional phone conversation, usually about work or daily happenings. Since he lost his job, our contact had diminished even more.

He was supportive of all I was doing, and he continued to tell me he loved me. But our time together had been reduced to a weekend get-togethers following each of my return trips from the States. We had become like high school sweethearts who meet up later in life only to tumble into bed, knowing that we would never have a true relationship together.

Even so, I wanted to share the good news with him. He felt like the closest thing to family that I knew in Mozambique. He had been the "constant" in my life since I met him in 2004.

Daniel's brother Santos was another important part of the home-and-family feeling I had developed for him. I really enjoyed meeting up with Santos and his family in Beira for dinner or a drink whenever I happened to be there. Those visits had become increasingly important to me since Helen had moved out to the bush. Santos made the best stuffed crab (fresh from the ocean) in the world… at least in my humble opinion.

I rarely had time to spend with the PEDRA girls' clubs in Chimoio because I was busy handling administration, so I always looked forward to getting away from my administrative tasks on my trips to Quelimane. There, I was able to connect with the PEDRA girls and actually teach classes.

I also enjoyed working with Bill and Karen Butts at the Quelimane girls' club. Karen had taught me the discipline and reporting aspects of her program while I shared the accident prevention and first-aid aspects of ours. I admired her and her husband, Bill, and I loved her projects' homey feeling. Her students clearly loved her and loved being there.

I knew she was running on a shoestring budget and that our more complex projects (like the anatomical dolls) wouldn't work for her girls because they were a bit younger than ours.

Still, I wondered if she could build in an older-girls' component so she could generate additional funding for her programs through product sales. The older girls in Chimoio participated in income-generating projects to gain a skill while earning funds for the school. The generated income allowed us to pay rent—which most funding agencies would not cover—and reasonable salaries. Karen did not seem to think the idea could work in Quelimane.

Nevertheless, we did manage to have our fun. We used the dolls to do theatre for our own entertainment, which helped keep us laughing through many long conversation-filled evenings.

We did not, however, let the girls play with the dolls. We found that the girls from the north were very innocent and timid, and we didn't want to start a "What is this?" conversation about penises. Indeed, Mozambique north of the Zambezi River was a different world from Chimoio. In Quelimane, Karen had to deal with a lot more superstition and ancient customs.

One custom was particularly difficult to fathom. At their coming of age, young girls were sent to their grandfathers to learn how to please a man sexually. The very thought sent a shudder through me time and time again. In my culture such things are considered sexual abuse, and in these cases, many of the girls would probably become infected with HIV as well, in which case they would have no chance at a full life.

I had an idea. "What if you introduced our dolls, Karen? What if you could convince a couple of the grandmothers that it isn't necessary for a man to teach the girls directly? The grandfather—or anybody—could illustrate the information for the girls using dolls. And then the girls could demonstrate their understanding using the dolls."

"That might work, Amy. Things are always so complicated and it takes such a long time to introduce anything new."

The idea seemed a bit crude to me, even though it was my idea, but it was certainly an improvement over the current arrangement. Unfortunately, nothing really came of my idea to introduce the dolls to the grandparents—at least not as far as I knew.

Setting all of that aside, Quelimane was the one place that I really got to interact with the girls. They even taught me a couple of African dances, something I never had time to indulge in at the schools in Chimoio. In Quelimane, I finally indulged in the cultural fun that Pazit had known.

In fact, Quelimane had come to feel like a vacation spot for me. I never vacationed there per se, but the breeze off the Indian Ocean, those incredible capulanas, and the mouth-watering fruit market reminded me of those wonderful first days with Daniel. Together, we had always appreciated Quelimane's calming and lovely environment. He had once told me Quelimane was a place to go for retirement as it had a slower pace, no chapas, and no tourists to speak of. The trips to Quelimane made it seem as if some part of the love Daniel and I had shared was still alive and well.

# 38

Another place I was drawn to because of its calming influence was my friend Mandy's home. Sometime around 2008 she and her family, along with their adored rescue horses, had moved from the Textáfrica property next to me, farther south to Vilanculos. The move had been a nightmare, fraught with countless logistical details and with emotion. The family's harrowing journey to get the horses over the Zimbabwean border and into Mozambique was still fresh in their minds.

They made the best of it because the move to the coast had to happen. Chimoio lacked enough grass to feed the horses, and the climate there left them plagued with parasites. Last but not least, veterinary care for horses was virtually nonexistent in Chimoio.

By moving their operation down to the coast, they were able to run the horses in the saltwater of the ocean to remove parasites, rather than having to chemically "dip" them at great cost. They also found the tourism community would happily pay a reasonable fee to ride horses on the beach and in the ocean, which some support for the ongoing operations of the rescue. In addition, the beautiful beaches and climate in Vilanculos, combined with the horses themselves, were very appealing to volunteers, who paid to come work with Mandy's horses. I was thrilled that she had found a way to provide a reasonable living and that things were going so well for her, her family, and her horses.

Mandy had invited me to visit many times, and the day had finally come. Four new volunteers were flying into the Maputo airport, and my new director, René, and I were combining their arrival with some time at Mandy's.

I had recently hired René to take David's place. He and his wife had helped us out by translating some of my HIV training courses for the road workers back in my early days. His English was impeccable; we were lucky to have him for that reason alone. Add in his excellent driving skills, so important on those roads, and he was like a dream come true.

The entire time he was with us, René would go with me to pick up the volunteers, and he was the one who usually coordinated their activities and participation in our projects. He even showed them Mozambique's sights along the way. Taking care of the volunteers was more important than you might think. These were paying volunteers, and their money was used for items that program funding wouldn't cover—like a new vehicle and fuel to fill it. Gas in Mozambique always cost more than $3.00 per liter, or more than $5.00 per gallon.

Some of the volunteers paid a few thousand dollars to come to Mozambique to help our projects. We ensured their safety, gave them meaningful work during their stay, and showed them some of the country. René took care of all of that, which was great because I sure didn't have the time.

The reunion with Mandy was as warm as ever. "It's great to see you!" I told her as I got out of the SUV.

"Darling, it's been ages!" She beamed from ear to ear.

The grandness in her voice took me back to the first day I met her, when she had walked up my driveway one sunny day in Chimoio, saying (with great drama!), "Darling, you really must come to dinner. And bring some pudding! You Americans make fabulous pudding!" Then, after handing me a flyer for an art exhibit to be held at her house, she'd whisked her way back up the driveway and whirled out the gate like a dervish. I hadn't even caught her name.

Now I knew who she was, and she was wonderful. She was an important friend to me and supporter of my projects. Since her move, I'd missed her. I missed the flourish with which she lived, and I missed the activity of her family and her horses. Most of all, I missed the wonderful evenings we spent at her house, enjoying dinner, drinks, and great conversation with her husband, Pat, and their guests. Those evenings had become a relied-upon bright spot in my always hectic, often difficult days. But I was thrilled to learn that her horses and her family were adjusting well in Vilanculos.

"Listen," I told her. "We've got to get René checked into his hotel and get the girls from the airport. Then later we'll meet up for a sundowner and dinner, yes?"

"Sure thing, Amy. Pat will be thrilled to see you, and I have some friends who want to meet you as well.

"Also, I wanted to tell you. You're famous! There were some American kids here last week from Youth With A Mission, and they had read an article about you in *Easy Chair* magazine. They were hoping to meet you." She laughed, I assumed at the absurdity of me being famous, but maybe with joy for my success. It is hard to say because Mandy laughs easily, finding joy even during difficult times. During her life, she has shown herself to be very resilient; maybe humor is her secret.

"Did you bring your dolls with you?" she asked.

"Of course I did. In fact, I brought you your own personal set that you can keep here so you can explain the dolls."

"Wonderful!" she exclaimed. She pranced off to tell everyone about the gift and to be sure she'd have a proper audience for the unveiling.

Three of our new volunteers were from the UK, and the fourth was from Sweden. They hadn't known each other before, but they had communicated and coordinated their travels via email. Allison, who came from the Isle of Man, was not staying very long, so we wanted to give her as much of an experience as possible right from the beginning. Heather and Pippa would be staying for a month, as would Julia, the Swedish girl.

We got the girls from the airport and hustled back to the lodge to drop off their bags and get settled in. The girls and I were staying in a 3,000-square-foot British cottage, with two bedrooms downstairs and an open loft upstairs that included a huge living room. This Zimbabwean-built house showed its roots; it had a beautiful, wide-open staircase and screened

233

windows that allowed the breeze to blow through nicely, keeping the humidity down and keeping us all cool.

"I know you're all probably excited to be here," I told the girls, "but we've got some time before dinner, and I would highly encourage you to take a siesta. We aren't really in malaria country yet, but we will be in Chimoio. The fastest way to get it is to be overtired or run down from your flight." The girls took my advice and settled in to nap until I woke them for dinner.

Early that evening, several people from many different countries gathered for dinner and conversation. There were about twenty people at our table enjoying grilled chicken and chips. I noticed a man who was a bit younger than me sitting at the next table. He had bright blue eyes and longish blonde hair. *He looks like he's from Colorado.*

After we finished serving ourselves, he managed to wedge himself between the older gentleman sitting next to me and myself. "Would you mind moving over one?" he asked the man.

I thought it was a bit bold and René, across the table, cracked a grin. The man introduced himself as Clay. A nature photographer by trade, he had come to Mozambique on a photo survey. He and his team were flying over the open areas of Mozambique to count the wildlife that was living outside of the game parks.

My intuition had been right—he had come from Colorado. I fed on those kinds of coincidences! We discussed those signs then chatted about his work with the survey team. He was thinking about leaving the job, but he didn't have much money and wasn't sure what his options would be.

"The kids must be all over you with your cameras."

"Yeah. They like having their pictures taken for sure."

"I have a small orphan school up in Chimoio, and the kids there don't know what they look like. Whenever we put pictures up on the wall, they line up and point each other out."

"Really? Clay asked.

"Well think about it, they don't have mirrors, let alone cameras, so most of them don't know what they look like. It's kind of sweet. I'll see one little girl pointing at a picture and then her friend's shirt, saying, 'This is you. See your pink shirt?'"

"Wow, that's something to think about. You know, I've wanted to start a small project called 'Giving Photos.' The idea is to teach kids how to take pictures and then get them digital or disposable cameras to tell their life stories. Especially when there's a disaster, the professional news photographers show up and take pictures and make lots of money; I'd rather the kids could take their own photos—tell the stories of their lives through pictures. If a photo is valuable, the kids make the money."

"What a great idea! I'm all about vocational skills for kids, and I like your idea a lot. Shame you won't be able to come up. It would be fun to have you in Chimoio." My conversation with Clay added to the enjoyment of the evening, and by the time the girls and I got back to the lodge, I was ready for bed.

The next morning the girls and I made lye soap with Mandy. I was teaching soap-making in my girls' clubs, so I was paying particularly close attention. Mandy guided us step-by-step on how to make soaps that would be anti-itch, anti-bacterial, and good for burns or bug bites. The girls and I were fascinated by the process, and the girls were fascinated by Mandy. This day would be part of the girls' memories of their volunteer experience, and I was grateful for that.

Mandy and I had wildly various volunteers—from the very best and most hard working to those who were disengaged and lazy and probably should have never been granted a passport. There were many reasons to want to have volunteers come help. Most of them were young and strong, curious, and passionate enough to travel hundreds or thousands of miles in order to be useful. But on the other side of the coin there were reasons for trepidation. Cars had been damaged, volunteers had gone missing (but were later found!), girls had gotten pregnant, babies had been delivered. Young people may be strong, but they can also be unpredictable!

That day, it was "so far, so good" with these girls. After our soap-making class, René picked up the girls to take them to Chimoio, while I continued on for a brief meeting at the U.S. Embassy in Maputo.

When I got back to the school a few days later, I discovered that one volunteer (Pippa) had settled into making wildlife paintings on the exterior of the building to teach the children and the local people about wildlife, as well as to teach them Portuguese by stenciling the names underneath. Allison had gotten busy with the safety school, as had Heather and Julia. René was a godsend. He had them settled right in and had even taken them out exploring.

The next morning, I heard a tiny tap on my office door. I knew it was one of my employees. Mozambicans always knocked very lightly. I guess it was an act of discretion, but I found it annoying. I told them over and over to "KNOCK on the door," but nothing changed. I was the one required to adapt.

That morning it was Tendai, one of our safety-school teachers. He had come with Lina, who was now baking for us, to tell me that we were out of flour.

I didn't even try to hide my annoyance. "How are we out of flour? Why did nobody bring this to my attention sooner— like soon enough for me to do something about it?"

Lina should have been making bread for the last three hours. If she'd had no flour, what had she been doing for all that time—stewing in her little bread kitchen, not wanting to come tell me?

"Okay, Tendai, *you* are going to tell the kids there is no food. This is not my doing; it is yours. You go. You tell them." My voice had become a bit shrill as I pushed this disaster back into his court.

I watched out the window as Tendai, who was only about twenty years old himself, broke the news to the children. He made some cute little face as he held out his empty hands saying and showing "No bread today." I was certain he was heading toward "Fazer o que?" But I knew that sentiment wasn't going to cut it with these hungry little children.

I had known there would be tears. Many of the children ate only when they attended our school. Our kids were divided into two groups: the morning kids who were served hot porridge, and the afternoon kids who were served hot bread. For many of the kids, this was their one bit of sustenance because their parents were not feeding them at home, saying or at least thinking, "You'll get fed at that TIOS School."

Ultimately, Tendai's punishment came from a three-year-old girl who burst into uncontrollable sobs. He continued making cute little faces and trying to soothe her as if he were picking up a girl in the market. But this little girl would not be distracted from the pain in her belly, a pain called hunger, undernourishment, even starvation. That desperation lived in her little body as she went about a daily search for enough food to survive. Her need would not be pooh-poohed by this ignorant young man. I was relieved when Lina got the desperate little girl a piece of bread that one of our older girls had brought to work.

If Tendai had come to me even half an hour earlier, I could have run to town or the market to buy bread, but he waited until class was over, and there was no time to get them fed now. I went to the market to get flour so the situation wouldn't repeat itself the next day.

As I rounded a curve on my way to the market, I saw a little girl, not more than six years old, stoop down. She was taking a drink from the slimy water that was coming from the Textáfrica drainage system. My pulse quickened as I hit the brakes and shoved the car into park. *"Não. Não pode! Não pode beber daquele!"* ("No. Don't do. No. You can't drink that.") The little girl ran away in fear, probably with no idea what I had said because such young children very rarely speak Portuguese. As soon as the scary Muzungu was gone, she would probably be back for another drink.

# 39

The next morning I headed out early to the Beira airport to pick up Gemma Bulos and Mariah Klingsmith. I had met Gemma in Minnesota on one of my fundraising trips. Since meeting, we had been corresponding by email about her upcoming trip and how we would be bringing safe water to people in Mozambique and job training to my girls.

Gemma was maybe thirty years old and a Filipina, with thick black hair all the way to her bum. In fact, it was so black it was almost midnight-blue. She was quite an extraordinary person and a gifted musician who recorded the hit song "We Rise." She had won considerable awards—one from Queen Latifa's foundation and one from Maybelline Cosmetics—for the work she was doing with clean water. She worked very hard to coordinate these projects and to involve many different and necessary organizations.

Unfortunately, our reunion at the Beira airport was anticlimactic. On the way there, I felt my fatigue catching up with me. It was as if my life was slowly draining out of me. I realized on that drive that I almost certainly had some African bug, although the malaria and bilharzia tests kept coming back negative. I remembered hearing of celebrities going into the hospital with "exhaustion," and I wondered if this almost paralyzing fatigue was what they were talking about. I also wondered if maybe I was depressed.

I didn't have much time to speculate, let alone mount an investigation.

I asked God for a sign about the problem, and on that trip to Beira, as I walked by an empty storefront, I saw two tse-tse flies on the glass. In fact I saw tse-tse flies three or four times during that brief trip. Since tse-tse flies don't live in Beira, I suspected this was a detail I needed to pay attention to. I had been bitten a number of times a couple months earlier, including a bite near my tear duct that had left my eye swollen shut for four or five days. I wondered how I would ever get tested in Mozambique for sleeping sickness, which is carried by tse-tse flies, but then realized the answer was simple: I wouldn't. I would wait for my next trip to the States or at least to Zimbabwe to confirm if it was sleeping sickness stealing my energy.

At one point, as I walked away from Gemma and Mariah, I heard Gemma say, "Wow, what a disappointment. She doesn't even seem to be excited that we are here." My heart sank. I really was doing the best I could, and I knew the work was so very important. But I had no energy to express the enthusiasm that I remembered once feeling. During those days, I often nodded off to sleep, even in broad daylight, and the tremors in my legs had become normal. In addition, I couldn't stay engaged in a conversation; no matter the topic, my mind would wander or go blank.

I tried to set all that aside and think about my part in Gemma's project. Gemma had worked in many countries, and she was rightly proud of the work she had done. Her success with the programs outlasted her time in-country; that is to say they were sustainable, and I knew by now that sustainability was the real trick.

She and Mariah, who had helped her with previous projects, would teach us how to create cement bio-sand filters that would remove 98% of the viruses, parasites, and bacteria from water. For many, these filters could make a difference between life and death. I especially liked thinking of how much they would help the grandmothers, many of whom had very difficult lives carrying water, farming, and raising grandchildren whose parents had succumbed to one of the "all-too-many ways to die" in Mozambique.

A donor in the States had funded the bio-sand filter project in Chimoio, and we were going to share the technology with OSEO, which at that time was under Jorge Lampião's direction. I always loved the opportunity to work with Jorge and his projects. He had been my mentor all these years, and I respected him very much. I still had much to learn from him, especially along the lines of building projects that were more disciplined. My projects flew by the seat of their pants much of the time. For example, we created the safety class using only what I had learned growing up and some common sense. But Jorge's projects were different. He started with the end in mind and plotted a clear path to get there.

In a day or two, Evans Chigenye was coming from Zambia to help teach about bio-sand filter production. He was one of Gemma's contacts, and she had arranged for him to come to help her with the training. He would be bringing the mold for making the filters with him on the bus so it would be sure to arrive safely. I was humbled. All of my whining about three days of traveling back and forth to the States, in the comfort of airports and airplanes. Now Evans was coming by bus from Zambia, toting this 170-pound steel mold. I could only imagine the discomfort of that trip.

We had a lot to get ready. We cleared an area in the back room of the TIOS School for constructing the filters. We met with Jorge to coordinate our activities with a number of rural extension health workers. Using the mold and materials that were readily available in Chimoio (except for the steel mesh for sifting the sand), one bio-sand filter could be made per day. The mold was about the size of a dining room chair standing on the ground, and of course the filters made from the mold were about that same size.

After the filters had been built and distributed to villages and towns, they would need to be monitored to make sure none turned into flower pots or trash bins. Projects not monitored after their initial installations tended to fall apart. We were trying to make sure this didn't happen, so Jorge had arranged for a number of students and activists from rural locations to come participate in the project. They would monitor the use of the filters in villages.

Within a week after we met, Clay surprised me by coming to Chimoio. He had quit his position on the aerial survey team and had come to help at our school. Something about Clay was refreshing and homey. He had a practical and gracious nature, along with the greatest heart for children. His first project at TIOS was to take a picture of each child—a real portrait, with a background of trees and plants to enhance the children's coloring. Our conversation had made an impression on him, and he wanted each child to have a photo showing what they looked like.

Next, Clay filmed our program—"The Five Components of HIV"—so that we could capture our methods for teaching HIV prevention in one shareable place. Unfortunately, the video showed me teaching the class in English with someone translating it into Portuguese, which made it not a very usable product, but it did allow interested people to see our approach.

I was glad Clay was able to get out about town. Chimoio was beautiful that time of the year—lush and green with mangos and litchi trees. Clay loved kids, and they loved him back. They would gather around him and hold onto his hands as he walked down the street. Part of the reason the kids were drawn to him (in addition to his other charms) was his unique look. He probably didn't look like anyone they had ever seen (unless they had maybe seen a picture of Jesus).

Clay was such a good guy that I was a bit surprised to get his call. "Uh, Amy, I think I've got a bit of a problem. I'm down at the police station and they are questioning me about what I'm doing here."

"The police station! What happened?"

"I don't know. I was walking with some kids down the street and then some adults started circling us. The next thing I knew, I was here."

"Don't worry, I'll send René down." I had René go because he was fluent in both English and Portuguese. René said that it had been his TIOS card that had done the trick. Apparently when the police saw that, it was over. He was back at the school with Clay in about an hour.

Clay hadn't done anything wrong, but the adults thought he was up to no good. Being a man—a white man with long blonde hair and a couple of cameras around his neck—they were worried those kids were about to become the stars of the next American porn video. They had heard of such things.

I often found the improbability of the rumors spread about Americans to be humorous. We were rumored to be putting HIV in condoms as a way to kill Africans. Nobody was ever able to explain to me exactly why we would want to kill Africans. Rumor had it that we were kidnappers, too, at least many of us. And, according to their sources, child sexual abuse was common in the United States. That was one of the many reasons that *Acção Social* required parents to stay in-country for six years after adopting a Mozambican child—to protect the child from human trafficking. Last but not least, all Americans are born rich, which incidentally lets American men have a woman on each coast. No wonder Mozambicans were slow to trust Americans!

It wasn't anything about Clay that caused him to be arrested; it was cultural misunderstanding. Clay was an amazing photographer, equally gifted at capturing people and nature. He had a huge heart and really wanted to help kids become photographers and journalists, particularly in Mozambique, where he felt the world needed their young perspectives.

I was thrilled that Clay was able to spend time with us. He helped us in so many ways. He not only took a portrait of each child; he also took a number of photos that we were able to use for pamphlets, brochures and PowerPoint presentations, and a TIOS promotional calendar.

Perhaps most prestigiously, one of Clay Hall's photos became the front cover photo for the 2009 PEPFAR[*] calendar, which was produced by the U.S. Embassy in Mozambique. One of my greatest mistakes in Africa, and one of my ongoing regrets, is that I forgot to put Clay's copyright information on his photos when sending them off to the embassy. As a result, he didn't get credit for his wonderful talent, skill, and hard work.

---

[*] President's Emergency Plan for AIDS Relief

Shortly after Clay's photo was selected, our new Peace Corps volunteer, Alexa, generously agreed to take one of the lead positions on our team, training the girls how to make the filters. She would be with us just a few months, so the plan was that she would pass the information on to the next Peace Corps volunteer, who would pass it to the next Peace Corps volunteer, and so forth into the future. I had some misgivings about how well this would go, but once again, I was trying to make the most of available resources.

The bio-sand filter project was complicated not only by my low energy but also by a scheduling snafu. I had arranged for us to make a safety video with the film team from Quelimane, and it had been scheduled for the month before Gemma's arrival. Due to a conflict on their side and a budgeting issue on ours, the film crew was coming at the same time Gemma and Mariah would be doing the bio-sand filter training. Add to those people Clay and the British volunteers, and you can start to see how hectic things were. The cherry on top was that renovations were still underway at the farm. God was having a good belly laugh at my plans this time.

But Gemma didn't think it was funny at all. She was disappointed and angry. "Amy, you have to be in charge of this project. You have to be the one who makes sure it is properly handled. You cannot leave this to a Peace Corps volunteer. It's your school and your project, and you have a duty to make sure this project is run effectively into the future. We agreed to come here because we believed *you* would run this project! You need to be more involved."

I was in full agreement, but my schedule was now on overload. "You're right, Gemma. Unfortunately, I got caught with this safety video project at the same time. The videographer had to reschedule, and this was the only time he could do it. I can't be in your class the entire time, but Berta will be my right hand on this project. It will be easier for Berta to do the bio-sand filters than the safety video."

In fact, it was Berta, along with Alexa, who really bore the brunt of the heavy workload and its coinciding with my waning health. They were taking over the bio-sand filter program, and they had been working side by side at the girl's projects in Chissassa, Macate, and here in town.

I continued to be buried in administrative tasks—keeping up with media, the accounting, program reporting, and donors. I was seldom able to work directly on the projects, which bothered me the whole time I was in Mozambique. The situation reminded me of the aid organization that had brought me to Mozambique, whose directors I had been quick to criticize for being unavailable and for dashing from one funding project to another. I soon developed a personal quote: "What you criticize, you will become."

The film director and his assistant from Quelimane arrived to make our long-awaited safety video. With everyone there at once, I was just as unavailable for the film team as I was for Gemma and Clay. Still, the film director did his very best to try to produce the video I had described, with vignettes of children falling into wells, picking up land mines, getting bitten by a dog, etc.

At least I was able to be there the day we filmed the crocodile-bite scenes. Some of the kids from the safety school enacted the scene, using a donated plastic crocodile. We had held screaming competitions to see which child could scream the loudest and the best. I have to say that scene came out great, though I'm sure my neighbors must have been talking about me and what in the world was I doing with those children who were screaming on my farm.

This safety video had been my baby—the very crux of what I had hoped to accomplish in Mozambique—but I could barely keep my eyes open after 4PM, so I wasn't available at the end of the day to oversee the film edits. I felt terrible that the film director had to do almost everything alone.

At least he would have a copy for the girls' clubs in Quelimane, and Church World Service could distribute it to their projects. But I felt we had really missed the mark with that video. It did not match my intentions. I had in mind a cohesive and frightening look at the dangers surrounding

Mozambican children, something that might scare them enough to make them change their behavior. But instead, the film came across as playful. For example, in the dog-bite scene, the film featured a child playing the part of a dog, and the scene came across as two children playing. I realized even before the film crew left Chimoio that I would have to remake the safety video with a proper budget and the necessary time to get it right. Bill was an accomplished video maker, but the project suffered because of my lack of participation.

The same week we were making the well video and creating filters with Gemma, a friend of mine, whose name was Pine, came out to the farm to help me divine water and find the best place to dig a well. Pine was a South African who had grown up in Mozambique on his family's farm. His family, like the Portuguese, had been run out during one of the wars but had returned later. He and his wife, Sue, had been supportive of my programs and had become good friends.

I'd had the opportunity to go divining as a kid, with a wishbone-shaped willow stick. I'd also tried a method using wires. But I have to say I had never seen it done the way they did it in Mozambique. Pine carefully balanced the one-liter bottle of water on his hand and began to walk about, like a waiter with a tray full of drinks. He explained to me that he was walking a gridded pattern and that when the bottle jumped off of his hand, it would indicate there was water below. Sure enough, as he walked patiently back and forth, the bottle jumped. He had told me that the force or the pull of the bottle off of his hand would be the indicator of how much water was below. He found two locations; he didn't feel that either one was particularly strong, but one was strong enough to at least dig a well.

I hired two Mozambican brothers to do the digging, and they showed up with their hoes and buckets the next day. In about a week the well was finished, and the day had finally come when it was time for me to move from the house at Textáfrica to the farm. It was a long last night at my Textáfrica house. All of my things were boxed up and sitting haphazardly around the living room, waiting to go to the farm. I was sitting on the brown vinyl sofa working on my laptop as the night got darker and the rain came down. Suddenly there was a movement from my right, where my attaché case was. I had been at the school that day and so had my attaché, which I used for carrying papers and my laptop.

The bag seemed to shuffle around a bit, and then it slid down into the sofa a bit more. There was no question; something alive had gotten in there, or worse yet come home with me in the car. I quickly shoved it off the sofa to the floor and saw a big hairy, blonde spider scurry out. My new puppy, Bella was on it immediately, chasing it around the room. Honestly, the thing was big enough it could have been a newborn terrier puppy, and I wondered if Bella intended to play with it. It raced along the perimeter of my living room until it met me with my can of Raid in the doorway. I sprayed it a solid white, and still it kept coming. I grabbed a shoe and quickly squashed it dead. Ugh.

The next day the rain broke long enough the guys to load the truck and drive out to the farm. They looked at me dubiously as it became clear to the driver and helpers that I was going to live on the farm alone, that there was no man at this house. The words of the Zimbabwean cops at the checkpoints echoed in my head: "Where is your man?"

As we arrived at the farm with our first load, I paused briefly to take it all in. This would be my new home and the new home for the safety school and bakery, as well as a new home for the volunteers that would come. I was fully committed, and given that moving day was also New Year's Eve (December 31, 2008), this really did feel like the ending of one era and a fresh beginning.

I began the job of unpacking, together with some help from Lina. She had left the TIOS School a month or so earlier, after giving birth to my namesake, Baby Amy. After a short time at home caring for the new baby, she had been anxious to return to work and a regular salary. I was thrilled when she said she could work at my new farm. I needed someone reliable and trustworthy.

One afternoon, Lina was working in the garden out back, and I was touching up the paint in the living room. I could not have been more shocked when my new Mozambican neighbor from across the road ran right into my living room, calling out *"Boas Festas."* In direct translation the phrase means "Happy Holidays." In Mozambique, however, the phrase is laden with subtext. The first Christmas I spent in Mozambique, I went around greeting everybody, "Boas Festas, Boas Festas," until one of my Mozambican guards corrected me, fairly abruptly, saying that it was "ridiculous" for a white woman to greet a Mozambican that way.

Much later I learned that the phrase is almost exclusively used in Mozambique by employees approaching employers and subtly (or not so subtly, depending on the situation) asking for a holiday bonus. By greeting all of those people with that phrase, I had essentially been asking for money.

When the woman stormed into my living room, then, she was asking for money, which I did not really realize at the time. The main thing I understood, which was also true, was that she had known she would startle or perhaps even frighten me, and she knew what she had done was beyond rude. I admonished her in my broken Portuguese and sent her away.

Even after she left, I remained troubled by what she had done. Where had her boldness and rudeness come from? Had this still been Monteiro's place, she would have never barged in like that. If my housekeeper had been inside or if a guard had been out front, she never would have tried it. If a Mozambican had bought this farm, she never would have tried it. I was pretty concerned. I was grateful that my things had not been unpacked because it meant she had not been able to "case" my house.

The rain started up again as the sun was setting, and it looked like I would have an all-nighter ahead of me if I wanted to prevent the house from flooding. The guard, who had been in the back of the property when the crazy neighbor barged in, worked with me to sandbag the driveway as best we could, but it quickly became clear that the house was right in the path of a watershed. At some point very soon we would have to dig a ditch along the road, and I would need some kind of steel to build a bridge to get to the garage.

Later we ended up solving the drainage problems, first with a ditch to divert most of the water and then with an old grain truck that had been left on the property. The truck had long since died of old age, so it was exactly the steel I was looking for to make that bridge. My guys dug a big hole and pushed the truck into the hole so that its top was just above the grade. They shored up both ends, and voilà—an erosion-proof bridge!

After I gave up trying to control the floodwaters that first night on the farm, I crawled into bed, leaving the kitchen light on. Boxes were everywhere, and after the previous night, I was painfully aware that any one of them could have picked up a hairy, scary hitchhiker. I wasn't quite ready for a pitch-black night.

Around 1AM I woke up, apparently because of the rain, which was still coming down outside. I decided it was probably for the best in spite of the flooding. During the previous October the farm had burned, which was common enough. Unlike a lot of other places, fires here usually raged through, killing only the grass and plants, not destroying the houses or trees. But the farm had been left in the middle of a dust bowl. This rain meant we'd have to deal with some mud for a while, but lush green would soon make up for that.

A few hours later, I was pretty sure it wasn't the rain that had woken me, and with Bella sleeping on the floor by my bed, I was pretty sure the crazy neighbor had not returned. Then I heard it. *What was that skittering sound?* Then I saw it. It was the spitting image of the six-inch hairy spider I'd killed the night before, and it was between the door and me. Not only that: Bella was between the spider and me, and I really didn't want to lose her to a spider bite. I jumped out of bed and worked my way around the spider to the kitchen for the can of Raid.

Like its twin the night before, it was barely slowed down by a white coating of poison. But the Raid at least bought me time to get the heaviest shoe I could find to squash it. I left it on the floor that night as a warning to any other bug that might think to wake me. Bella slept through it all.

# 40

My association with the Dutchies, as my friends from the Netherlands sometimes called themselves, had started way back in my early days at the Pink Papaya. The first time Helen had taken me to Mario's Place, I had met Henry, René Diks, Nico and Berend, and all of the others with Vitens, a Dutch organization committed to providing clean, safe water.

Many times the Dutchies came to help me at the school. They made tables for the children and came to our safety classes to sing "Head, Shoulders, Knees, and Toes" in Dutch with the kids. Our kids knew the song in Portuguese, and all of our foreign volunteers sang it with the kids to give them the opportunity to explore other languages.

The previous year, Henry had introduced me to Casper van Ommen from the organization *Water Is Our World*. He told me that this organization could put a borehole (a drilled deep-water well) on the farm. He also suggested that I make an application to another organization, Wilde Ganzen (Wild Geese) in the Netherlands. Wilde Ganzen's funding process was to match the funds of other agencies; Henry's thinking was that combined funding from the two organizations might finance a borehole.

Henry was right, and we got the funding. The farm sat on the edge of town, but right on the edge. More than 7,000 people surrounded the outer perimeters of the farm, and this borehole would change their lives by bringing them safe, nearby drinking water. Unlike the water they'd had in the past, which they often had to travel miles to fetch, this water would not have to be boiled, which meant that trees would not have to be cut down for fuel.

It was August 2009 when we decided to seek funding for the borehole, and I was about to leave for a four-continent tour. First, I would travel to the Netherlands to visit my friends and raise funds for our programs. After that, I would proceed to the United States to meet with my board of directors and make some fundraising stops. Then I would travel to Guatemala to explore the possibility of replicating our projects there. After Guatemala, I would head back to the States for more fundraising, and finally I would return to Mozambique through Zimbabwe. Most of my fundraising trips up to now had lasted about five weeks and involved traveling to churches and other fundraising locations in the States. This would be the first time my fundraising would be so international.

Casper and his friends in the Netherlands were preparing a gift for us. They had an organization that purchased large forty-foot shipping containers (like the ones on the back of a semi-truck) and filled them with all kinds of donations for children in developing countries. The TIOS School had been chosen to receive one of these containers. The loading had begun just after I purchased the farm, and as I headed toward the Netherlands, the final space was being filled. I was excited to be spending some time with the people who were making this generous gift possible.

While in the Netherlands, I was going to make a presentation at Henry's church and meet with him and Wilde Ganzen to discuss our programs. I had never traveled to Europe, except for passing through Heathrow Airport in London and accidently taking a train into and then back out of the city. Before Mozambique, I had never traveled anywhere, other than crossing the border into Mexico or Canada.

Henry met me at Schiphol Airport in Amsterdam. I was surprised to see that in Europe most of the signs were printed in English as well as the local language. It was really helpful. We went to the parking garage to get Henry's car and then drove off to Hasselt, where I would be staying with a family from Henry's church. The church was called *Ontmoetingskerk*, "The Meeting Place."

Dita and Charles and their two teenagers welcomed me with open arms into their lovely home. I was amazed to see how small and efficient most of the homes in Hasselt were. I

251

thought it curious that nobody's windows had coverings. You could look straight through the houses, as if to keep a good eye on your neighbor's backyard.

The first night there was a meeting of people from Henry's church who wanted to hear my story—how I had gotten started with so little and now had created orphan schools and girls' clubs, how important it was to collect used donations, and how much could be done with very little. Though I was sleepy, I did my best to be entertaining with stories and examples of how we were empowering Mozambique's youngest citizens with lifesaving skills. At the end of the night, I fell into bed and was asleep in a minute.

The next day the ladies took me on a bicycle tour of the area. I'd not been on a bike since Dombe (and before that, elementary school). We parked our bikes in a ten-story garage built for just that purpose. (Dutch people ride bikes everywhere.) We saw huge old barns, where the people live in the front half and the animals in the back. We went boating on the canals of Giethoorn and to the wax museum in Amsterdam, where I had my photo taken with the Dalai Lama and Oprah, or at least their wax images.

One day, Henry took me to meet with the program director at Wilde Ganzen. The director had visited Mozambique the year earlier, and she had a big heart for the Mozambican people. She was very excited to help bring clean water to people in Chimoio.

To me, the Netherlands seemed very engineered. I found the carefully arranged countryside very soothing after the haphazard and often dangerous conditions of Mozambique. The Netherlands had no potholes that I observed, let alone one big enough to break an axle. Water meandered through canals, roadways were well maintained and easy to navigate, and the small food markets were perfectly placed. I learned that entire lakes had been drained to make towns. (They say, "God created the world, but the Dutch created the Netherlands.") Near the airport, huge wind turbines stood in the sea, reaching toward the sky. I also saw windmills everywhere—the kind that bring to mind Don Quixote.

Dita invited me to speak to her second-grade class at school. The children asked very poignant questions about aid work in Africa, like, "How can they take a bath if they don't have clean water?" and "Why aren't there enough schoolteachers for the children?" These questions were very different from those asked by U.S. second graders, whose curiosity tended toward things like, "Did you see elephants?" and "Do the people have rings in their noses?"

In both countries, the children were most amazed and grossed out by the keyhole latrines and the idea of squatting and trying to pee in a little hole. Adults in both countries tended to be most grossed out by the possibility of maggots burrowing into their skin.

Sunday came, and the church was packed. In addition to my presentation, the church was hosting a fundraising carnival. Most of the proceeds were going to be used to pay for transporting the container full of material donations to Mozambique. The church held about 300 people. All available space was filled with linked padded chairs, and all the seats were filled with congregants. I took my place up front with Dita and Charles and their kids. To the right I saw Henry, holding his Bible and sitting with several other men, who like Henry, were dressed in dark suits. My mind flashed to the elders of the Lutheran Church, and I realized that's who these men were, the church elders. I barely recognized Henry, sitting up there in his black suit. It was like meeting a whole new person.

During the church service Henry stood to speak, and Dita quietly translated as much of the talk for me as she could without interrupting the service. Finally it was my turn to speak; I was to deliver the sermon, which I had built around the poem I had written, how little money we had started with, and how much could be done in Mozambique with meager resources. As I took my place behind the pulpit, I immediately made my first faux pas by mispronouncing Henry's name. The congregation was delighted; they roared with laughter. By this time I'd spent five years in Mozambique, and I'd only recently been able to pronounce *Grant* "Graunt," and to develop my British English. Now I had muffed it again. But getting a laugh was not the worst way to start things, so I pressed on.

After the service, I gave a PowerPoint presentation in order to kick-off the fundraising event that was going on outside. I delivered my presentation in the "Souse," which, I was surprised to learn, was the church's bar. I recalled how my Grandma Clara had talked about getting "soused," and now I understood the expression. A bar in a church! It was ironic from my American perspective, but I had to acknowledge that it was a clever idea. At weddings and other church-related events, the church rather than the local bar made money for the liquor that flowed. Plus clergy could keep a closer eye on their congregants.

I had prepared my presentation, with the help of Dita and Charles's son, Jaap. We had arranged numerous photographs to illustrate my presentation of the story of TIOS, focusing on how it took very little money, but rather basic, material donations to improve lives in Mozambique. I also explained how I had formed a connection with this church via Henry.

My talk was sparsely attended compared to the group that showed up for the carnival. Perhaps people were there mostly for the fun of it, or maybe they just trusted that the project was in good hands. At any rate, there were maybe only thirty people at my PowerPoint presentation.

To be honest, I didn't blame anybody for choosing playtime over a PowerPoint presentation. Outside there were homemade pies and other baked goods, even a stand selling homemade ice cream. There was a car wash, a bounce-house, and about twenty different carnival games. One woman was dressing women and children in capulanas and taking digital portraits. None of the activities or goodies cost more than about three or four Euros, and the money was flowing. I looked around the room, thinking, "Even if every person just gives a little bit. . ." I had learned to never underestimate the power of small money, especially when fundraising. Small money—grass roots support—was the cornerstone of our finances.

At the end of the day, Henry shook his head in amazement, calling the result a true miracle, unprecedented in all his years at Ontmoetingskerk: they had raised more than 7,000 Euros.

The next day, Henry picked me up at Charles and Dita's house to take me sailing with his friends. When he was in Mozambique, he had often said, "Amy, sometimes you just need to go sailing," which had always made me think of my own "need" to soak in the hot springs. Now that I was on the water with him and his friends, I was starting to realize how much I missed having free time. When I later saw photos of that relaxing day, I was startled to see exhaustion etched across my face. The work without break was taking a toll, even when I managed to get some down time.

On my last night in the Netherlands, I went for tea and dessert at Casper's house. I nursed my tea, surrounded by the foreign-language drone that had become so common in my life. Casper shared with me that the container was nearly full. It was almost ready for shipping! He boasted of welders and steel pipe and scaffolding and other large items, and I wondered how we could use those things in our girls' programs.

Then Casper told us about his daughter's lavish wedding, which had included a Romeo and Juliet balcony scene. At that point, one of the ladies leaned over to tell me you can get married for free at 9AM at the court building in Hasselt. I just smiled. *Good to know. Good to know.*

Those beautiful days in the Netherlands had passed so quickly, and too soon it was time for me to leave. But I will never forget that trip or the generosity of my friends there. I felt more relaxed during that visit than at any other time in that entire decade of my life. I remember thinking many times: *This is so soothing.* I left there with the opinion that God lives in the Netherlands—or at least vacations there.

As I settled in for my flight, I reflected on the trip ahead. In the States, there would be the normal whirlwind fundraising tour, jumping from organization to organization, location to location.

Then I would head to Guatemala. One of our donors wanted to see if our program could be replicated, and I wanted to know that as well—with one alteration. I wanted the program in Guatemala to be developed with our cooperation but operated from the start by local people. Aside from this one change, the Guatemalan program would be a replica of the Mozambican program.

If I could create a replicable framework, I could deliver it to a number of organizations that were already working around the world. For me, this would be the ultimate success for my programs: duplicating them around the world, using local staff without my direct involvement. Success in this endeavor would mean that one day I could retire from my mission, allowing local organizations to step in.

In Guatemala I met up with Pahola, the local woman who was leading the project, and we went to meet the women who would sew dolls, as well as the seminary students who would be trained to deliver our HIV prevention curriculum.

After we presented our HIV class, one of the donors who attended said, "Amy, the thing I noticed is that usually after a half hour or so, people are fidgeting, texting, wanting to go to the bathroom. Yet you held them mesmerized for two hours. Nobody moved; nobody texted. They really wanted to know this information."

"We have a similar experience in Mozambique," I said. "When I hear people say, 'Oh, the locals just don't care. They keep having unprotected sex.' I know they are wrong. People do want the information. I've seen it time after time. They want to understand the facts so they can make clear choices, even if their choice is to continue having unprotected sex."

After Guatemala, I headed back to the States for more fundraising events. By the time all was said and done, I was beat. I had been on four continents, in six states, and slept in five strangers' houses. I had spent at least fifty hours inside of airplanes—all in just five weeks. The most defeating part was that, though the event in the Netherlands had been financially successful, the rest of the trip had generated only about $12,000.

Though we were receiving funds from the U.S. Embassy and Church World Service, those funds were awarded and distributed on a timetable that made long-term planning difficult. I was worried about trying to run the projects for an entire year on so little. Our overhead, the bulk of which was rent and salaries, had increased, and I was running classes at the farm, classes at the TIOS School, and all the girls' clubs. But I had been down to just a little money many times by then, since the day I decided to start my nonprofit, when I'd had only $150 in my pocket. Or the day I actually started creating the nonprofit when I'd had only $70. I could not clearly see how we were going to make it. The ball was in God's court.

# 41

I was beat from the trip, yet I was excited to be landing in Zimbabwe, where I had not been able to visit for several months. Americans had been booted out of the country because of national elections, but the borders had recently been re-opened. Still—even when the country was open—visitors had to have a letter of invitation from a Zimbabwean, along with a notarized copy of their passport, their address, contact information, and a few other documents. During elections, they tightened their borders even more, especially when it came to Americans—especially the press. I was looking forward to indulging in the Zimbabwean culture once again.

Daniel was meeting me, and I was looking forward to seeing him again as well. As I exited the plane, I realized he was not there and headed off to get my immigration stamp, figuring I would find him in the parking area. But, no, he wasn't there. The airport was so small there was no way I missed him. I sat down to wait and wondered what to do if he didn't show.

Our plan was to spend a couple of days at Leopard Rock, which was once described by the Queen Mother of England as the most beautiful place in Africa. I can't recall who had originally told me about the wonderful hideaway in the mountains, but I had stayed there one other time, and I was excited to share it with Daniel.

Many Zimbabweans were making money during the economic crisis by renting out rooms or little cottages on their properties. They especially enjoyed guests who brought the treasured U.S. dollar or South African rand, which were the only functioning money in Zimbabwe at that time. They had completely given up printing Zimbabwean money.

I waited forty minutes before I considered heading back into the airport to make a call (because my cell phone would not work in Zimbabwe). But to whom? If Daniel was across the border already, his phone wouldn't work either. And I didn't have a single phone number for anyone I knew in Zimbabwe. I could get a taxi to a hotel and sort it out the next day, but how would I get word to Daniel? Another thirty-five minutes passed. A couple of taxi drivers came up to me, but I assured them I had a ride. I started to get worried. We needed to get going if we were going to make it to Leopard Rock before dark. *Where is he?*

I kept trying to formulate a plan, finally deciding that if worse came to worse, I could just stop a passing Zimbabwean (a white person because they'd be more likely to know one of the Zimbabweans from Chimoio) and ask if they could help me figure out a place to go or what to do—or at least let me use a cell phone.

Just as I decided the time had come to lug my five bags back into the airport and carry out this plan, I saw Daniel's familiar form moving across the parking lot to greet me. He gave that shrug of his shoulders as he explained that he was late because it had taken a while to get across the border. I had forgotten to give him a letter of usage that said he had permission to cross the border with my car.

"I explained the situation, and gave a little money for appreciation." Daniel said. *Great, that's all it takes to steal a car and hustle it across the border.*

He barely gave me a butterfly kiss, then tossed my bags in back. He seemed stressed and distracted, and he didn't say why. I planned to simply wait and keep watching.

We stopped at a store for some groceries and anxiously watched the setting sun. I had been to this guesthouse at Leopard Rock only one time. I wasn't sure I could find my way to it from the city of Mutare in the daylight, let alone in the dark. Mutare was still two hours ahead. It was a hectic way to begin a vacation.

As we were leaving the grocery store, Daniel opened the car door so that I could load our provisions, and the handle broke off in his hand. He was startled and his frustration showed through. Since Daniel rarely showed any emotional upset, his frustration peeking through added to my sense that something was "off." After just a beat, though, he shrugged. We tossed the groceries in, and we were on our way—and although the door never opened after that, at least it stayed closed.

As we drove, Daniel was quiet and evasive, and his breathing was fast and shallow. He was also jumpy, which had never been part of his persona. We drove along in silence, as I wondered where we would go from here, and I wasn't thinking about the highway.

Daniel had always taken great pride in his work and his income, and he was responsible for his younger brother, Geoff, whether he had a job or not. In addition, it was easy to see the light competition among the siblings in Daniel's family. Daniel had two siblings in the country's Finance department, one in Customs, one at an airline, and one at the port. Then there was Daniel, who was used to having an equally respectable career directing aid agencies—but who was now laid off. I knew it had been weighing heavy on his mind and heart. I was worried about Daniel.

It was fully dark when we got to Mutare, and we still had another forty-five minutes of winding mountain roads to get to the guesthouse. Along the way, we had to ask for directions. Even though Zimbabweans speak English, when it comes to giving directions, they speak African. "You go down there and then when you see the tree you go over and you will come to a mailbox..."

"Daniel, please. I need a translation."

"But they are speaking English, Amy."

"Yeah, but I need lefts and rights and straight-aheads. You do logistics. Please can you get the instructions from him?"

Daniel spoke briefly with the Zimbabwean, and the man led us with his car to the turn-off. Daniel gave him a cheerful wave as we headed up the mountain. I knew there was a blue reflector on the tree where we would turn off the main mountain road and was pretty sure I would see it, even in the dark.

Sure enough, it was there. Daniel wove us through the dirt path in the heavy forest in the dark, our lights sometimes catching the reflection of a wooden fence or glowing eyes. After carefully counting past the third barely discernable path on the left, we found the one we needed. At last. The stars seemed thick and close enough to touch but provided little illumination in the African night.

"Don't go in too fast, Daniel. This place is built on the edge of the mountain. I think it would be easy to go over the side." Thankfully he took my advice and slowed down a bit.

Eventually we pulled up to the little cottage and got out. Two big dogs came out barking, but they did not bite. Soon our hostess appeared with a gas lantern and showed us into the cottage. She encouraged us to take a shower before the night air cooled the solar-heated water and to then come up for a proper Irish whiskey with her and her husband.

We had our showers and chose the big bedroom to the left. This was such a lovely cottage and reminded me so much of mine in Woodland Park, except of course mine had twenty-four-hour electricity and hot water. This little cabin had just a wood burning stove, which our hostess had kindly lit, and lanterns. The city generators were unreliable. Like my former cabin, this one had a small central living and kitchen area with a bedroom/bathroom suite on each side.

I began to unpack, digging for the things I had brought back for Daniel. He smiled, but I could tell he was here out of obligation. The way he avoided eye contact and showed so little affection told me he had a big secret on his mind and in his heart. I knew he must have another woman, but for some reason he was making an attempt to also stay with me.

I started to think the farm had something to do with it; since buying the farm, I had become a source of possible wealth, one that his family members would encourage him to keep whether he loved me or not. Love often had nothing to do with Mozambican alliances, many of which were built on economics and survival. Perhaps because Daniel had brought me into his family, he was now obligated to keep me for the potential assistance I could bring to the others. We were like long-ago lovers who had become friends. We continued to support and feel a strong bond for each other.

Still, it was difficult to be in bed with a man who didn't want to be with me, so the next day, I brought it up. "Daniel. I know you love me but perhaps you don't like me so much. Maybe you should say your goodbyes to me and move on to a woman who you do love. One who sets your heart on fire."

"Amy, I love you. It's not half. It's full. I need you in my life. Things are difficult since I don't work at WFP, and I am trying to get by. I need you in my life."

So we spent a couple of days in the incredible beauty of the Bvumba Mountains, sometimes going for lunch or a sundowner at the Country Club at Leopard Rock. Then we headed back to Chimoio. My heart told me this was all wrong, but he insisted he wanted me in his life. Looking back, I see that I never even asked myself what *I* wanted. On the other hand, that probably did not matter; Bruce died so soon after I sent him away that I was not in an emotional place where I could take a stand with Daniel. He could pretty much come and go as he pleased.

As we started our journey back to Chimoio, Daniel seemed to perk up a bit. "Amy, did I mention we dug a borehole on the farm while you were away?"

The man knew how to pull out a carrot. A borehole! I pretty much jumped up and down, as much as I could in my little Suzuki. Daniel hadn't done this; I knew it had to have been Casper or John Bunnik or one of the other Dutch guys from *Water Is Our World* or Wilde Ganzen. But Daniel was the one telling me about it, and I was very grateful. Clean water on the farm! This was a wonderful thing for us and a miracle for the surrounding community. Finally I was doing something substantial—and *lasting*—for the Mozambican people.

# 42

Daniel dropped me at the farm and headed back up north. I was anxious to catch up with René. With him on board, I finally had a director who could manage things while I was out of town. Thank the Good Lord for that.

René and I had lots to discuss, and I didn't have much time to do so before I had to go to the Beira airport to pick up a new volunteer. I wanted to send René instead, but I had promised Daniel's brother Santos and his wife Helena that I would stop by.

Before I headed out, I took a peek at the bank accounts at the TIOS School, now that the money from the fundraising trip had been deposited. "Where are this month's bank statements, René?" As he showed me around the school, catching me up on the events of the past five weeks, I repeated the question at least four more times without getting a response. Then I went to the bank to get the statements myself. There was a deposit for 40,000 meticais, about $1,300. That was a huge deposit for us, and I had no idea where it had come from.

My stomach sank as I began to dig through the receipts and petty cash documents over the next couple of days, trying to understand what had gone on in my absence. Unfortunately, the new volunteer was there when reality soaked in. René had apparently manipulated funds by "borrowing" money.

I lost it. This was full-blown anger. I had kept my cool in countless situations that would have really pissed off most Americans, but I was finally, fully, and completely furious. My slow burn had turned into raging fire. Where had the money gone? It was donor money, and I was responsible for it.

"You need to take a couple of days off," I told René, "while I sort through this. Give me your keys to the car and the school, please." Looking pensive, he took a deep, slow breath as if considering his options. Then he gave me the keys and left.

As near as I could tell, $1,000 of the missing money had been spent on fuel. René was a clever man, and I could see he had thought things through. The odometer on the Toyota was busted, so he probably figured I wouldn't be able to tell whether he'd driven enough to use the reported gas. But I had investigated insurance fraud, and I knew the tricks.

A thousand dollars' worth of fuel equated to something like 300 liters of gas, which would have fueled something like 4,500 km, which would have taken fifty hours to drive. Nobody else at the school had a driver's license. Ironically, his plan to submit gas receipts from his taxi service in order to explain the missing money was the very thing that tipped me off that a theft had definitely taken place and that he had done it.

Eventually, the final total was in. He had run $10,000 through petty cash in five weeks. The strange deposit had been from René, his attempt to put some of the money back.

I met with him in Sheila's old office and confronted him about the receipts, the gas, and the deposit. He said that his father had needed surgery, so he had taken the funds and that he had returned some of them, and would soon return the rest. I asked him to take some time off so I could figure out what to do. Because his father-in-law was the head of the national police, this could be a very dangerous situation if René wanted to retaliate. So I did not involve the police.

But I had to fire him. To not fire him would have meant keeping an employee who I knew had stolen funds and taken advantage of Berta, who was a required cosigner on the account. I would have lost respect in the community if I had kept René on; I would no longer have been perceived as serious. Donors would not respond well if they found out their money had been stolen and nothing had been done about it.

My employees had known he was taking money; even though Berta was the second signatory on all checks, she said to me, "What could I do, Amy? He tells me to sign a check. He is the director. You put him in charge." She was right. I did put him in charge.

A week later, one of René's former employers told me that he had released René under similar circumstances. The news was incredibly frustrating. Why tell me now, after he had taken money? Why not tell me when I had called for a reference before I hired him?

I am guessing this employer was also aware of René's position as the son-in-law of the head of the national police. All one had to do was pull out a business card showing the uncle's last name, and people would retreat. That is how René had gotten Clay out of jail so quickly; he told me how he barely said a word, just handed them his card from the TIOS School. Now I could see that it wasn't my influence that had gotten Clay out; it was René's connection.

I began to take a deeper look at my mission. I recalled the words of the director at the training campus in the States: "If you are doing more work than the people you are helping, your ego might be involved." She further explained what she meant. If aid workers are more committed than those they are helping, then the project is more about the aid worker than the community. She used the analogy of a person pushing a piano to the top of the mountain—working so very hard to get it to the top, only to realize that nobody at the top of the mountain wanted to hear music. One person's initiative was simply that, one person's initiative.

In my case, I had heard a calling, and I could see that my mission was being supported. Each time I needed something, it had come. Sometimes it did not come until the eleventh hour, but it came. The one thing I was seeking but couldn't seem to find was a committed director, a local person who had a passion to bring safety to the country's children. Perhaps I needed to look more deeply into why I was staying. In some ways, René had done much more than "borrow" funds to pay for his father's surgery, he had stolen my hope.

Up until now I had been resilient and I had kept putting one foot in front of the other when I was tired, challenged, threatened, and sick. But here was another local person corrupting the work intended to help his own people. I understood his need to "borrow" money for a family emergency, but his actions had jeopardized everything. I just wasn't sure it made sense for me to stay. I had some feeling, thinking, and praying to do.

I sought a bit of support from Sharlene, a member of my U.S. board of directors. She had been with me since the very beginning, she understood my mission, and I trusted her. I tried to be tactful and open-minded in my email about the situation with René, but I was almost afraid to keep going with my projects. I couldn't control the actions of the director when I was out of the country.

At some point in our emailing back and forth I mentioned my concerns about my health and having been bitten by tse-tse flies. She urged me to get to the doctor before I ended up dying in Mozambique. Without even thinking about it, I had responded with, "You know, Sharlene, death would be a welcome thing right about now. There is just no life in my life."

I wasn't exactly suicidal, but right then I would have almost welcomed a lethal round of malaria. Even with all the wonderful help I was receiving from volunteers and funding agencies, I was completely overwhelmed running things, and there was nobody to fall back on.

But this was not the time to crumble. Two huge projects were on the horizon, thanks to my associations with my Dutch friends. First, Henry's daughter-in-law Hanneke was coming to help remake our safety video. Second, the container would soon be arriving; unpacking and distributing its contents would be a big job.

I was determined to produce an effective safety video. While I had been in the Netherlands, I'd spoken with Hanneke about my struggles with the project. She had made HIV prevention videos in Namibia, and she had worked in Bosnia. She said that she would love to come to Mozambique to help me remake our video. She also mentioned that her husband had done sports projects. Would our kids be interested in that? Of course they would.

Hanneke was a pro. Via email, she had been pushing me to finalize my scripts and organize my props. ("Hey, Dad, I need a rubber snake and maybe a couple of spiders. Can you get them for me and ship them here?") Because she directed my preparation from afar, by the time she arrived, everything was ready. With the help of a couple of our volunteers we had begun practicing the scenes with the street kids who were attending classes at the Formigas do Futuro School, as they were a bit older than our students and had a lot of theatre practice. I had barely participated in the development of the first video, but this time I was fully engaged. I saw this video as one of the things that had to be done, and done well, before I left the country.

Once again, I would have two big projects going (the video and the container), but Hanneke's husband, Rik, would be keeping the kids busy doing sports projects, and he was going to help us sort out the inventory from the container. So I felt like I could concentrate on this safety video. I prayed that it would enable me to reach millions of kids, as I had originally set out to do.

# 43

Three years had passed since I first rented space for the TIOS School at Textáfrica, and the time had come to have an exposition for the community. All of the preparations were in place. We were ready to show the community what their youngest children and growing girls could do.

The kids outdid themselves, truly. The presentations of safety skills and self-defense were impeccable. People in the audience nodded and pointed as the children bandaged and wrapped wounds and explained how to splint an arm.

The kids had prepared a demonstration of first aid. They confidently put on their rubber gloves and explained how they were wrapping pretend wounds. One of the men in the delegation asked one of the boys, João, why he was putting on gloves.

João explained, "Sometimes there are germs or diseases in the blood. We don't want to mix body fluids because it's dangerous."

The gentleman was astounded. "He knew the answer!"

His comment amused me. Of course João knew the answer; we were in the business of teaching first aid! With some satisfaction, I reminded myself that João's answer was only a small part of what he knew and that bandaging a wound was only a tiny part of what he could do.

The kids were pros by this time. One of the volunteers had taken the kids into the markets to do safety theatre. They had also done a few radio interviews. A number of our kids had even been on television demonstrating their skills. They were very proud of the work they had done, and I was proud of them. They were building a reputation in the community, all without me. Exposition day made me optimistic that our two teachers, Roberto and Berta, would soon be able to take over and own this project. As Berta's duties had begun to include administration and more work with the rural clubs, we had needed a sewing teacher to continue with doll production.

Roberto was a Zimbabwean, meaning I wouldn't need to lean so heavily on an English-speaking director, and he had experience in electronic embroidery, which would help us with the dolls and even be able to create commercial dolls with company uniforms and logos. We soon envisioned making tourist dolls as a means of income. Of course those wouldn't be "anatomical."

Before moving on to create safety skills and roll out this project in other countries, I needed to make arrangements for each project to continue. So I started talking with Roberto and Berta about the possibility that they could create a Mozambican association that would continue the work of TIOS. They agreed, but were very nervous. We got to work on the filings and registrations necessary to create their organization. When we were done, they were ATM, (Associação TIOS Moçambique). Next they needed to find a location where they could run the school.

They would need a fairly sizeable building because they were going to carry on most of the projects. They would still be training girls to manufacture the dolls, which meant they needed space for the sewing and embroidery machines. And they would still be training girls to manufacture bio-sand filters as well, so there needed to be space for the manufacturing equipment and for storing inventory.

Finding the new location had been quite a trick. Berta and Roberto had looked at several places before finding the building for ATM. First they went high-rent and found a place for $500 per month, nearly twice what I'd been expecting. All I can figure is that they saw how much money was moving through the organization and thought more should be spent on rent. But I had never paid that much for a location for TIOS, and that was a big part of the reason we had made it this long. We controlled expenses, while generating income and supplementing our income with available funding in-country.

269

Finally they found a house that was $350 per month. I was willing to help them support it, but I still didn't like it; there were plenty of good houses available in town for $250–$300. However, I agreed to pay rent on the new place for six months. I also agreed to give them the materials and equipment from TIOS. The rent was paid, they had a new location, and I was passing to them all of the inventory—the bio-sand filter mold, all of the sewing machines, computers—everything.

The documents we signed said that I would continue to own the materials the new organization would be using. After all of the corruption I had seen and experienced, I knew better than to simply sign over thousands of dollars' worth of equipment to a new NGO. If I had, the stuff could have been liquidated on my first trip out of the country. I'm not saying they would have done that, only that they could have done that. On paper, all of the equipment headed for ATM would continue to belong to TIOS, America, with me as designee. If they were going to sell anything, they would need to contact me in writing first.

Not long after the exposition, I sat down with the community in Textáfrica to tell them we would be closing this school at the end of our lease in the spring. I presented my plan—moving the school to a location in the bairro, where it would be run by our Mozambican staff as ATM. I pointed out that it was just our big "R&D" TIOS School in Textáfrica that was closing. The projects would continue in new locations.

Later that same day, Madelaine (a volunteer from Austria) came to my office and delivered a speech that was eerily similar to the one I'd received from Gemma the year before. "Amy, these people are not ready to take over this project. *You* wanted this. This was for you. They only wanted to be employees. For you to expect them to take it over is rude and inconceivable!"

She was angry, but it had always been my intention to hand off these projects to the local people, before I ever started the first orphan school in Mudzingadze. I had done all I could to find somebody who was willing to take over the work. Maybe in that effort I had failed, but Roberto and Berta were willing to try, and that was something. I would support them in any way I could, but the time was fast approaching when I would need to head out doing safety-skills training for other projects, and even replicating this one.

In truth, there were many reasons to close the TIOS School, not only because it was time to hand off our programs to local people. In part, it had served its purpose. It had served as a research center for us to teach our kids safety and to test the programs as we created them. And though the location had been fabulous for making the bio-sand filters because there was so much space, we needed more water than the school's small well could provide. Besides that, interrupted electricity had always been an issue.

Though the new ATM location had less indoor space for storage of the filters and tools, there was at least adequate water and a safe electrical supply, and hopefully they wouldn't blow up any more computers because of power surges.

Another reason it was time to close the TIOS School was that, though the project had been created for orphans, very wealthy families were bringing their children to us rather than sending them to school and paying school fees. That was not working for us or for those children. We weren't teaching Mozambican curriculum, just health-safety classes and art-and-craft skills. Kids should never have been kept out of regular school to attend TIOS, just so their parents could avoid school fees and the kids could get free porridge or bread. Besides, our resources needed to go to the children most in need—like that little girl who had cried in hunger.

I remembered a conversation with Mom two years before. Her health was being challenged, and she had chastised me on the phone: "Amy, I don't want to use my health to influence you, but you know stress is not good for my condition. Don't you think it's time to come home?"

Her question made me recall one of the earlier messages I had received regarding my work with children: *You will find a way to go on your mission. It will be challenging. The greatest trial of your life. It will be different for your family and friends to let you go. You will fight Goliath and win for the children.*

How could I have gone home to Mom? Was I supposed to tell God, "Sorry. My bad. I'd love to help you out, but I've got something else going on"? That message had pushed me through many a challenging moment in Mozambique, and it was with deep knowing that I had responded to Mom.

"Mom, I haven't even had a flat tire. I haven't had any run-ins with the government. I haven't even had a cell phone stolen. God isn't exactly packing my bags!"

But by the time the TIOS School was closing, I had indeed lost a cell phone to theft—and a whole bunch of money. Every part of the project, it seemed to me, was running up against considerable problems. Maybe I needed to surrender my attachment to running a school. God had certainly taken my suitcases out of the closet.

# 44

—◦◦◦◦—

Mozambique had a huge problem with land mines, and Chimoio was no exception. The fact that there were land mines in such a peaceful place was just one more paradox of Mozambican life. The mines had been buried in the war years and had been displaced by time and by flooding. Now, thirty years later, it was quite a task to track down the missing mines and accidents were common. While I was at the teacher-training center in Chimoio, a land mine hidden beneath the market had killed two children.

We taught land mine safety and had taken some footage to include in the original safety video. Land mine safety training is pretty straightforward. We showed the kids photos of things that might actually be land mines and told them never to touch them, to stay away from the area, and to tell adults what they had found. Normally mines are completely buried, but flooding had displaced many mines. Now they could be found anywhere: buried, half-buried, or out in the open. I once heard a story about a tree that had grown with a land mine in the fork of its trunk.

The HALO Trust, a British NGO specializing in deactivating mines and removing other types of war debris, works around the world to save countless people by safely detonating land mines. (In the words of one worker from The HALO Trust, "It's much easier to just blow them up than to try to remove them. Besides, what would we do with thirty-year-old mines if we dug them up?") I still want to cheer whenever I hear The HALO Trust mission: "Getting mines out of the ground, now." They are an organization after my own heart.

The HALO Trust was in our area, and it was a pleasure getting to know those generous, hardworking people. One of The HALO Trust's Scottish employees, Helen Tirebuck had arrived in town sometime around 2009. Since Mandy and Helen Large had left town for their new homes, I was excited to develop new friendships. Helen Tirebuck was slim and tall, with shoulder-length blonde hair, and we often shared a beer or two. She seemed to enjoy rural life and maybe even farming, as she had started a garden with all kinds of plants at her house, and she would often come out to the farm to escape the city.

I met up with The Halo Trust team in Maputo one day, and they took me out to see their operations. The land mine site they were working on was right in the bairro. There, just on the edge of the hut-lined dirt road, land mines were being marked for detonation.

They actually let me detonate a mine. Safely encased in my Kevlar jacket, behind my plastic shield, I pushed down the handle. As the land mine exploded fifty feet away, I felt like I was in a scene from *Hogan's Heroes*. Helen was right. It was fun.

We had done some HIV training courses for Helen Tirebuck's mostly male de-miners in Chimoio. As always, there had been snickering when we broke out the dolls, and this group was exceptionally gifted with theatre. A wave of laughter rang out as the men demonstrated how a guy picks up a woman to have sex. They were very talented, and I laughed right along with them.

The partnership we had formed with The HALO Trust was incredible. We were an unlikely pairing—an orphan school and a de-mining organization, but we found ample opportunities to work together. Helen and her drivers were instrumental in helping us deliver clothes to children in rural areas for Christmas. Seeing the happiness and wonder on kids' faces in Macate and Sussundenga brought the holiday to life. Who knew "Santa Berta" could arrive in a HALO Trust Land Rover?

Now I had an idea for extending our partnership a bit further, and I broached it with Helen over a sundowner at Mario's Place one evening. "Hey, Helen, don't you ever need a place to blow things up? You know, for training purposes?"

"Yeah. We do quite a bit of our training at camp, but then we do need an actual site where we can train guys to do the job. We need to show them how to grid and sweep an area. Why do you ask?"

"Well, if you could grid something on the farm before I finish building the preschool, it would be really helpful. I'd be happy to do some free HIV prevention training for your guys in exchange."

"That won't be necessary. We have a budget for the HIV prevention, and we like your training. But we might be able to use your property for our gridding training. I just don't see how that would benefit you."

"The farm sat empty for so long that the locals got used to crossing right through it. That wouldn't be so bad, but they come across right at the middle, next to the house, the garage, the transformer, the well. It makes for a heck of a guarding situation."

"Why don't you just put up a sign telling them to keep out?" she asked.

"We've tried putting in signs, asking them nicely not to cross there. The guards even got some horrible dog that attacked a couple of volunteers. We had to shoot it."

"How can we help?"

"I'm okay with them crossing the farm, but not in the middle, past the electrical transformer and the school. They need to cross down at the other end. Past all the buildings, there are four more acres where they can cross. I don't even care if they take some of the bananas that are growing out there."

"Wow, Amy, it's weird they don't just go further down if they know that's all you want them to do. I wonder what the problem is?"

"They feel that since they've been crossing here for years, they should be able to continue. If I were a Mozambican they would have stopped the day I moved in, but I'm not. So I've been planting thorny bushes all along the property line to make a live fence. It has helped a lot, but it needs a few years to grow before it will completely solve the problem. I also planted bamboo down at the river to minimize the number of crossings down there.

"Anyway, I was thinking, if your guys grid the farm, and we put up warnings that there are mines, they would probably be happy enough to cross further down. What do you think?"

"Oh my God, that's funny. Ya. I've got a group that will be ready for grid training in a couple of weeks. We can go out to the farm to do the rural part of the training. We had been looking for a site that wasn't too expensive."

"Well, feel more than free to use the farm. I won't charge you, and I can at least host some of your HIV training class here, even if you pay. Be sure to blow something up—anything but the transformer or well. That way the whole community will know that it isn't safe to cross the farm where it's been gridded."

"Sure, I'm on it."

True to her word, Helen showed up a couple of weeks later with the big white HALO Trust vehicles and her team. Suited up in Kevlar and masks, the trainees began the tedious work of stringing grids across about an acre of the farm, midway behind the new preschool building and the well and transformer. They put on quite a display, using every caution for this very dangerous and difficult job.

I smiled from ear to ear when I saw the grid work they had created. The next day they would begin moving about with their metal detectors to sweep for mines. I had found all kind of coins around the farm when I first bought it—old money from before the war years. I hoped they would be lucky too.

My guards looked anxious at having so many people on the farm, and they couldn't figure out what those people were doing. They all knew there weren't any land mines on my farm.

Lucky for me, there was a lot of old buried metal fence, so the metal detectors kept going off with a high-pitched whine. Discreetly, Helen had her team bury and then detonate a land mine. Well, the detonation wasn't discreet—a huge *kaboom* rang out through the bairro.

The day was a huge success! When the HALO Trust trucks pulled out of the driveway, the bairro was silent. I could almost hear the whispers: "Stay off the farm. There are mines! Cross on the other side. Nobody really knows what the crazy Muzungu did."

It worked! People stopped crossing through the middle of my property. And I inadvertently gained the respect of several Mozambican directors—the director of the electric company, the phone company, and other aid organizations—for the playful and creative way we solved the problem.

# 45

———⊶∘C∕⊃∘⊷———

Word was coming back from installation sites that there were quality issues with the bio-sand filters. When I checked our records, I could see that the ongoing monitoring of the installed filters was starting to slip. The filters were not collapsing or failing, but there were too many surface bubbles, which made the filters look like they were thrown together or shoddily made, potentially causing people to doubt whether the filters actually worked.

When one of the volunteers mentioned these issues to Gemma, she called me, very angry. "We have never had a project where the quality of the bio-sand filters has gone down. Yours is the first! I am embarrassed to be involved in a project that is so poorly maintained." I felt guilty and embarrassed by her admonishments and for letting the quality slip under my supervision. Gemma ended the conversation by saying that she would be sending Mariah back to Mozambique to repeat the training.

She would be arriving in just three weeks, and since René was gone, I needed some backup to make sure the retraining would be effective. I knew that Daniel was not working, and I knew he would be a wonderful help during this hectic time. I picked up the phone. "Uh, Daniel? I could really use a hand on the farm right now. Mariah is coming back to do another bio-sand filter training; we are moving the big TIOS School; the container is coming from the Netherlands, and we are about to start a second try at the safety video. Would you think about coming to help me? I can pay you René's former salary."

"I can come help you, Amy. But I will still have some commitments here in Nampula and Nacala, so sometimes I will need to come back here."

I was hugely relieved. I had lost René at the worst possible time, and Daniel already had the skillset to help with my

278

projects. I needed Daniel, and I knew that Daniel needed an income too.

When Daniel arrived, the farm was beautiful, and the projects seemed to be running fairly smoothly. I felt proud to show him around. Recent improvements had been focused outside. The drainage problem had been fixed. Gardens had been planted. The preschool and bakery were done. The avocado trees that I had germinated at the TIOS School were growing, and several trees that Allan Schwarz had brought me were beginning to grow, despite the fact that the guards kept forgetting to water them.

When Gemma and Mariah had come to do the initial training, Gemma had helped us install a safe-water storage tank on the farm that included a cistern to collect rainwater runoff from the garage. We now had the river, the original dirty well down by the transformer, and the well that Pine had divined, which had problems of its own. I had been hopeful the day we divined that well, but the water always had a slick, oily film on top. So we still had to walk more than a mile to get clean water for cooking and bathing.

Because of the situation with the water on the farm, Lina left us. Walking to work on the farm and then walking another two miles for clean water was too much for her. I couldn't blame her and gave her a great reference when she sought employment with another family.

Even though the borehole had been dug back in September, it had not yet been attached to plumbing. But soon—soon!—we would be able to pump the water up to a water tank that would supply clean, running water both in the house and outside. Best of all, a pump attached to the borehole would be built at the mosque across the road to provide clean water for the whole area—over 7,000 people!

Mariah arrived, and we conducted the week-long training with Daniel and the health extension agents from OSEO, who were serving nearby rural communities. Even Jorge Lampião came back and conducted a few classes for the training. Daniel drove Mariah and the girls out in the bairro to check the water filters that had been installed. They efficiently checked and even reinstalled a number of filters in the communities and rural health clinics.

Those first days with Daniel on the farm were calm. In the mornings, we started our day with fresh eggs from our chickens. Often I made grilled egg sandwiches with ham, egg, and cheese, like in the States. Those sandwiches would hold us for most of the day, at least until our lunches of *mutapa* (a dish of collard greens, peanuts, and coconut milk) and rice at the school.

All of the employees and students seemed happy to have Daniel there. I'm sure they were thinking that not only was he fun and interesting, but maybe he would calm down Dona Amy just a bit. "Nobody can live without sex. It's not possible." The words rang in my ears as my staff gave me knowing smiles when they saw Daniel and me together. Ernesto tiptoed around like a five-year-old, and I believe he was hoping to catch Daniel and me in a kiss that he could turn into gossip.

In the evenings, Daniel and I took turns preparing dinner or different parts of dinner. Sometimes we would go to town to shoot a game of pool. Once or twice we played soccer in the front yard. Those were good times for us—normal happy times. Conversations were light. We discussed our projects and other events happening in Mozambique.

"Amy, did you hear the news about Beira?" Daniel asked one evening.

"No. What's going on?"

"Santos called. There has been a rash of crime. You know, it is not uncommon for someone to wake up to robbers in their house. The thieves steal everything. People sometimes wake up to a thief telling them to get out of the bed so they can steal it. The people always do it, and there is no fighting. What would be the point?"

I remembered my Zimbabwean neighbors at Textáfrica having this experience a couple of times.

Daniel went on. "The unusual thing in Beira is that these were armed robberies."

"Where did they get the guns?"

"Well, at first the police thought they had gotten them the same way Mozambicans always get guns—by going to the police station and checking them out, like a library book in America."

He was right. Each year before the holidays, crime always increased, and the Zimbabweans often spoke of getting guns from the police to protect their farms, especially because people knew they had a lot of cash during that time in preparation for paying Christmas bonuses.

"After some days investigating, the police discovered the guards at the prisons had been giving their guns to the inmates and sending them out to rob houses and bring the goods back."

"What! You mean the prisoners had done it using the guards' guns and then came back to prison? Why would they go back? The airport is right there."

"Yeah. Right there."

"Why would the prisoners do it?"

"I don't know. I suppose it was a combination of the guards beating them if they didn't do it and the prisoners getting some kind of extra perks or part of the take if they did."

I hoped the idea wouldn't catch on in Chimoio.

Often Daniel and I would eat our evening meal at the table by the garage and enjoy a Manica beer or a glass of wine. I would sometimes turn the tarot cards, and we would talk about the day. Our backdrop was the deep orange burn of what we had come to call "second sunset." It was an odd thing that I hadn't seen until moving to the farm. The sun would go down, and it would get dark. Then about twenty minutes later there would be a deep orange back-burn. It was a stunning end to the day. The farm also had what are known as fire rainbows. Fire rainbows are a rare phenomenon that only occur when the sun is higher than fifty-eight degrees above the horizon and its light passes through cirrus clouds made of ice crystals. I sometimes wondered if the two phenomena were related, or if the farm was just magical.

I was thankful for the calm and quiet of the farm at night. I began to call it "The Oasis Farm."

Daniel would come and go, always with a new reason. "I have to run up north to do a job in Nacala." "I have to run to Beira to see my rental."

He would come and work with me on a project, and then he would disappear for a week. Alface seemed to eye him with the same wariness he had given the director from the labor department. I wondered why.

One afternoon, Daniel and I went to Beira to get our latest volunteer, Fiona. She was coming from the UK in order to help us with the safety-school kids. She was a writer, and I was excited to have another writer in the house. She'd had rough times while traveling up the coast; a friend of hers had died, and she was taking a bit of a time out in Mozambique to assuage her grief.

When we got back to the farm, I stopped to pet Bella and noticed that she was covered in lumps—putse flies! Who had been taking care of my dog? Was it really so difficult to remove a maggot? I sat on the floor to undertake the exceedingly gross task of popping the maggots out of her skin. Before the job was done, poor Fiona nearly passed out. I guess I could understand why my guards wouldn't do this part, but I still hated the fact that my dog was full of maggots.

Fiona enjoyed being at the school with the kids, but she was not excited about spending the next weekend on the farm alone while Daniel and I drove Mariah back to the airport in Beira. Before we left, I cautioned her about coming and going. "Listen, Fiona, whatever you do, if you go away, don't tell the guards that you're leaving or when you're coming back. Just lock the door like normal and leave with your little day bag, not a word about where you are going or when you will return."

Daniel and I had a quick snack on the outdoor veranda of the airport and thanked Mariah for all of her help. We waved from the balcony of the airport to say our last goodbyes to her before heading back to the farm.

As Daniel and I arrived at Inchope, the phone rang. It was Margareta, my new housekeeper, and she was upset. "Amy! We are robbed."

"Okay," I said, keeping my cool like a true Mozambican. "How bad is it?"

"It's pretty bad. I think everything is gone."

"Okay. Well, I can't do much from here. We'll be there in another hour or so." The prison break-ins from Beira (or maybe they would be more aptly called "prison break-outs") came to mind, and I wondered what had happened on the farm.

I relayed the news to Daniel. "Maybe we should stop at the police station on the way to the farm to report it."

"Amy, sometimes these police can have some other interest. Maybe this time it would be better not to contact them."

"Well, Daniel, we can't get our things back if we don't go report it," I said, knowing that might not altogether be the case. This had to be an inside job; when white people were robbed, it always was. Either my guards had done this, or they had been asleep while someone else had done it. I remembered the night Daniel and I had pulled into the driveway and discovered our newest guard sleeping in the wheelbarrow. Even the lights of the car had not wakened him.

Daniel and I arrived at the house to find Fiona and Margareta quite upset. Fiona suggested that I prepare myself, as the house was "pretty bad."

When I got inside though, I realized it could have been much worse.

I did not find the empty-house scenario that many people discovered upon returning to a robbed house. These thieves had taken the chicken from the fridge but not the condiments, the mattress from the bed but not the sheets, the white wine from the cabinet but not the red. All of the beer was gone, of course. In addition, the big water bucket was gone. Whoever had robbed us had spent a lot of time in the house and made sure not to take anything identifiable.

My room had been left somewhat alone. My bank cards, cameras, and jewelry remained. The robbers had gone through every DVD case but left the DVDs. Had they been looking for money? There was no way to tell. What they did get was my luggage—my big, rolling bags that could have carried five orphans were gone, probably filled with our stuff.

Worst of all, Fiona's bag was gone. They had taken her money, her ATM card, her camera, everything. She called her insurance company and card companies to report her loss, but her documents would have to be replaced before she could leave the country.

I knew the robber was someone here on the farm. The question was who. Fiona admitted telling the guard how long I intended to be gone, but this theft was not Fiona's fault. A thief might be encouraged to have information like that, but a thief with any determination could have easily just waited until any time that everyone was out.

I decided to get the police despite Daniel being against it. There's no calling the police in Chimoio. I had to collect them from the police station and bring them to the farm.

Bringing the police to the farm turned out to be a bad decision, just as Daniel predicted. Not only were they completely unable to help, but as a result of this visit, the police now knew everything that was left in my house. A fear started to grow in my belly that they would be back for it later. Looking back, I wish I had listened more closely to what Daniel was implying when he said, "Sometimes these police can have some other interest." As a plain-speaking, up-front person, I always struggled to understand the *unsaid* in Mozambique.

The police were crammed back into the car, ready to return to the police station, and we were heading toward the gate when Bella took chase. The guard ran to stop her, but to no avail. As I swerved to miss a rut in the road, she got caught under the tire and yelped. I saw her tumble away. I stopped to see how bad it was, practically pushing the policemen out of the car so that I could open the hatch and have room to examine Bella. She was dead, a victim of my panic and of my refusal to listen to Daniel's advice.

Daniel remained silent as we packed up once again to head to the police station. Though he was riding along, he still refused to drive. The trip seemed interminable, and probably to avoid thinking of Bella and crying, I kept thinking about Daniel's refusal. He knew I was upset. He knew how I loved my dogs, even if he did not really understand it. I just kept thinking: *Why doesn't he offer to take over and drive the car?*

When I got back to the school, I placed Bella in our trash hole and instructed the guards to fill it in. She was gone.

# 46

Though well worth it, getting the bio-sand filters to the villages was a logistical problem. I was glad Daniel was there to get our shipment of 100 filters to Chinde, a village 200 miles to the northeast. If anyone could do it, Daniel could. He had the necessary logistical expertise, and he had led the second bio-sand filter training with Mariah, so he understood the installation process.

There was no denying that Daniel excelled with logistics, but even he had some trepidation about the job in Chinde. "Amy, when your boss is very, very angry with you he will say, 'If you do that again, I am sending you to Chinde.' It is a terrible place. You must go by boat and truck and foot to get there." I wasn't worried, though. Daniel could move things from point A to point B like nobody else. He worked with Concern Worldwide on this joint project to install 100 bio-sand filters to Chinde, and the whole installation had happened without any problems. I was so grateful for his help with these things. He and my students Marta and Nerzita worked very hard to get the filters installed properly with the reinforced knowledge they had gained from Mariah.

Marta took her work very seriously. She worked hard at the school and sometimes even came in on weekends to learn crafts. For the trip to Chinde, she had coordinated the assembly of all the bio-sand filter installation kits. She had carefully crated all of the cement filters, along with the necessary sand and rocks to fill them and the metal filters and lids. She made sure they had all the equipment they would need for the installations. I think Daniel might have made sure they had enough Manica beer. He was always good in the bush.

Every time the girls returned from a new installation, they were full of stories and excited about the impact these little cement boxes were making in people's lives. They were also teaching dental care after each installation, and they enjoyed that, along with the gratitude they got for it. Yet somehow their enthusiasm wasn't applied to the production and monitoring of the project. Getting them to clean up the construction area or maintain the paperwork was like pulling hens' teeth.

Even though we were having issues with the bio-sand filter project, Helen Tirebuck could not say enough wonderful things about the filters and how, nearly overnight, they had turned around a serious health issue at The HALO Trust camp.

"Amy! I'm not kidding you. We were averaging ten people a day out sick with stomach problems. Once the filter was on site, we started drinking that water. We knew we were supposed to wait twenty-one days for the filter to be fully functioning, but after all, we'd been drinking the dirty water all along. From the first day, our time-outs were reduced by more than half. By the second day, we had everybody back at work. Your girls did a wonderful job! Thank you so much!

"My director was so impressed that she contacted our central administration. Now The HALO Trust wants to put your bio-sand filters in every camp *and* put a couple in each of the communities where we work, as a good-neighbor gesture to the people."

Her approval made me happier than she could have known. I thought back to how I had let Gemma down during the training and how we had limped along with the project, especially with respect to monitoring. Again, I thought I just needed one efficient person in the office—and a break. I needed to go breathe, to get some rest, and to find some way to hit my reset button. I needed my staff to be able to run this project so I could go do what I was best at: creating dynamic training programs and materials.

When Daniel returned from delivering the filters to Chinde, we sat down to look at photos of the installations. I hated to criticize him, but *really?*

"Daniel, is that you pulling water out of the hospital's well with a used paint can?" I said it with a smile, to keep from hurting him too much after all he had done. But I knew there was no fixing his mistake. Daniel—to the villagers, the expert—had just shown them that it was okay to use an old paint can to get water out of the well. After all, the bio-sand filter would remove the lead, right?

Wrong! Bio-sand filters are brilliant for parasitic and bacterial issues, but they do nothing to remove chemicals like lead, which was still used to manufacture Mozambican paint. I reached out to Concern Worldwide, who had funded the installations and might be able to replace the paint can with a proper, clean bucket. I also created a new scene for the safety video about using a clean bucket to haul water. But with communication the way it is in Mozambique, they might still be using that paint can at the hospital in Chinde.

By this time, *Fazer o que?* was making some sense.

Over time, Mozambique presented me with many opportunities to understand and apply *Fazer o que?* One afternoon, I was in my office at the TIOS School and Daniel was working in the back with the girls when Margareta called to say the farm was on fire. "How much is burning?" I calmly asked.

"Everything," she said.

"Okay. Well, let me know how it goes." I slid the phone closed and turned to Marta. "Would you get Daniel for me please?"

When Daniel came in, I gave him the news. "Margareta phoned. The farm is on fire. Can you check it out?"

He grabbed one or two teachers and they sped off, kicking up a cloud of dust as they raced out the driveway.

As the dust settled, one of the volunteers looked at me incredulously. "How can you be so calm?"

"Before I came here, I did disaster relief for an insurance company, so I was surrounded by fires and tornadoes and floods. Since coming to Mozambique, I've learned that when something is small and theoretically under my control—like an employee being late or quitting—I can get pretty strung out. But with big things that are completely out of my control—

like a fire—well, that's God's department. There is nothing for me to do, nothing for me to get upset about."

She stared at me blankly and fidgeted at her computer as I went back to work. I finished entering the accounts and started working on the newsletter. From the corner of my eye I saw her look up at me once in a while, probably checking for signs of emotion. But I stayed calm, and in about an hour Daniel returned. The teachers jumped out and hurried to the back of the school, evidently wanting to share what they had seen.

Daniel walked into my office, shaking his head. "How was it, Daniel?"

"It's all gone, Amy. Everything is gone. It's burnt." He chuckled, his way of dealing with stress.

"Well," I told him, "I guess we can deal with that later."

When I got home at the end of the day, the house and buildings were surrounded by charred grass, but all of the trees were intact, including the sixty we had just planted. Still, I knew the farm would return to its "dust bowl" look.

Though nobody came forward with a confession or an accusation, my guards had probably lit the fire to knock the grass down and control the snakes. "It's easier to get forgiveness than permission" is as true in Africa as anywhere else.

In any case, I almost never had time to dwell on things that had already happened. I was always busy with the thing that was coming at me—usually urgent paperwork. I was like a pastor who thought he was hired to preach but ended up buried in paperwork and committee meetings. Every once in a while one of the kids would come to my office, and we would chat about the dogs or the school or something that happened in the bairro. But for the most part, I was an administrator and only got the chance to be with the kids when we were having an exposition or when I showed a visitor around.

So I was excited that not long before the TIOS School closed, we were hosting some exciting visitors. I took time to enjoy them with the kids. A group of three men led by Roger Scheffer had put together the project "Motorcycles from

Durban to Dublin" to raise funds for the Pebbles Project, a South African charity focused on the issue of Fetal Alcohol Syndrome.

This was the first leg of their journey from South Africa to Ireland, and they stopped at our school to meet the kids and to give them a gift: South African flag bandanas. The visit seemed to really open the kids' eyes. Our kids sort of knew where South Africa was, but Ireland had probably never occurred to them until that day. And although the kids had seen small motorcycles, like dirt bikes (which were the main transportation for many Mozambicans), they had never seen big touring bikes like Roger's. The visit was a grand success.

Our kids beamed with pride as they donned their South African bandanas for the first time. After that, they wore them during all of their safety presentations to signify that they were TIOS Safety Kids. Never mind that the bandanas were South African and the kids were Mozambican. There were no Mozambican bandanas.

# 47

Word had come that the container from the Netherlands was on its way! Daniel was going through paperwork, trying to lower the value of the shipment so we could avoid paying a huge import tax. With his family connections, if anybody was in a position to get this container through, it was Daniel. Still, it took him at least six trips to Beira to get it done, and I felt blessed that he got it through at all.

Our Textáfrica landlord ran a trucking company and would transport the container from the docks to the school in Chimoio. Then we would need to get it off the truck right away because we were hiring the truck by the hour. I figured it would be pretty manageable; we could just lower the full container at the school and unload it after the holiday break. Unfortunately, I was wrong. The container had to be unloaded completely before it could be lowered to the ground with a crane.

That is why we had decided to bring the container to the school instead of the farm; there was more space inside at TIOS, where we could store the contents of the container. Some of the larger construction-type items like scaffolding and plumbing pipe, which we wouldn't be using for teaching, could be put back in once the container was on the ground. We decided to sort at the school; later we would take to the farm only what was needed there.

We still had to figure out how to get the empty container to the farm, where we would use it as an additional outbuilding (a common practice in Mozambique). But first, it had to be unloaded, which in itself was a daunting task. While the container was still on the back of the semi, it was above most of the girls' shoulders, and we knew it would be as packed as a sardine can.

Daniel warned everybody to get back as he swung the door open, in case the load had shifted and came tumbling out.

Nothing fell out, but Daniel was right when he said, "Not even room for a mouse, Amy." The container was full from floor to ceiling, side to side, and front to back. There were wonderful items like sewing machines, desks, reusable water bottles, and cans for transporting water safely. There were also plenty of things we wouldn't be using ourselves, such as excess pieces of steel and a 300-pound welding machine.

The three days it took us to unload were like the longest Christmas. We opened one gift after another, thinking of what we could do with this, what we would do with that. We put the things we could use in the middle room and the things we thought we might sell in the back room. Both rooms (totaling about 400 square feet, under a 12-foot ceiling) were pretty full.

I looked at Daniel, starting to get a bit anxious. "What are we going to do with all of this? I don't even know what some of it is."

"Henry said you could sell some of it, didn't he?" Daniel asked.

"Yeah, he did. Let's take the desks and the welding stuff to my new office in the bairro and then figure the rest out after Christmas when you get back from Quelimane."

After Christmas, we would be moving the TIOS School to the new ATM location, and I would not have office space in the new building. So I had rented a *dependência* (a small, very simple building, like a garage) for only $150 per month, and I would have my office there. It was great timing because we had that space now to store things that I wanted to either sell or distribute to other children's programs.

Around this time I found a folder in my laptop that somebody else had created while I had been in the Netherlands. It was filled with photos of people I did not know—women, children, and a few men—who seemed to be having quite a grand time in my farmhouse. I took a closer look and realized that three different children I did not know appeared in the photos, and I knew right away that these children belonged to Daniel. They all resembled him, and the littlest one, about three years old, was his spitting image. Daniel had told me early on that he had one son, and later he told me about his daughter. But he had neglected to mention his newest little one.

I was not too surprised to see this third child. I knew that his wife Beth had returned to his home when I was at the Pink Papaya four or five years earlier. (Being the mother of his children makes her known as his wife in Mozambique, where weddings are not required.) Daniel had told me there was no relationship between him and Beth; she had simply come home to be with her children. Had I given it any thought, I would have gathered that they were sleeping together, but four years ago Daniel and I had been seeing each other only rarely.

So the fact of this little boy did not upset me, but the photos reinvigorated my suspicions about *now*, about Daniel's behavior with women *now*, while we were living together. He consistently claimed that he had no other women. But he received texts late at night and constantly. And photos he'd downloaded from dating sites sent a pretty clear message. He was seeing others. My staff insisted I was wrong, and they were at my home twenty-four hours a day, which I was not.

I had been questioning my staff for months before, trying to see if they could confirm my suspicions that he was involved with other women. I got the same answer, with slight variations, from everybody I asked: *I have seen nobody; he does not have women in your house; there are no girlfriends.*

My heart, every cell in my body, my entire existence told me otherwise. But these were my employees. If I could not trust them to tell me the truth, even if it hurt Daniel, who had no part in employing them, who could I trust?

I decided to try one more time, this time approaching Lina, who I thought most likely to tell me the truth.

"This little boy, he looks just like Daniel." And he did. He was a Xerox copy, right down to the way he shrugged his little shoulders. I showed her the picture as I asked, "Is this Daniel's child?"

"I talked to the little boy, Amy. He said his name was Mario, and that Daniel was his father."

Of course he was.

I decided I needed to show Daniel the photos and listen to his explanation. He said the ladies were "cousins and old friends." I guess that could have made sense, though they certainly were not "old."

When I showed him the photo of the little boy, he said only, "He is not my son, Amy. I have two children."

"Whose son is he, Daniel?"

"He is Beth's, yes, but he is not my son."

"Daniel, he is the exact image of you. Of course he is your son."

"No, Amy he is not."

My heart sank.

As Daniel was getting ready to leave to spend Christmas in Nacala with his (*three*) children, I decided he shouldn't come back to the farm.

A stampede of elephants went through my belly as I packed *all* of his things into the back of his car. The whole situation took me right back to fifteen years earlier, the last time I had put my needs in front of my man's, when I had sent Bruce away. A fresh wave of pain and guilt about leaving Bruce seared through me as I put the last of Daniel's items into the trunk of his car.

Daniel appeared lighthearted. He gave me a teasing look when he noticed what I was doing. "I am only going for a week, Amy."

I managed a smile, but we both knew a lot was left unsaid.

That afternoon, we headed to the TIOS Christmas party. The day was sunny and bright, with the light breeze Chimoio is known for. All of the teachers and administrators gathered under the shade of the thatch roof at Na Sombra Restaurant and toasted our Dutch friends who had been so generous with the gift of the container.

We looked back in awe at what we had accomplished in the three years we had been in the TIOS School, and yet were all a bit anxious about the future we were facing as we divided forces and worked together to set ATM up for success in 2010 without Amy at the helm.

A couple of Daniel's friends had come to the restaurant to meet him for the Nacala trip, and they were waiting for him when we arrived. So not long after the party got started, he left with them. I told him goodbye without much emotion. First of all, Daniel was never up for much of a goodbye; as a Mozambican, he wanted to avoid that kind of stress. But couples would never be demonstrative at an employee party.

When the party was over, I drove back to the farm in solitary silence. I straightened up the house. I had never gotten used to having housekeepers in my home, and I still kept my room as the one place they didn't clean. It wasn't a matter of trust so much as the shift in energy when people are in my personal space. Having a housekeeper in there would have left me feeling like I was in a hotel room rather than my home.

I looked ruefully at our bed. It was just a mattress on a small wooden frame. My normal, full-sized bedframe had been broken in September, during my Netherlands trip when Daniel had been here "alone." My rosary, which my grandmother had given me from the Vatican, had also been broken. I felt sick remembering. As I settled in for the night, I was glad he was off to the north. I figured it would probably be a couple of days before we would talk, and I planned to use them for deep thinking and prayer.

# 48

I was surprised the next day when Daniel called. We had a conversation like we hadn't had in... forever. We spent nearly an hour and a half on the phone, just chatting about life. I felt he had sensed my distance and was trying to draw me back. When I got off the phone, I wondered what had happened that suddenly he was the peaceful, playful Daniel I had met in Quelimane five years earlier. I wondered if his children had that effect on him.

Later that night, well after 1AM, my cell phone rang. I could see it was Daniel calling, but when I picked up the phone, "Alo?" the connection was gone. Still half asleep, I hit the speed dial a couple of times, but he wouldn't pick up. I figured it must have been a "butt dial." (One of the hazards of being named Amy is that I get a lot of those.)

Morning came, and I greeted a gorgeous summer day. The disconnected phone call wasn't so incredibly strange. Phone signals often cut out in Mozambique. Still, I had tried Daniel once in the morning and gotten no response. I thought maybe he was off with his kids or with another woman. That was a painful thought, one that I pushed from my mind.

I met Yunas for cappuccino at Elo 4 Café. The place had fabulous cappuccino, topped with cinnamon and with a cinnamon stick for stirring. We were chatting along when the thought, clear as day, came to me. *Call Santos.*

But I didn't have any reason to call Santos. I went back to my conversation with Yunas.

As we were saying our goodbyes, it came to me again: *Call Santos.* My stomach started to tighten. Something was wrong. I should know not to ignore these feelings, but lately I'd had to push away a lot of misgivings. It was getting in the way of my intuition. *I have no reason to call Santos.*

Santos was soft-spoken, honest, and strong. Daniel greatly admired and respected Santos, and I simply adored him. He was my rock in Mozambique. I always trusted Santos. He told me once about fighting with his father, who disagreed with his decision to marry Helena, a white Portuguese Mozambican. Santos had held his ground despite his father's strength, and Santos and Helena had raised three lovely daughters: Patricia, Tania, and Lara. I had visited their Beira home a number of times, and I always felt like family there.

The tightness in my stomach nearly doubled me over. *Something's wrong.* I stopped a young boy on the street to buy phone credits to load into my phone. Most things in Mozambique were pay-as-you-go. Even the electricity to your house had a code box to enter the credit. If the electricity shut off, it was because you didn't refill it, not because the electric company shut you off.

I put the plastic cards on the seat and drove home, where I intended to make the call. I was still a few miles from the farm, when, like a scream, the message came again: *Call Santos now!*

Oh, Good Lord. I had no reason to call, but it would be Santos's birthday in a couple of days, on December 26, so I figured I would use that excuse and just see what else came up in the conversation. I felt pretty stupid as I stopped the car, there in the street, and picked up one of the cards. I scratched off the number and entered the credits into my phone. Then I speed-dialed Santos, and he answered on the first ring. *"Alo?"*

*"Alo, Santos. Tudo Bem?"* (Is all well?)

*"Não, Amy. Não estamos bem."* I felt, then, like I had swallowed a big rock. Things were not well.

He went on to tell me in his perfect Portuguese that there had been an accident. It had been late, and Daniel and his youngest brother Geoffrey had been traveling to Nacala at night and… the line cut out as a semi-truck passed my car… Santos's next words were "and he was killed." *Morreu.*

I stammered, "Santos, he… he can't be. He called me. Last night."

"Did you speak with him?"

"Uh, no, Santos. The phone cut out."

"He's dead, Amy. I have to go to fly there now for the body." He ended our conversation and got off the phone.

I sat there on the side of the road, stunned. *No No No— this isn't happening. I sent Daniel away, and he is dead? This can't be happening again. . . .*

Wracking sobs rose up and out of me, Mozambican customs be dammed. People drove and walked past as I sat there behind the steering wheel, sobbing. Nobody stopped. Nobody asked. People stared at me from their cars, but nobody honked for me to get out of the roadway or waved in recognition. I must have sobbed there in my car for at least fifteen minutes before I was able to think again.

It didn't make sense. As many times as I had gotten "gut feelings" about Daniel, I would surely know if he had died. I would *know* in my body and heart if he were dead. But I told myself that I did know. Santos said it was so, and I always trusted Santos.

It took me several more minutes to pull myself together enough to start driving home. I had to get home. I had driven maybe a mile or two when another wave of tears took over. I pulled off the road and let them stream down my face.

I felt like floodgates had opened, releasing a lifetime worth of unexpressed grief. I grieved every person I had loved and lost: my sister, my high school best friend, my birthmother, and my husband. Grief for all of them seized me in that terrible moment, combining with the pain of losing Daniel. Every ounce of love I had ever felt for him, every wonderful memory, came flooding back to me with the tears. He became my beloved Daniel once again.

Another twenty minutes passed before I could again start driving. This time I made it home. I pulled in the driveway, hoping not to run into any employees. Lina (who was filling in while Margareta had a baby) was hanging clothes on the line. When I told her she should go home, she easily saw that I was shattered. "*Que foi,* Amy?" (What happened?)

298

I could only choke out, "Daniel died in a car accident," before the sobs worked their way up from my belly again.

She must have said it three times: "Don't be too sad, Amy."

The guards were walking by the windows. I saw their shadows as the tears overtook me. I knew my crying and tears were making them nervous, as they would any Mozambican. But I felt like they might understand. This was a death, after all; I wasn't crying over a lover or a fire or a theft.

I could not make sense of the news. I waited for a break in the storm of tears and tried Santos again. His phone was off. I figured he was on the plane to Nacala to pick up the body or to Quelimane for the funeral.

I could not convince myself that Daniel was dead. Daniel and I had always been connected energetically. Though I was genuinely grief-stricken, I was also puzzled because Daniel did not "feel" dead to me. I still sensed our connection.

I tried his other brother Mardiano. He tried to explain the situation and all that had happened. But I couldn't follow his Portuguese, either because he was too upset or because I was. Again I tried Santos, but still no answer.

Four long hours after I learned that Daniel was dead, I called Carlos, one of the members of my Mozambican board of directors. "Please, Carlos, could you call Mardiano and ask what has happened? They tell me Daniel died—that he drove under a semi-truck in the night. But it doesn't make sense. The accident happened before his last call to me."

Carlos said he would call. As I waited for his call back, I paced endlessly. It was the longest half-hour of my life. When he called back, he spoke slowly in English to me, explaining that Daniel had been driving and Geoff had been beside him in the car. Daniel had not seen the semi-truck until it was too late, and he drove under it. Geoff had been killed instantly when the top of the car was sheared off. Daniel was not injured, nor were the two children sleeping in the back seat.

I had misunderstood Santos when the semi had driven past my car, garbling his voice. After I understood my mistake, a brief, intense, guilt-inducing moment of relief was followed with concern for Daniel.

"Oh, no. Carlos! I don't know that Daniel can survive this. He's not made for this kind of disaster." Then I thanked him and hung up.

I finally understood my Scottish friends' saying, "I'm gutted." That is how I felt as reality sunk in. My head was spinning, and I felt sick. I desperately wanted to see Daniel. I needed to see him. I was so relieved he was alive… At the same time, this situation would destroy him. I was very concerned about the guilt I knew Daniel would be feeling.

I'd had to work through my guilt over my sister's death. I knew all too well the pain, guilt, and heartache that was building in Daniel's life. And I knew it would be even worse for him. Before he died, Daniel's father gave his older children instructions about raising the younger ones.

"Daniel, I want you to raise my youngest son."

"But, Papa, why not the others who are older, who are better situated?"

"No, Daniel, you are the one I trust to do this."

Many years had passed since Daniel assumed responsibility for Geoff. So Geoff had been Daniel's brother and his son— and of course also his friend. Daniel had lost so much!

Most of my friends were gone to their home countries to celebrate Christmas, and I really needed someone to talk to, somebody who could be at least somewhat understanding of my emotions. I called my friend Retracto from the road workers. He came to the farm and sat on the veranda area with me. "Amy, you have to calm down. You have to be strong for the family. I know this is so difficult but you have to pull yourself together."

"But, Retracto, he won't let me come to Quelimane. He won't let me be with him. He ignores my phone calls and only texts me."

It tore at my heart that Daniel would not let me come to him. I knew it was because his children's mother was there, which confirmed she was not an ex and I was not a girlfriend.

She was his wife, and I was some kind of mistress. Why else couldn't his girlfriend of five-plus years be allowed at Geoff's funeral? The distance between us now seemed entirely too vast to bridge. Our chance to be together continued to disintegrate.

Christmas Eve came, and Daniel texted to say that Geoff's funeral was finally over, and I offered comfort as best I could with a text, knowing that if he had wanted to talk on the phone, he would have called. The pain and guilt over involvement in a sibling's death was a strange thing for Daniel and me to have in common. I wondered what God had in mind putting us together.

Christmas passed, the school reopened, and Daniel stayed up north, still refusing to let me to come visit and refusing to return to the farm. I kept asking. "Come back, Daniel. Come to the farm. Come help me, and let me help you through this time. I need help at the school, and I need help turning the farm into a *machamba* (a garden producing plot). Please. Just come home."

Nearly two months later, at the end of January, he did come back. I went to pick him up at the same bus stop I had originally arrived at, near my former home at Textáfrica. I hoped for a kiss or a hug as he got in the car, but he sat sullen and gruff, as if he had gotten into a police car to go to prison. I couldn't say that I blamed him.

The guilt Daniel felt over his brother's death was taking its toll. The next few weeks were strained and awkward. I made our grilled breakfast sandwiches in the morning and served them with coffee or Coke. Then I would head to the school, and he might stay and work at the farm or come to the school to help me sort out the accounts. But even when we were together, he was not present, and the distance between us seemed to widen when he started dressing like a Nigerian or a Muslim, in a long dark robe. I wondered who this man was.

There were peaceful moments as we shared dinner and enjoyed second sunset. But especially during those times, I had my own trouble staying present. My thoughts were turning toward home. Work stress was one thing, but in addition to all of that (and whatever was going on with my immune system and energy levels) my personal life had been too complicated for too long. I needed a proper break, not a fundraising trip. I needed to be consulting and free of the school that I couldn't monitor when I was away.

Although Henry and Casper had told me to plan on selling some things, I felt a bit guilty when I made the plan to sell the beautiful Dutch children's desks to the International School. The buyer and I agreed to a reasonable and negotiated price, much less than they would have cost anywhere else in Mozambique and much more than they would have cost in the Netherlands, even on sale. I imagined that my Dutch friends had envisioned a school with space for a proper classroom full of desks. But a real classroom would require resources that would be better spent in other ways. We were too small and small-funded to create a full and proper school with fabulous little Dutch desks.

Perhaps they had sent the welding machine and steel thinking I would offer all kinds of vocational training, perhaps even for boys. We did not offer vocational training for boys because they already had so many opportunities compared with the girls. So we ended up selling those things, and it was wonderful to have the funds. But I wondered a lot what my Dutch friends would think of my decisions.

# 49

──────◦○◦──────

Hanneke and Rik were coming from the Netherlands in February to help us make the safety video. I gave them my bedroom and moved into the volunteers' room, where Daniel had been sleeping in a bunk bed since returning from Nacala.

So much between Daniel and me remained unspoken. He did not talk about his grief, which increased the distance between us, and I did not talk about my side of the distance either—my deep knowledge, confirmed or not, that he had lied to me about having other women and having a third child during our years together.

I just did not think it mattered anymore. Besides, he was in mourning for his young brother who he had pledged to care for and protect. His lack of fidelity to me was trivial in comparison.

I had been reading one of Doreen Virtue's books in which she gave many exercises that included asking your angels for guidance. I found an exercise to ask Spirit to show you about a past-life experience. Before I fell to sleep the first night on the bunk bed, with Daniel in the bunk across from me, I prayed, *"God, show me why Daniel and I were brought together. What did we hope to learn, experience, accomplish in this life? What had we meant to each other in the past?"* I went to sleep expecting to dream about it and wake up with my answer.

I dreamed that Daniel and I were somewhere in the Middle East in an ancient time, in a large room full of people. He was one of many dancers performing a very fast Egyptian line dance. The music was heavy drumming and Egyptian instruments.

All of a sudden, the music stopped and the dancers froze in place. All of us were frozen. Daniel was looking at me, not moving his face but piercing me with his gaze and trying to get

303

my attention. The whole room seemed to watch him conveying a message to me telepathically. *Look behind you.*

I looked over my left shoulder. Nothing. Then I looked back at him. *Look again.*

Over my right shoulder I saw a man who looked like a policeman or a customs agent with epaulettes on his uniform.

Then I fell out of that room, thousands of feet below to a life we shared during Biblical times. Daniel was Isaiah from the Bible, and I was his wife, the prophetess. We had a loving and abundant home. People came to our home to share stories of God and of God's love, and though we were not wealthy, there was always enough food and drink.

I sensed that life ending suddenly, as if we'd been pulled apart or one of us had been killed. And I saw that in our Mozambican life we were both angry that the other person couldn't fill the same roles we had known in our Biblical life. We could not be man and wife. At the same time, we loved each other too much to part. Falling suddenly from that dream, I screamed *Isaiah!*

Daniel rushed to my bed. "Amy, what happened?" He took me in his arms as I told him of the dream, how I had come to have it, and what I felt it meant. He held me gently, and I felt that the truth of my dream also reached him.

The rainy season started early that year and continued until after I left Mozambique. We relocated the TIOS School from Textáfrica to ATM's new location in Bairro 5 in the rain. Hanneke and Rik were on hand to help, which was a godsend. But none of it was simple. In Mozambique, things so rarely are.

In addition to moving the bulk of things from TIOS to ATM in Bairro 5, many things were being moved to the dependência I had rented in the city. The remaining inventory from the container was going there, and so were the electric sewing machines, a photocopier, and other valuables. Last but not least, my remaining personal items were going to the farm.

The move was exhausting, and whenever I had a moment, I continued to wonder what was going on with my health.

For the most part, though, I devoted myself to the safety video and relied on others to do the heavy lifting with the move. Thankfully, a few blessed breaks in the rain made it possible for us to film the video. As we had planned, we filmed our road-safety scenes first. I had asked an old friend from the teacher-training college, Antonio, to help me stage the scenes of children being struck by cars.

Antonio was great. Hanneke sat with her handheld camcorder in the front seat, filming Antonio's face as he supposedly struck a child who had chased a ball into the street. We "killed" child after child on the muddy roads.

Only after we filmed the last "take" of the scene, I discovered to my absolute horror that Antonio had left my car in gear every scene, having never driven an automatic car. Thank God, he had set the parking brake every time or the scene could have gotten a little too realistic.

Nevertheless, the scenes were beautifully done, and I was excited to move forward with the filming. In all we had nine scenes scripted and ready to film. After the road-safety scene, we filmed safety with wells, safety with dogs, and safety with fire. Daniel would intermittently play a role in the videos, still dressed in black in memory of Geoff. He played the man in the dog bite scenes and in the scenes showing children playing near an open well.

But on some days he would disappear. At one point, we needed to finish a scene and Daniel was gone. I knew with *my every breath* that he was with another woman, but I had no time for that.

I stopped my car along the road and grabbed a man in a pink shirt. "Would you like to make a movie?" For all he knew, we could have been making a porn film. But he was wearing a dress shirt and nice slacks, and he came along willingly—that was what mattered to me. That man is forever memorialized in our scenes.

The next day, we began to dig a cemetery behind the back bedroom on the farm. Beyond a sign that said, "The Cemetery of Children Whose Deaths Were Preventable," we created child-sized mounds of dirt. Daniel and I were both moved by that "pretend" cemetery much more than we realized.

For Daniel there was Geoff's recent death, still an open wound. For me, creating that cemetery brought to mind the images of funeral trucks driving in steady streams to the cemeteries. In all my years in Chimoio, that stream of trucks never let up. From the farm I could no longer see the trucks, but I could hear them... and the wailing.

I had considered using the real cemetery to film these scenes, but I did not want anybody to perceive disrespect. Besides, I was a big believer in ghosts and didn't need a new ethereal companion. I had enough going on with living people. So we had made this little replica on the farm.

Our prop cemetery did not go over well with the community. Alface, my guard, finally came to me: "Amy, the community is disturbed. They think you are burying dead children here."

I asked Alface to explain that the cemetery was only for a video and that we did not mean any disrespect. Since we were only filming for a week, we carried on. But as soon as those scenes were finished, we removed the cemetery. I trusted that Alface had helped the locals to understand.

Finally the day came that the video was done, and I was even happier with the results than I thought I would be. The results were professional and effective. I felt confident the video could help millions of kids in Mozambique, and I was excited to get the final edited copy to the embassy and Church World Service.

It was time to take Hanneke and Rik back to the airport in Beira, and I wanted Daniel to come along for the ride.

"No, Amy. You will all speak in very fast English, and there will be no place for me."

"But they like you, and you like them. We can visit Santos at the end."

"Couldn't you stay here, Amy, and send them back on the bus?"

"On the bus, Daniel? That would be rude. How would they get to the airport from the bus?" I knew from my own experience how easy it would be to get lost on a trip like that. "They don't have any training in Portuguese, Daniel. What if they get confused and miss their flight?" He only sighed.

"You go, Amy. Let me know when you are coming back, and I will meet you."

I had noticed a change in the way the community was responding to me. People were becoming more and more edgy, and there was an ominous feeling in the air. I had always been sensitive to energetics, and something felt off. I had a growing sense of unease.

One day while I was in town, I overheard a conversation between a young woman and a man. She was going on and on in Portuguese about how she had been with Daniel. That night, I brought it up with him. He told me I must have misunderstood and then cited a number of examples where my Portuguese had been incorrect or I'd misunderstood something. Then, I guess because I looked unconvinced, he said, "It was probably a different Daniel." *Right*.

I had the sense that the community's new… *distance* from me was related to Daniel and other women, but I knew it was also due to my own mistakes. I was feeling the guilt of not succeeding at my projects, at potentially having let everyone down—donors, employees, parents, friends. I was weak. These days I was past my breaking point—weak physically, emotionally, and spiritually. I was more aware than ever that the quickest way to lose respect in Mozambique was to lose your cool, and I held on by a thread.

Another part of the community's new attitude (which felt a bit like aggression to me) was due to the growing opulence of the farm. It used to be an abandoned wreck, but now there was a home, an orange grove, bananas, bamboo, papayas, litchis, coconuts, avocados, clean water, and the school. It looked like too much for one Muzungu.

Still, I sensed that the biggest reason for the hostility was that my man did not respect me. He did not show any sign that he would protect me or that he was on my side. To the local people, that indicated I was not such a good person. If my own man would treat me without respect, that gave them license to also treat me rudely.

One experience in particular made me feel like things were coming to a head. Because of all the rain, the road from the farm into town was more like a ditch with high banks running along both sides. One night, when I was driving home alone, two obviously drunk men jumped down on my car from above. My little Suzuki rocked and teetered, and I was horrified at myself for merely hitting the gas pedal and speeding away, which sent one of the drunken men toppling into the ditch. I felt like a calf being separated from the herd.

# 50

—◦◦◦◦◦—

March came, and one of the last things I accomplished before I left Mozambique was to have the borehole on the farm hooked to a public pump that had been installed at the mosque across the road. The borehole drilled by *Water Is Our World* and *Wilde Ganzen* would soon bring fresh water to more than 7,000 neighboring people. Finally.

One afternoon while I worked in the house, I reflected on the inauguration we would soon be having for the well. I was excited. This project was coming together to bring safe water to the people—and even though most of the credit went to John, Casper, and Henry—I had nevertheless taken part in a project that would unquestionably change lives for the better, and for a long time to come.

Margareta was out back doing the washing and Daniel was down at the new well when a strange car pulled into the drive. A Mozambican woman I did not know was driving. She was a bit older than I was, and her hair was brushed out. I recognized her from the photos I'd found on my computer. She did not seem very attractive. (She probably thought the same about me.) She asked to see Daniel.

*How did she find my farm out here in the bush?*

I sent Daniel a text, only to hear his phone ring in the volunteers' room. So I gave the woman instructions on how to get from the farm to the mosque. As she pulled out of the driveway, I remembered something Daniel had said long ago. "All women can be beautiful. Some are beautiful for their money or their power…"

As the woman drove away, Margareta, for some unfathomable reason, decided now was the time to tell all. As we stood in the hallway between the kitchen and dining area, she started speaking very matter-of-factly about Daniel's indiscretions—*in my house*—ever since coming to direct the school after René left. Her tone did not match her words, which was sort of disorienting. Judging only from the tone of her voice, you would've thought she was telling me that it was supposed to rain tomorrow and that we might want to bring in the laundry.

I walked to the volunteers' bedroom, eyeing Daniel's phone on the bed as Margareta continued, telling me about finding used condoms in the house while I was gone to the States on my last fundraising trip.

She would not stop. "You remember the day you took those Dutch people to the airport, after they helped with the movie? You weren't gone five minutes and he slammed the bedroom door. Ten minutes later he came out and told me to go home. He called a woman and locked the doors. The guards agreed, she came to the front door, and he did not come out until an hour before you returned.

She went on to tell that one day in the market she had met the black Zimbabwean woman that he had been seeing. "I told her, 'He's been lying to you. Miss Amy will be back soon and you had better disappear.'"

I knew it would be only minutes until he returned. Still, I turned to Margareta. "Why? Why, Margareta, did you not tell me while he was out of my house? I could have told him not to return."

Her shameful face was her only response. I picked up his phone and entered Daniel's security code. As I entered it, I swore to myself: *If I ever again feel the urge to look in a man's cell phone, our relationship will be over. If we have no trust, then we have nothing—absolutely nothing.*

In the phone, I found her. I showed the photo to Margareta to confirm it. His black Zimbabwean woman was the front screen saver. I opened the text messages.

Daniel had written to her: "*Meu Amor*... My love. I have to see you. Where are you? I need you!"

I heard a car and looked out the window. The woman who had stopped at the farm to see Daniel was dropping him off at the end of the driveway. He didn't look guilty, but then he had never looked guilty in five years. And after Margareta told me about the women he'd been with recently, I knew at my deepest level that he'd had other women all along, even in those sweet early days.

I quickly closed the phone and put it back on the bed. He would know. He was as intuitive about me as I was about him. He would know that I'd seen. He would know that Margareta had told.

If he knew, he didn't show it. I thought about talking with him, about really letting him have it. But I had already confronted him. I'd been confronting him for three years.

I hurried back to the middle bedroom, my bedroom, and began going through the closet. Suddenly it was time for some spring cleaning, one final purge before I packed to leave this place.

I was furious with every last one of my employees, and I could not stop reviewing the many conversations in which they had lied. Every one of them had lied! I became more and more angry with them, which insulated me from my anger for Daniel.

I tried to hide my stress, but I knew Daniel would see it. Obsessively, I looked at the situation from every possible angle. I knew *she* (*they!*) had been in my home and knew who I was, but I did not know who they were.

I thought of all the people who had warned me about moving to the farm—their fears of "people who come and kill you with machetes in the night." The irony made me laugh out loud. It is a silent killer that hunts in Mozambique: HIV and the secrets and infidelities that it feeds on.

Had my employees wanted me dead? Had Daniel? Why? Why did no one tell me the truth before now? Did they wish me not just gone, but dead? Had he offered them something for their silence? Had he threatened them?

Shame and betrayal overwhelmed me. I remembered every lie I had told in my life and felt this was my payback. Was God punishing me? I had come to try to complete His mission. I see now that it doesn't make sense, but at the time I felt like God was saying, "Time to pack, Amy." I needed to return to the United States and rebuild my life, my health, and my self-esteem.

I didn't want to abandon Daniel during this tough time, but it was time for me to start on the path back home to the United States. I had to be in Guatemala in June. Maybe it was time to change that to a one-way ticket.

# 51

—∘ᑕ᠍᠍᠍᠍ᑀᗆ∘᠍◡—

I decided to say a novena. For nine days, I would petition St. Joseph to bless me with a buyer for the farm. My flight was due to leave in just five weeks, on May 10. So I was going to bury St. Joseph head-down in the yard. Joseph is the Patron Saint of (among other things) house sellers, and I wanted to summon his help. I waited until Alface was guarding because he would question me the least.

I dug the hole. "God, I don't have a statue of St. Joseph. All I have is St. Joseph's prayer card. Please let this be enough! It's time for me to go home. I'm not well." I dug the small hole outside of my bedroom window where the neighbors wouldn't see. Then I began to pray the novena of St. Joseph to sell my home.

Not long after burying the prayer card, I shared with Daniel my intention to sell the farm and go home. His initial response was "We should keep a place here, Amy, for retirement. For when you come back." Daniel wanted to ignore the reality that I was leaving. He seemed distressed and angry when he overheard me telling people I wanted to sell the farm and asking if they knew anybody who might be interested. I can see that it might have been an embarrassing situation for him. I had made the decision to sell the farm without discussing it with him. He was trying to figure out what he was doing with his own life as he made trips to Maputo to look for a new job and a new life. I knew he was still reeling from his brother's death, and now I was leaving too. I wasn't the only one who was overwhelmed.

Just days after I buried the St. Joseph card, my phone rang with a number I did not recognize. It was Andrew, an acquaintance I had met at one of the local watering holes. He was British and ran a local eco-tourism project.

"Amy, we've got visitors. My wife's sister Mariana is here with her husband from Cincinnatti, and they are looking to purchase a place."

*Thanks, God! And, thanks, St. Joseph!*

"They are only here until tomorrow, when they're going to look at some places in Beira. Could we stop by?"

I was absolutely thrilled. God was supporting me and helping me pack my bags. "Yeah, Andrew. I'm here this morning. Bring them by."

Like her sister Milagre, Mariana had deep, mocha skin. She was tall for a Mozambican, around five feet eight inches.

Mariana's husband, Vernon was African American, and the difference between his energy and a native African's was palpable. He laughed loudly and spoke fast. In contrast, and true to her Mozambican roots, Mariana had calmer energy. "I always wanted to come back home to take care of my people," she said.

She liked the house, especially the MC Escher tile floor in the bathroom, which had somehow survived the years of war and abandonment. Both Mariana and Vernon were gracious enough not to mention the "happy paint" on the exterior of the house—yellow with purple trim. I had allowed my volunteers pick the colors because I had always felt that this place belonged to the program, the children, and the volunteers. I only lived here.

Mostly, Mariana loved the abundance of the farm. By now, it had more than twenty-five orange trees, three coconut trees, three mango trees, five papaya trees, three avocado trees that were producing, twenty-five new avocado trees, three peach trees, maybe 100 banana trees, and a forest of bamboo I had planted.

This was all in addition to the hibiscus bushes and sixty or so non-fruit-bearing trees that Allan Schwarz had given me to reforest the farm. It was what a Zimbabwean might call a plot because it was relatively small (only about 11 acres, compared to the average Zimbabwean farm which is around 160 acres). But I called it a farm. It was late March and the rains should stop soon, and as soon as that happened, we could (or whoever bought the place could) begin planting a second crop of green beans, cove, cabbage, and tomatoes.

Vernon and Marianna went to see some houses in Beira the next day, but they came back to my property. Mariana was excited that the project was already on the farm and that she could just step in and start working. She said she would love to keep the sewing project going and continue to work with Nelson to run the safety school and the bakery. She also would be happy to work with Berta on the girls' clubs. She was excited to do these things with her daughter and expose her to Mozambican life.

We agreed to the price of $35,000. Then we went to my lawyer in town so Mariana and Vernon could sign papers giving Milagre power of attorney. That way they could go back to the States to wait for the insurance check that would fund the purchase. When that check came, we could close on the house, with Milagre signing in their place. Mariana planned to come back and take possession before I left May 10.

We signed the papers on March 20. The inauguration of the well was scheduled for the first week in May. The way home was becoming clear.

A few weeks ticked by, and I noticed I hadn't heard from Mariana. Pretty soon, I started to worry and began emailing.

There had been a couple of other interested buyers, but my conversations with them had stopped when Mariana and Vernon agreed to a price and made the documents for the purchase. I sent another email to try to find out what was going on.

Daniel seemed stressed as he said, "Amy, why don't you go to America and then come back to finish selling the farm later?"

"No, Daniel. The flight is very expensive, more than $2,000, so I must handle the farm sale before I go. I'm sure I will hear back from Mariana soon. If not, I will continue to see if there is another buyer here."

315

It was nearly the third week in April and my concern was growing. I rebooked my flight for May 30 and sat down to write emails to my other prospective buyers. When I opened my email account, I noticed an email from Mariana. She confirmed they would return to Mozambique to close the deal on the farm at the first of June. *Thanks, God.*

A few nights later, I woke to a chorus of children singing in the night. It was quite disorienting. I could hear the children singing, yet it was two o'clock in the morning. Once I was awake, though, I realized the voices were coming from the mosque. The children were preparing for the inauguration of the public water pump that would provide water to much of Bairro 5 and Bairro 4. I was pleased the pump would be on public land, because it meant that it would serve the local people in perpetuity and that nobody who bought this farm might think it was theirs alone.

The inauguration would further clarify any confusion that may have existed about its ownership. It belonged to all!

The inauguration was fabulous, perhaps even more so because I had finally heard from Mariana and Vernon. For me, it was a real celebration of all that had come from my efforts in Mozambique—all the programs, schools, products, girls' clubs, and now this—the water pump that would serve thousands of people. I had not done it alone, but that day I had a sense of satisfaction which was wonderful. I hoped that I had redeemed myself, and I believed that my efforts had come to something.

We showed the safety video on a big sheet inside the mosque. We inaugurated the water pump with a toast of champagne. Even Senhor Pinto had come; he was our local version of a regulo and was known to be quite a player. Still, it was fun to have our official at the ceremony, and he was so charming that I nearly forgot that he was one of the more corrupt local officials I had met.

Many of my Dutch friends came, which made it glaringly obvious that Daniel wasn't there. It's hard to say where he spent that day or who he spent it with, but I didn't give it much thought. By this time I had one foot out the door. Daniel could do what he wanted. I wanted only to get home, and until I could, I was going to do my best to enjoy my last days in Africa.

My friends John and Tjitske's two-year-old son Tristan was at the inauguration. He was as tall as some of the eight-year-olds. He had fiery red hair, which always made me think of my little sister, and he led the girls to do their dance. It was almost painfully cute.

Then the kids demonstrated first aid and first response. The little kids (ages four–eight) demonstrated basic bandaging. The older kids (ages nine–thirteen) showed the bio-sand filters and their health-safety products. Berta showed everybody the dolls and the other girls' club projects, and we served bread from the bakery.

The women at the mosque had been baking and cooking all night. It was a simple meal of chicken with tomatoes and vegetables served over rice. But it was good, healthful, hearty food, and everybody enjoyed it. It was a great joy to fund one more community meal before leaving my Mozambican home—especially because the meal was a celebration of the pump, one of my proudest accomplishments.

I shared my chair with the old caretaker from the mosque. He had been neighbor and monitor of the farm for many years before I had purchased it, and occasionally he still came down in his long robe to steal mangos. It was rumored that he was more than ninety years old, which was almost unheard of in Chimoio. Slyly he would walk away with his arms crossed behind his back, a mango in each hand. When I saw him like that, I would say, "Alface, pick him a few mangos." Alface would smile in agreement and approval as I recognized that we should share with our neighbor.

# 52

———⊸o⟨⟩o⊶———

Dividing the TIOS programs before leaving Mozambique had been a big project, but the final details were falling into place. In addition to directing the new ATM school, Roberto and Berta were going to continue teaching girls' club on the farm. I hired Nelson, the street kid who I had met so long ago at the teacher-training campus, to stay on at the farm to teach safety class. Nelson had come a million miles from the street kid I had originally met four years earlier. Now he was a young man—and a good man. When Mariana arrived at the farm from America, she also would help with the programs at the farm.

But for so many reasons, I was still anxious. The work of many people had to be coordinated. The new Peace Corps volunteer would be arriving the month after I left, and she would need to be trained. A family from Portugal had offered to check on the projects in late June or early July. In fact, several people would monitor their success and their need for assistance. Jorge and Yunas were both keeping an eye on the programs, and Vasco and Daniel were both ATM association members and would know what was going on.

All it would take was a little self-confidence and faith on the part of those at ATM. I had started with nothing but faith and $150; compared to that, I was leaving them in a great situation. They had facilities and equipment and even contracts for work. Plus, they could speak the language. I thought I was leaving them with everything they needed, and I knew I was leaving them with everything I could give.

Honestly, if I'd had a partner, either in life or at TIOS, I would likely have stayed. I thought about what it would have been like if Daniel had not felt shame over working at our center, which he interpreted as being employed by me, his woman, instead of being my partner in the work. What if he had instead seen it as a great opportunity to help the children that he loved? What if we could have paid René enough to win his heart to help the children?

I did not know, and of course what ifs don't really matter. I only knew I wasn't well, and I was getting worse. If I stayed much longer, my life would be in danger. None of the tests available in Chimoio had found anything, but I suspected, and later confirmed, that parasites—specifically the aftereffects from a tick and some tse-tse fly bites—were draining the life from me.

I had only a few more duties to attend to before I could leave. First, I needed to calculate and pay my employees' severance. In Mozambique, employers are required to pay severance to all employees when they are let go. The amount to be paid is one month's salary for every year of employment. These payments are called indemnities, and they are highly regulated. The amounts I needed to pay my employees had been figured up by my Mozambican lawyer—$10,000 in all.

I would pay those indemnities willingly, and I hoped to do more. I wanted to find work for my employees so that they and their families would be okay when I left. I had arranged for Alface and Ernesto to return to the employment of Textáfrica. I wanted them to have a stable future, and they would have that there. (I was concerned that they may or may not have security with the new owners of the farm.)

I left Margareta in the employment of the new owner of the farm, and of course I paid her indemnity. I also paid an indemnity to Berta and for Roberto, even though they were getting most of TIOS. I knew that ATM could fail, and I wanted them to have the indemnity just in case.

I had been very careful to make sure my employees got every penny they were due as per my lawyer's computation. I thanked God for having the funds to pay the severances and asked Him to bless my Dutch friends. Doll sales and HIV training covered part of the total $10,000 that I owed in indemnities, but it would have been a stretch without the sellable items from the container.

319

Not long after I had paid the last indemnity, my employees got together and reported me to the Labor Department, stating I hadn't paid them enough! I was summoned at short notice to appear in court to face the charges. The first case was Roberto's—yes, Roberto, who had received the indemnity due and TIOS, was one of the petitioners. My lawyer could not attend Roberto's hearing, so I had to appear before the judge and prove this case.

Every one of the charges laid against me, including Roberto's, was thrown out. The judge said he wished he had been given such a generous break as my staff had received. Still, lawyers are not free. I spent a lot of money on the court cases, money that would have been better spent supporting the ongoing work of ATM. By taking me to court, Roberto and Berta were whittling away at their own funds.

I had one regret about Berta that was difficult to reconcile. I felt that I should have trained her to be the director of my programs from the start, but I had let the language barrier get in the way. (I couldn't understand her Portuguese.) Well, during the hand-off of TIOS to ATM, one of the volunteers told me that Berta speaks English. She had never spoken a word of English with me or even in front of me. We would have been a much more effective team if we had been able to communicate freely. I felt betrayed. I still do not understand.

Madelaine, my Peace Corps volunteer, made one more attempt to get me to stay in Mozambique. "They can't run it without you, Amy. It will fall apart, and all of your efforts will be gone." But I knew that didn't have to be true.

"I am offering them everything they need, Madelaine. I'm even paying their rent through the end of the year. There is no reason for them to fail unless they don't believe in themselves. I certainly hope they believe in themselves more than you believe in them!

"You can help them decide if they will succeed or fail, Madelaine. Encourage them to keep doing what they've been doing—making the safety programs, doing the HIV training for payment, and making and selling dolls and bio-sand filters.

Their success depends on what they are willing to do for the children of their own country. What happens will depend on what people *do*."

I had arranged for Daniel to have an interview for a prestigious job in Maputo and had given him a rave review—"Yes, he was a great employee. No, he didn't lie or deceive. He was a good man and a good person."

In fact Daniel was a good person—he *is* a good person. Yet I felt like Simon, who had betrayed Jesus; I knew my opinion was valued by the organization, and I knew that I had been deceived by Daniel. Those were personal matters, though; without question Daniel would do an excellent job for them. And I needed him to be well when I left. I cared—and I still care that he has a good and abundant life.

I saw that I was partially responsible for the situation with Daniel. For years I had known deep down that I was not the only woman in his life or in his bed. Yet I had continued on with him. I'm not even sure that I had asked him to be faithful to me before he came to live and work at the farm. We sometimes only saw each other twice in a year.

But his recent behavior was something else. It hurt me in a way that my vague sense of his other involvements had not. And in addition to my personal pain, I'd lost face—in the final months of my six years working here. It stung.

I knew that when the trauma of Geoff's death had passed and Daniel got settled in his new job, he would once again become the wonderful and balanced guy I had met years earlier in Quelimane. But that did not change the fact that I needed to put physical distance between Daniel and myself to protect my resolve and rebuild my self-esteem. I needed to get away from him, and I needed to cut my strings to Mozambique.

As I drove Daniel to catch a bus to Maputo for his interview, he returned to what had become a familiar topic. "Amy, I need you to come back. I want to marry you."

I recalled Daniel's text message to his other woman. Very gently, I repeated what I had said on Leopard Rock: "I can understand that you love me, but you don't like me sometimes."

He got out, gave me a kiss through the window, and responded the way he had at Leopard Rock. "I love you, Amy. It's not half. It's full. I need you to come back."

Word had gotten out that I was returning to the States soon—and for good. The staff had started matter-of-factly looking around my place and telling me what they wanted. Margareta made a play for my extra sheets: "I suppose you won't be needing these..." I let the remark slide without an answer, but this was just the first such question I would face.

It's the way things are done in Mozambique. As a Muzungu heading home to the United States, I was seen as a very rich person on her way to a rich homeland. I would not need my things where I was going, so I *had* to give them away—and not to other white people.

In the final days, threatening and drunken policemen visited my farm, perhaps as many as six times. They came in pairs and arrived in the early morning with AK-47s, saying that I had to pay in order to leave and suggesting that all of my possessions were to be given to them.

One of them said to me, roughly, "You are not supposed to leave. You are supposed to pay or stay." It was a rather indirect translation, but it was the bottom line meaning of his Portuguese.

Even after six years in Mozambique, my Portuguese was not great. At one point in a conversation with the police, I made a comment about my dogs, and the policeman misunderstood, thinking I had called him a dog. Luckily, Daniel was at the house. I don't know what he said, but he smoothed things over.

The last time the police walked away from the house with their guns slung over their shoulders, Daniel looked at me.

"Amy, we need to leave. It will not be good for us to stay here." He started packing.

His idea was fine as far as I was concerned. I was already nervous. I continued to feel that the sentiment of the local people had turned against me. In fact, now that I was leaving, their attitudes toward me seemed to harden even more.

Daniel had rented a dependência in town to use after I left and until he got confirmation on the start date of his new job. After the last visit from the police, we started quietly moving our possessions to his place in town, day by day and bit by bit. I wondered at my own skills of deception and at how much I had changed. I also struggled to imagine how my life would be back in the States.

As I walked out of the house to leave the farm for the last time, my staff did not seem at all suspicious. They knew I wasn't scheduled to leave Mozambique for three more days, and my favorite purple dress and orange capulana were hanging on the line. They were my final deception: Who would leave home forever with her favorite clothes blowing in the breeze?

Trying to appear calm, I got into the car slowly and deliberately. But my body was flooded with adrenaline, and my head was spinning. This was it, the last time I would see the home and the orphan schools I had helped create. Would the school continue? Would it make good on the promises I'd made to the donors? Would the well continue to provide clean, safe water? For how long? Had I done enough?

On a more personal note, would my friends forgive me for leaving without saying goodbye? Would Mariana and Vernon love my dogs as I had? They had always been my guardians, and I'd kept them nearby during those final days.

Most painful of all—what would become of Daniel? What would happen between us? Probably nothing. This was the end. We drove silently away from my efforts, my work, and my home in silence. Daniel was angry with me because I had no plan to return. We sat silently as he drove us to town.

As far as I was concerned, my losses—even Daniel—were the price I had to pay to get safely out of Mozambique. The time had come. God had packed my bags. I would not be back.

# 53

My friend Tjitske gave me a ride to the Harare airport, which no longer intimidated me. I was surprised to see an ATM machine in the airport. I heard they had been declared illegal years earlier, and there had never been one in the airport before. Changes were coming to Africa, with or without me.

As I settled into my seat on the plane my adrenaline started to ease. I knew the efficient British Airways staff would soon inject us with a heavily sugar-laden dinner, followed by a couple of complimentary bottles of wine—their attempt to bed us down for the night. I liked the routine, and I would miss this part of international travel.

Soon after dinner the plane was dark, with only a few reading lights on. I felt oddly disoriented. In all of the years I flew to and from Mozambique, every time, my seat had been on the wing, and my right shoulder to the window. On this flight I was in the aisle. I struggled to get comfortable.

I was exhausted—but not in a drama-and-trauma kind of way. It was more the kind of exhaustion that seeps into your cells after a day working in the barns and fields; the exhaustion of a good day's work completed.

I had made it out of Africa alive, after six years teaching survival skills to children in a place where it was entirely too easy to die. I wondered… Had I succeeded? Had lives been saved? Had I set a footprint for others to follow?

The years had been rugged, sometimes stretching me to the edge of snapping. But I had also experienced moments of shocking success. I felt humbled. And I also felt proud.

I had done my best to apply spiritual principles in my everyday life in Mozambique, but much of the time I got swept up in stressful details instead of remembering, as the review had taught me, that all the gifts are right at our feet if only we trust and know.

I only knew that for the last five or six months I had felt like an hourglass that needed to be tipped back over. Time had been running out. But enough about that.

With my head swimming with sugar and wine, my memories blurred together—so many major events in so few years. My mind wandered back to those few days in Dombe, sitting in front of the school building and repairing the children's clothes as they sat patiently in my lap.

Could I have used my time better in those six years? How I had loved Mozambique! But I had not allowed myself to fully enjoy it. I ruefully remembered how I had turned down helicopter rides over Kilimanjaro and up to the game parks of Morremeu; I had turned down invitation after invitation to Cariba to experience elephants walking up to houseboats pulled up to the shoreline. And why? The offers had been free. I would not have used donor money. They were lovely invitations I had turned down because of lingering ideas from my younger years, such as, "You're not supposed to have fun while doing work for God" and "Gaining redemption for your mistakes in life requires hard work." Instead I had kept my nose to the grindstone, with the exception of sundowners and braiis with the international community, people I would sorely miss.

I searched my mind to recall conversations with the children. I reached and stretched and could not think of a single one. In the vague recesses of my mind I remembered one little boy, Leo, coming to my office one day to ask me about something. We hashed out some kind of conversation, but my limited Portuguese, combined with his blended dialect of Portuguese, kept us from having a real conversation.

In an effort to keep my emotional balance, I had avoided close contact with my Mozambican employees, children, and teachers. I had left that pleasure to our volunteers. Many people I knew died while I was in Mozambique, and I never attended a single funeral. I had left that sadness to my friends. I was always two steps too close to the edge.

As the plane made its way safely to London, I had to consider that of the four orphan centers we had created, two remained. Mariana was going to take over the safety school and sewing at the farm. All of the girls' clubs were still intact under Berta's watchful eye. ATM had all the equipment they needed and Madelaine to guide them along. Had I helped the children of darkness I'd been called to serve?

I hoped my presence had facilitated some improvements for some people. How many of our students would grow up to be diplomats because they met people from the U.S. Embassy? How many of our kids would go on to some kind of health-safety career because of the training they received at the TIOS School or even the girls' clubs?

How many kids would now grow up healthy, rather than contracting HIV? How many dogs would not suffer? How many kids would see our safety video? How many kids would not be killed in traffic accidents? I was always more focused on getting things done than keeping careful statistics. And really— careful statistics? In Mozambique? That futile effort would probably have been a waste of time.

I will not know the answers to my questions about my usefulness until I go through my own review at the end of my life. There were so many things left undone that I wanted a do-over, but it was time to let go. I would simply have to live and learn from my mistakes.

I was so tired, but my mind couldn't stop rambling. I went back to the galley of the plane to stretch my legs and get a juice. This part of the ten-hour flight was all at night, but it was so long that I had to get up and move around. When I returned to my seat, I laid my head back and tried to unwind. I considered how I had come to this calling, how this journey had begun with a divorce, a car accident, a forest fire, and a bankruptcy.

Like the phoenix rising, I had sought redemption for my sins and mistakes in life by asking God's direction. I recalled the many late nights and early mornings when I would sit down with a journal and pen held loosely in my hand. Then I would begin to take down what I would later call "dictation."

I closed my eyes and tried to sleep, but images and visions from the past began to zoom and expand as the visions had done in my early childhood. The girl—that little girl whose portrait I had left packed away with my things—how she had called to me from my room! At the time I had thought it so bizarre, so "Twilight Zone," and yet I couldn't deny it had been a real experience.

I had asked my guides for some insight about the girl. "What about the little girl in the drawing?"

*She waits for you.*

"Will I live overseas?"

*Quite likely.*

"What is most important for me to know?"

*You just walked through the gate to your life. You are now directly on the path you came to live...*

The messages were often vague and obscure, yet in the months leading up to my going to Mozambique, I had diligently written them down in journal after journal—thirteen journals in all. As the journals had once called me to Africa, it seemed the journals were now calling me home.

Message after message kept floating through my mind in bits and snippets. When the messages first started coming to me, it was the strangest experience of my life. I knew I could never explain the experience to my parents. They would think I was plumb crazy, hearing voices out of nowhere and writing it all down.

Yet I knew many people whose parents had dubbed them crazy who had grown up to be incredible authors. Even my patron Saint, Theresa, had experienced visions and Divine messages. The only way I could ever explain to Mom the journals and their importance in my decision to go to Africa would be to bring out the journals and compare them to things that had been foretold to me and then came true as I walked the path of listening.

One of the last messages I had written seemed to appear before my closed eyelids as though it was beckoning me to remember the journals:

*As for you, a day is coming soon from which you will not turn back. You will awaken to that which is only yours to do and you will see no other road than the one which has always been laid at your feet... There will be some obstacles; some moments of truth and some of fears. Know your heart and your faith. They're stronger than you imagine and you're protected more than you realize. Take care of you, Little Annunaki. The world awaits...*

With that, sleep finally found me. I'd had enough experience of the *review* and other Divinely delivered messages to know that everyone at ATM and in Mozambique were exactly where they were meant to be on their life path. I had been a contributor, an instigator, and sometimes even a hindrance, but in truth we were all just learning and growing and moving along. All was well in the universe, and I could rest now... at least until the next dictation.

# Epilogue:
# June 10, 2014

This spring of 2014 marked twelve years since I started receiving spiritual messages during automatic writing sessions. In the early days, I doubted most of the messages until I saw indications that they were true.

Amy: What about my insurance job?

*It will go away in time, but all will be well.*

I was at the height of my insurance career on the prestigious Cat teams at that time. The message made no sense. Another that made no sense was:

Amy: Will I live overseas?

*Quite likely.*

Amy: This is a life beyond imagine. So, I am correct in these messages?

*Yes, they are your gift. Find your Passport! All that is in your life now will seem moot.*

At that time I was sliding into bankruptcy court, had never been out of the country—other than to barely cross the border into Canada or Mexico—and I certainly had no language skills... Or money.

Had I listened to some of them a bit sooner, my journey might have been smoother. For example, I could have started putting some money away or packing my house when I was told my job would go away. But what rational person would decide "I had a message in my head that said my job was going away, which means I will lose my house, so I'm going to start packing."?

It took me some time to let go of "rational" and simply take the messages to heart. About the time I left for Africa, I had developed the ability to do that—to trust the spiritual guidance that I was receiving—but that was not a straight path; my trust was built in fits and starts.

The children of darkness had called to me, and I had answered. Had I found them? Had I helped them? I believe I did find them. Working with the good people I met along the way, I believe and hope that I did help them. Some of the programs I started continue under ATM's operations. The girls' clubs continue. Because of the afterlife review that my birthmother brought to me, I trust that everyone in Mozambique is on their own path, exactly where they are meant to be.

I understand that each person who was part of my experience came into my life for a benevolent purpose, to help me grow and become more than I was the day or the moment before. I believe I came into their lives for the same purpose; I hope they would agree.

When I returned to the States, I reread my journals. I also began my studies in epigenetics (the study of our ancestors' experiences on our DNA), and I received new information about how life works. My most recent automatic writing sessions taught me that the little girl in the intuitive drawing by Deborah Hanna in 2003 represented me. The information I've received recently brought me to my current work, which involves helping teenagers find an early life purpose and passion by evaluating the imprints in their eyes (where epigenetic information can be found) for clues of their gifts, talents, and ancestral belief systems.

Ten years ago I arrived on Goliath's doorstep, seeking the children of darkness and along the way I found myself... What will you find on your journey?

—Amy G.

# Acknowledgments

Wow. Where do I begin to thank everyone who has supported me on this journey? First would have to be God—because God brought each of you into my life in a certain "Divine Order." As we say at Unity ~ Thank you, God, Thank you, God, Thank you, God.

Then there's my editor, Cheri Colburn. This book would not be in your hands if it weren't for her—and of course, Zora Knauf, her graphic designer. Cheri sorted out my fumbled chapters and disorganized notes until my story came through for you in a way that made you want to read the next page, the next chapter—maybe even the next book. Zora crafted and designed the cover, dealt with low-resolution photos, and laid out the final manuscript for final publication.

I thank my family (especially my parents) for their patience, for their resilience, for putting up with me, the oddity in the family who went to Africa chasing a whisper and returned a different person.

From there I thank every donor, every volunteer, every minister, every director... every one of you who challenged me, pushed me, accelerated me, defeated me, inspired me, and supported me on this crazy mission to Mozambique to find and help the children of darkness.

I could not have gotten much done in Mozambique without the help of the U.S. Embassy in Maputo. I am also greatly indebted to a number of organizations: fhi360, Concern Worldwide, The Halo Trust, Church World Service, Ontmoetingskerk, *Water Is Our World*, Vitens, Wilde Ganzen, CNCS, ICAP, Columbia University, Johns Hopkins Bloomberg School of Public Health, Johns Hopkins University School of Communications, The Presbytery, Unity Churches across the United States, *Easy Chair* magazine, *The Fairmont Sentinel*, *The Mankato Free Press*, U.S. Air Force Academy, OSEO, ADPP, Peace Corps, HorizonT3000, Madelia Rotary

Club, Colorado Public Radio, Minnesota Public Radio, and JICA.

Thank you to my reviewers who gave their time to edit my rewrites and rewrites.

I'll name a few names from the international community; some I only know by first name and these are in no particular order, except the order of my fragmented memories.

My U.S. Board of Directors and other supporters: Sharlene Yabe, Amy Alsum, Joan Lomas, Dave Bryan, Eric Berolzheimer, Clay Hall, Carol Kelshaw, Will Flanders, Bob Simpson, Kate Snyder, Lois Bascom, Mike Foos, Bill Clarke, Bonnie Clarke, Lindsay Wells, Chris Wells, Dr. Ty Flewelling, Rev. Lawrence Palmer, Alexa Banks.

Everybody in the Netherlands who helped with donations and hospitality: Henry Jansen and his family, Rik & Hanneke Jansen, Nicole and Nico and Jeoren Gaal, Casper van Ommen family, Dita and Charles Romelaar and Jaap and Hanneke, Nathanje Jansen, Berend and Elsa Bruins, Rene Diks.

All of the other folks who came to my projects to lend a hand: Az Daniel, Helen Large Jarman, Briana Lisignoli, Rachel Bachiller, Helen Tirebuck, Vasco Galante, Berta Sixpence, Allan Schwarz, Yunas Vally, Alfredo Gonçalves, Frederico Magalhães, Nicole and Paulo Azevedo, John Bunnik and Tjitske Leemans, Gustavo Galante, Jorge Lampião, Gemma Bulos, Mariah Klingsmith, Monica Treipl, Kristina Smets and Stefaan Dondeyne, Wolfgang Peuerbach, Alfredo Ferreira, Christina Pimenta, René Nhantumbo, Corinne Boehm, Simon and Carol Nelson, Bob Squeri, Michael Squeri, Karen Angeles, Jenni Bekker, Helen Gray, Karen and Bill Butts, Leonel Miranda, Hajime, Anne Ola, Corinne Boehm, Madelaine Willeit, Ricky Monopoly, Greg Carr, Steve Calasse, Mandy and Pat Retzlaff, Yuri Vitolo, Nik, Nelson, Ernesto, Alface, Manuel, Lynne Joshua, Alan Nicholson and his family, Amy Rullkoetter, Fiona Benson, Evans Chiyenge, and Darci Broich.

Thank you to the "behind the scenes people" who helped in ways they might not even realize: Naomi Scott, Aissa Ibraimo, Victor Dantes, Santos and Helena Assunção, Christie

Zelling, Sea Stachura, Wendy Burt, Maria Holt, Michele Von Memerty, Todd Summers, Wendy Prosser, Steve Low, Bob Poole, Roberto Zolho, Fred Wise, Richard Hanes, Canaan Valejos, Will Flanders, Eric Whitney, Joe Uveges, Tammi Mott, Rev Barb Jung, Robert and Peggy Weed, Sofia Lightfield, Maj. Tim Frank, Lorée Rider, Cindy Korteum, Ahrianna Platten, Heather Stocker, Stephanie Lerner, Paula Connelly, Matthew Gormely-Fisher, Satoko Hashimoto, Todd Chapman, Robin Goff, Mike Weddle, Anthony Wessel, Robyn Dixon, Deb and Chris Mitguard, Doca Paulo Mussororo, Jytte Martinussen, Lilli Scheiterle, Barbara Roellkoetter, Simone Severo, João da Cruz, Joe Morris, Sergio Pereira, Antonio, Vasquinho Moisés, Angelo Gerónimo, Mia Yankow, Tammy Mott, Susan Sherman, Susan Krenn, Dr. David Holtgrave, Zandra Moffett, Paula Connelly, Zara Balouri, Cerene, and Libor Duffka.

Last but not least, I want to thank *you* for reading my story. I wish you a very blessed life.

# ABOUT THE AUTHOR

As a 38-year-old woman who had never traveled abroad or even learned a foreign language, Amy Gillespie beat the odds. Working on the ground in Mozambique, Africa, she started a nonprofit with $150 and the idea that all children deserve the right to keep themselves and their siblings alive. Her programs with children and her work for greater HIV awareness and prevention were successful; she was nominated as a finalist for CNN Heroes and received accolades from embassies and aid organizations.

Now, nearly ten years after her arrival in Mozambique, Amy Gillespie tells the full story of her experience answering a divine call. She reveals the secret that much of her mission and her success were guided by mysterious messages, chance encounters, and nebulous symbols.

She describes how an old-school farm approach to aid work was often the most effective. She speaks of her own lack of preparedness and failures, and how, ultimately, her lack of experience and education became her greatest gift.

Amy is currently working on a project involving epigenetics and iris imprints with teens and young adults to reveal their greatest talents, gifts, and genetic belief systems. She helps teenagers and young adults choose an early life purpose and vision for their future.

If you would like to learn more about Amy's work in Africa, see her book page "Six Years in Mozambique" on Facebook. If you would like to know more about her or her current programs go to www.TIOS.us.

Made in the USA
Las Vegas, NV
16 May 2023

72144652R00193